Intermediate Language Practice

MICHAEL VINCE

 HEINEMANN ELT

Heinemann English Language Teaching
Halley Court, Jordan Hill, Oxford OX2 8EJ
A division of Macmillan Publishers Limited

Companies and representatives throughout the world

ISBN 0 435 24121 4
        0 435 24120 6 (with Key)

First published 1998

Designed by Newton Harris

Illustrated by Philip Emms

The author would like to thank the editor, Sarah Curtis, for all her
help and comments. I would like to thank in particular Susan
Derry-Penz for commenting on earlier versions of this book.

The publishers would like to thank Costas Gabrielatos, Diane
Stewart and Marion West

Printed and bound in Great Britain by Scotprint Ltd, Musselburgh, Scotland.

98 99 00 01 02 03 10 9 8 7 6 5 4 3 2 1

Contents

Grammar

Vocabulary

Unit 1 Introduction

How you can use this book.

This book is for practising grammar and building up a wider vocabulary. Practising might involve working on your own or with others. You can study the explanations and then do the activities, or you can do the activities and check the explanations when you need them. You can use the units in any order. You can either work through the whole book, or focus on areas which you find problematic.

Thinking about grammar

1

Can you name the tense underlined in each example? What kind of time does each one describe?

a) I've been studying English for two years.

   Present perfect continuous/progressive. Continuing time up until the present.

b) Helen is leaving first thing in the morning.

c) If I had a helicopter, I'd get to school more easily!

d) I get up at 7.30.

e) By the time we got to the station, the train had left.

2

For each situation, decide which expressions are possible in the context. If you choose more than one, what are the differences?

a) It's your birthday on Saturday. Invite a friend to your party.

   1) I'll have a party on Saturday. You will come.

   2) I'm having a party on Saturday. Do you want to come?

   3) I have a party on Saturday. Are you coming?

b) You are on the bus. Ask a stranger to open the window.

   1) Could you open the window, please?

   2) Open the window.

   3) Excuse me, but do you think you could possibly open the window?

c) You arrive late for class and apologize to your teacher.

   1) I'm late, I apologize.

   2) Sorry I'm late.

   3) Please accept my most sincere apologies.

d) You are a witness to a minor accident. Explain what you saw.

   1) This car comes down the road and hits a tree, bang!

   2) A car had come down the road and had hit a tree.

   3) A car came down the road and hit a tree.

3
Compare each pair of sentences. Decide if they are both possible.

a) 1) I'm living in Paris.   *possible*
   2) I'm owning a motorbike.   *not possible*
b) 1) We went there by car.
   2) We went there in Helen's car.
c) 1) Where is the bank? Do you know?
   2) Do you know where the bank is?
d) 1) I used to like history lessons.
   2) I was liking history lessons.

Language comparisons

What problems do you have in learning English? How is your language different from English? Tick the points which are problematic for you.

a) the articles
   a/an, the
b) tenses
   Talking about the present, past, future, etc.
c) prepositions
   at, to, for, etc.
d) auxiliary verbs
   do, have
   slowly, well
e) modal auxiliaries
   can, must

f) conditional sentences
   If I …, I will/I would …
g) passive voice
   It is made of wood.
   The book was written in 1997.
h) forming questions
   Who are you? Where do you live? etc.
i) adjectives and adverbs
   happy, important
j) phrasal verbs
   get up, look up a word

Other ways of learning

Which of these ways of learning do you think are useful? Which ones do you regularly use?

a) Reading widely for pleasure.
b) Translating.
c) Making lists of words, or problem points.
d) Using a dictionary.
e) Listening to songs.
f) Keeping a diary.
g) Reviewing your written work.
h) Listening to the radio or watching television.

Which English?

English is a world language, and the English spoken in the USA or Australia differs from the English spoken in Britain. There are also differences between speakers from Scotland, Ireland and England, and between different parts of the same country. This book uses what is generally called Standard British English. References are also made to some differences in American English.

Unit 2 Present time 1

Explanations

Present simple:
formation rules

- Present simple is formed with the bare infinitive form of the verb.
    I like   You like   We like   They like
  We add *s* in the third person singular *he/she/it*. Verbs ending in *o, s, ch, sh, x*
  add *-es*. Some verbs are irregular: *have, be*
    She likes   He goes   She watches
    She misses   He wishes   He relaxes

- *Do* and *does* questions
  Present simple questions are formed with *do* and the bare infinitive form of
  the verb. We form third person singular forms with *does* and the bare
  infinitive form of the verb.
    ***Do** you like?*   ***Does** she like?*

- *Do not* and *does not* negatives
  Present simple negatives are formed with *do not* and the bare infinitive form
  of the verb. Third person singular is formed with *does not* and the bare
  infinitive form of the verb.
    *I **do not** like.*   *She **does not** like.*

- *Do* and *does* contractions
  In speech and informal writing, *do not* becomes *don't*, and *does not* becomes
  doesn't.
    *I **don't** like.*   *She **doesn't** like.*

- *Do* and *does* Wh- questions
  We also use *do/does* when we form questions with *when, what, why, where,*
  how, etc.
    ***What do** you want?*   ***Where does** she live?*

Meaning

- We use present simple to describe:
  Habitual actions
    *I usually **get up** at 7.30.*
  Personal facts
    *Liz **plays** in the school basketball team.*
    *We **like** ice-cream.*
  Facts which are always true.
    *The sun **rises** in the east.*

- See Unit 3 for future meanings.

Pronunciation

Verbs which end in /z/, /dz/, /s/, /sh/, /tsh/ and /ks/ make an extra syllable in the third person, pronounced /ɪz/.

    watches   misses   relaxes

After /f/, /k/, /p/, /t/, third person sound is /s/.   *hits*   /hɪts/

Other third person /s/ are pronounced as /z/.   *sees*   /siːz/

Does is normally pronounced /dʌz/ and *says* /sez/.

Present continuous: formation rules

- Present continuous is formed from the verb *be* and the bare infinitive with *-ing*.

      *I **am relaxing**.*   *He **is relaxing**.*   *She **is relaxing**.*
      *You **are relaxing**.*   *We **are relaxing**.*   *They **are relaxing**.*

  Present continuous is also called present progressive.

- Spelling

  Verbs ending *-e* drop the *-e* when they add *-ing*.

      like **liking**   *decide* **deciding**   *write* **writing**

  Verbs with one syllable, ending in one vowel and one consonant, double the consonant when they add *-ing*.

      sit **sitting**   *swim* **swimming**   *dig* **digging**

  Verbs ending *-ie* change *-ie* to *-y*.

      lie **lying**   *tie* **tying**   *die* **dying**

- Contractions

  In speech and informal writing, the verb *be* is contracted:

      ***I'm** writing*   ***He's** writing*   ***She's** writing*
      ***You're** writing*   ***We're** writing*   ***They're** writing*

- Questions

  We form present continuous questions by inverting the verb *be*.

      ***Am I** writing?*   ***Is he** writing?*   ***Is she** writing?*
      ***Are you** writing?*   ***Are we** writing?*   ***Are they** writing?*

- *Wh-* questions

      ***What** are you writing?*   ***Why** are we writing?*

- Negatives

  We form present continuous negatives with the verb *be + not*.

      ***I'm not** writing*   ***He's not** writing*   ***They're not** writing*

Meaning

- We use present continuous to describe:

  Actions happening at the present moment.

      *Sorry, I can't speak to you, **I'm washing** my hair.*

- See Unit 3 for future meanings.

Practice

1
Choose the correct phrase underlined in each sentence.

a) What time go you/(do you go) to bed on Saturdays?
b) Why <u>are you waiting/do you waiting</u> outside the door?
c) Don't ask Tim. He <u>doesn't know/not knows</u> the answer.
d) <u>I having/I'm having</u> my lunch at the moment.
e) When <u>you leave/do you leave</u> the house?
f) I don't understand. What <u>is happening/is happen</u>?
g) Excuse me, <u>does you know/do you know</u> the time?
h) This is a great party. <u>I'm having/Am I having</u> a lovely time.
i) We can't use the lift because it <u>don't works/doesn't work</u>.
j) What <u>you are doing/are you doing</u> here?

2
Read the answers and then complete the questions.

a) Where ...*does Sue live*........................ ?
   Sue? She lives at the end of Axwell Road.
b) Do .... ?
   Jim? No, I don't know him.
c) What .... ?
   At the moment? I'm doing my homework.
d) Are .... ?
   Here? No, I'm sitting over there.
e) Do .... ?
   Here? No, we change trains at the next station.
f) Why .... ?
   I'm wearing two pullovers because I feel cold!
g) Is .... ?
   David? No, he's not staying with Tom.
h) When .... ?
   Kate? She comes home at 6.30.

3
Rewrite each sentence so that the verb underlined is a negative contraction.

a) Naomi and Bill <u>are watching</u> television.
   ...*Naomi and Bill aren't watching television*..........................
b) Peter <u>likes</u> chocolate cake.
   ....
c) Carol <u>drives</u> a little red sports car.
   ....
d) <u>I'm using</u> this pencil at the moment.
   ....

5

e) The children <u>are having</u> lunch in the kitchen.

....

f) The sun <u>sets</u> in the east.

....

g) I <u>get up</u> early on Saturday.

....

h) Kate <u>is writing</u> a novel.

....

i) Sue <u>lives</u> in London.

....

j) We<u>'re waiting</u> for you.

....

4
Complete each sentence with a present simple or present continuous form, using the words given.

a) ...*Do you like*........................... cheese sandwiches?
   you like

b) What time .... ?
   the sun rise

c) What .... at the moment?
   you read

d) Sorry, I can't talk. .... a bath.
   I have

e) We .... at school.
   not watch videos

f) Look out of the window! ....
   it snow

g) This is an examination! Why .... ?
   you talk

h) Ann .... to school by bus every day.
   go

i) .... a uniform at your school?
   you wear

j) Pat has got an interesting hobby. .... a boat.
   she build

5
Choose the correct spelling from each pair of words.

a) (writing)/writting
b) diging/digging
c) takeing/taking
d) deciding/decideing
e) swiming/swimming

f) having/haveing
g) lying/lieing
h) readding/reading
i) using/useing
j) waiting/waitting

k) washeing/washing
l) riding/rideing
m) flyeing/flying
n) studing/studying
o) going/goeing

Unit 3 Present time 2

Explanations

Present simple:
frequency
adverbs

- Frequency adverbs are often used with present simple. They explain how often someone does an action, or something happens.

always	✓✓✓✓	I **always** get up at 7.00.
often	✓✓✓	Pat **often** goes to football matches.
usually	✓✓✓	It **usually** rains when I go on holiday!
sometimes	✓✓	We **sometimes** eat pizza for lunch.
rarely	✓	Jane **rarely** listens to jazz.
never	–	My bus **never** arrives on time.

- Note that the frequency adverb goes between the pronoun (*I*, *she*, etc.) or person and the verb. Other frequency adverbs are: *seldom* (✓), *hardly ever* (✓), *occasionally* (✓✓), *normally* (✓✓✓), *frequently* (✓✓✓✓).

- Frequency adverbs used with the verb *be* come after the verb.
  *Jim **is usually** late.*

State and event
verbs

- Some verbs are usually used in present simple and not in present continuous. These are sometimes called state verbs, because they describe continuing states, not sudden actions.

- *having* and *being*
  belong to, contain, cost, depend on, have, own

- *thinking* and *feeling*
  believe, forget, like, hate, know, prefer, understand

- Some verbs are more common as state verbs in present simple, and change their meaning when they are used as event verbs in present continuous. Event verbs describe actions.
  *I **have** two sisters.*   (permanent)
  *I'm **having** problems with this computer.*   (a temporary action)
  Examples include *be, have, taste, think*.

- Some state verbs can be used to describe temporary feelings.
  How are you getting on at your new school?
  *I'm **hating** it!*

| Simple and continuous contrasts | Simple forms usually describe states which are permanent or a fact. Continuous forms describe events which are happening at this moment. They will not continue for ever, or are not complete, and are temporary or in progress. |

>
> ***I live*** *in Budapest.*   (permanent)
> ***I'm living*** *in Budapest.*   (temporary)
> *This plane* ***lands*** *in Frankfurt.*   (a fact)
> ***We're landing****.*   (in progress)

Future reference

- Present continuous is also used to describe a future arrangement. There is usually a future time expression. This reference to the future emphasizes an event already arranged.

> *Paul* ***is leaving*** *early tomorrow morning.*
> *My parents* ***are buying*** *me a mountain bike for my birthday.*

  This future reference is common when we describe social arrangements.

> *Are you doing anything on Saturday?* ***We're going skating****.*

- See also Unit 8.

Other problems

- *feel*
  Sometimes there is only a small difference of meaning between simple and continuous.

> *I* ***feel*** *awful!   I'm feeling awful!*

  When we use present continuous, it suggests that we are asking whether any change has occurred.

> *How* ***are you feeling*** *now?   Are you any better?*

- Present perfect
  Check with Unit 6 about uses of present perfect tenses for situations which might seem to refer to present time.

> *Sue* ***is staying*** *with Jill.*   (temporary situation)
> *Sue* ***has been staying*** *with Jill since March.*   (time until now)

- Present continuous with *always*
  We can use *always* with present continuous when we are complaining about actions which we find annoying. We emphasize *always* in speech in this case.

> *You're* ***always*** *forgetting your keys!*

- Historic present
  In informal speech or in telling jokes present simple is used to describe narrative events in the past. This is also used in written summaries of film or serial plots.

> *A man* ***walks*** *into a bar and* ***asks*** *for a glass of water ...*
> *The story so far: Michael* ***meets*** *Susan in the library and* ***tells*** *her about the missing earrings ...*

- See also Unit 4 and 5.

Practice

1
Choose the correct sentence in each context.

a) You want to invite a friend to your party on Friday. You say:
  1) I have a party on Friday. Do you want to come?
  2) <u>I'm having a party on Friday. Do you want to come?</u>

b) You find a wallet on your desk and ask the people nearby:
  1) Who does this wallet belong to?
  2) Who is this wallet belonging to?

c) A friend invites you to a snack bar at lunch time. You say:
  1) Thanks, but I always go home.
  2) Thanks, but I'm always going home.

d) A friend opens the door and says: What are you doing? You reply:
  1) I work as a secretary.
  2) I'm repairing the computer.

e) A friend asks: Do you like lemon tea? You reply:
  1) I prefer tea with milk.
  2) I'm preferring tea with milk.

f) You haven't decided yet about buying a new bike. You say:
  1) I think about it.
  2) I'm thinking about it.

g) A friend asks you if you have finished the book she lent you. You say:
  1) Sorry, I still read it.
  2) Sorry, I'm still reading it.

h) It is a hot day, but a friend has a heavy coat on. You ask:
  1) Why are you wearing a heavy coat?
  2) Why do you wear a heavy coat?

2
Choose the correct word or phrase underlined in each sentence.

a) That can't be right! (I don't believe) I'm not believing it!
b) Carol can't swim today. She <u>has/is having</u> a cold.
c) See you in the morning. <u>I leave/I'm leaving</u> now.
d) What <u>do you do/are you doing</u>? If you drop it, it will explode!
e) Stop doing that, Billy! <u>You are /You are being</u> very silly.
f) <u>I drive/I'm driving</u>! You can sit in the back with Martin.
g) What <u>do we eat/are we eating</u> this evening? I'm really hungry!
h) You're a great cook! This cake <u>tastes/is tasting</u> wonderful.
i) Where <u>do you go/are you going</u>? I haven't finished speaking to you!
j) Chemistry is hard. <u>I am not understanding/I don't understand</u> it.

3

Put each verb given into present simple or present continuous.

a) Ugh, don't show me that picture! I (hate) ...*hate*.................... spiders!

b) Who (you, go with) .... to the match on Saturday?

c) In the winter, what (you, wear) .... ?

d) I can't stand horror films. I (think) .... they're really silly!

e) Diana (not, usually, sit) .... next to Ellen.

f) Why (you, look at) .... me like that? Have I done something wrong?

g) Excuse me, but (this bus, stop) .... outside the Post Office?

h) I (not take) .... the bus to school today. My mother (give) .... me a lift.

4

Choose a sentence from a) to h) which is the best continuation of the conversations beginning 1) to 8).

1) What do you usually do on your birthday? ..*a*.

2) Would you like to meet again on Saturday? .....

3) What do you usually do when there is an earthquake? .....

4) Have you finished your homework? .....

5) What are you doing? .....

6) What are you doing on Friday? .....

7) Are you in the school basketball team? .....

8) What do you do? .....

a) I have a party.

b) I lie under the table.

c) I work in a travel agency.

d) Yes, we play every Friday.

e) I'm still doing it.

f) It's hot in here. I'm opening some windows.

g) I'm going back to Canada tomorrow.

h) I'm having a party.

5

Put each verb given into present simple or present continuous.

a) What (usually, you, do) ...*do you usually do*.... at the weekend?

b) Don't worry about the cat. It (only eat) .... once a day.

c) I can't work out the answer. (you, know) .... what it is?

d) What's the matter? Why (you, stare) .... at me like that?

e) Excuse me, but (you, speak) .... English? I'm looking for a hotel.

f) Helen (stay) .... with her brother while her house is being repaired.

g) You should go on a diet. (you, put) .... on weight.

h) (they, speak) .... French or German? I can't tell the difference.

Unit 4 Past time 1

Explanations

Past simple:
formation rules

- Regular verbs
  Past simple regular verbs add -*ed* to the bare infinitive. Verbs ending in -*e* simply add -*d*.
  > *I **enjoyed** the film.*   *I **loved** the music.*
  All persons have the same form.

- Spelling problems
  Verbs ending in consonant + -*y* change -*y* to -*ie*.
  > *try* **tried**   *cry* **cried**
  Verbs ending with one vowel and one consonant double the final consonant.
  > *regret* *regretted*   *fit* *fitted*

- Irregular verbs
  The most common past simple irregular verbs are listed on page 246. It is necessary to learn irregular forms.
  > *eat* **ate**   *drink* **drank**   *wake* **woke**

- Questions
  Questions are formed with *did* and the bare infinitive.
  > ***Did you enjoy** the film?*   ***Did you drink** all the milk?*
  > *What **did you do** yesterday?*   *Why **did she leave**?*

- Negatives
  Negatives are formed with *did not* and the bare infinitive. This is contracted to *didn't* in speech and informal writing.
  > *The coat **didn't fit** me.*   *Carol **didn't eat** very much.*

Meaning

- Past simple is used to describe definite events in the past. A definite time expression can be used with these events.
  > *I **enjoyed** the film we saw **last night**.*
  > *We **listened** to some new CDs **yesterday afternoon**.*

- Past simple is used to describe habitual actions in the past.
  > *Every day we **got up** early and **went** to the beach.*

- See Unit 7 for contrasts with present perfect simple.

Past continuous:
formation rules

- Past continuous is formed with the past of *be* and the bare infinitive with
  -ing.

*I **was sitting** by the door.*	*He **was sleeping**.*	*She **was driving**.*
*You **were laughing**.*	*We **were crying**.*	*They **were eating**.*

  Past continuous is also called past progressive.

- Questions
  We form past continuous questions by inverting the verb *be*.

***Was** I sleeping?*	***Was** he reading?*	***Was** she driving?*
***Were** you waiting?*	***Were** we writing?*	***Were** they leaving?*

- *Wh-* questions
***What** were you writing?*	***Why** were they waiting?*

- Negatives
  We form past continuous negatives with the verb *be + not*. *Was not* is
  contracted to *wasn't*, and *were not* is contracted to *weren't*.

*I **wasn't** listening.*	*He **wasn't** playing.*	*They **weren't** looking.*

Meaning

- Past continuous describes a continuing situation. This is often contrasted
  with a sudden event.

Continuing situation	Sudden event
*I **was having** my lunch*	*when **Ruth phoned**.*
*While **I was waiting** for the bus,*	*I **met** Karen.*

- Past continuous is used to describe a number of continuing situations, as
  background description.
  > *The airport was full of people. Some **were sleeping** on benches,
  > some **were shopping**, others **were reading**. Everyone was waiting for
  > news of the delayed plane.*

- It is also used to describe two continuing situations, which are happening at
  the same time.
  > *While Jim **was cooking**, David **was phoning** a friend.*

Time expressions

- With past simple
  > *I arrived here **two hours ago/in September/last week/at 6.00.**
  > Helen lived in Madrid **for three years.***

- With past continuous
  > ***While** we were waiting for the train, it started to rain.
  > I cut my finger **when** I was peeling the potatoes.*

- Narrative time expressions – see Unit 29.

Practice

1
Choose the correct word or phrase from each pair underlined.

a) While I washed/(was washing) my hair, the phone (rang)/ringed.

b) How <u>did you felt/did you feel</u> yesterday afternoon?

c) When I <u>reached /was reaching</u> home I <u>received/was receiving</u> David's phone call.

d) Last summer I <u>was going swimming/went swimming</u> every weekend.

e) When the dog <u>bit/was biting</u> Laura's leg, she <u>screamed/was screaming</u>.

f) We <u>sang/sung</u> some songs and then <u>ate/eat</u> some sandwiches.

g) When you <u>fell/felt</u> over the cliff, what <u>happened/was happening</u> next?

h) While Mary <u>washed-up/was washing-up</u>, she <u>broke/was breaking</u> a cup.

i) I <u>didn't see/didn't saw</u> where the bus-stop was, so I <u>was missing/missed</u> the bus.

j) What <u>did you do/were you doing</u> when I <u>phoned/was phoning</u> you last night? There was no reply.

2
Rewrite each sentence according to the instructions given.

a) I enjoyed the concert.   (negative)   *...I didn't enjoy the concert...............*

b) Sue liked the party.   (question)   ....

c) You ate all the bread.   (question)   ....

d) Did Tom spend a lot?   (affirmative)   ....

e) I felt well yesterday.   (negative)   ....

f) Ann didn't buy a car.   (affirmative)   ....

g) They won the prize.   (question)   ....

h) Paul doesn't speak Polish.   (affirmative)   ....

i) I paid all the bills.   (negative)   ....

j) Ruth made a mistake.   (question)   ....

3
Complete each sentence with a suitable time expression from the list. You can use an expression more than once.

ago   in   last week   at   when   while

a) Two burglars broke into the house ...*while*....... we were watching television.

b) .... I met an old friend of mine in the city centre.

c) What were you doing .... the police officer knocked on the door?

d) Jan met Sarah .... half-past eight outside the cinema.

e) .... Dick was preparing lunch, he cut his finger badly.

f) I first came to this town more than twenty years ....

g) Jim was studying to be a doctor .... he met Sally.

h) Tony bought his first motorbike .... 1992.

i) .... did you start playing basketball?

j) Most of the young people left this village a long time ....

4

Choose a sentence from a) to h) which is the best continuation of the conversations beginning 1) to 8).

1) What was Carol doing when you knocked on the door? ..c..
2) How did Brenda spend her holiday? .....
3) What happened when the lights went out? .....
4) When did you meet Cathy? .....
5) What did Jean do when Tony called? .....
6) Did Ann hear what David said? .....
7) What did Pat do when the bell rang at the end of the lesson? .....
8) Why did Helen leave so early? .....

a) She went sailing most days, and sunbathed at the beach.
b) She put the phone down.
c) She was listening to the radio in the kitchen.
d) She went to meet her parents at a restaurant.
e) She came to my brother's birthday party.
f) While Tina was looking for a torch, they came back on.
g) She wasn't listening.
h) She put her books away and left.

5

Put each verb given into either past simple or past continuous.

a) When Harry (wake up) ...*woke up*... , we (tell) ...*told*..... him the good news.
b) Where (you leave) .... your wallet when you (go) .... swimming?
c) Everyone (wait) .... for the concert to begin when a message (arrive) ....
d) When Tom (finish) .... his letter, he (take) .... it to the post office.
e) Pam (want) .... a relaxing holiday, so she (choose) .... to stay on a small island.
f) When I (study) .... abroad, my parents (phone) .... me every week.
g) I (find) .... my lost pen while I (look for) .... my pencil sharpener.
h) Ann (watch) .... television when Julie (arrive) ....
i) When the lights (go out) .... , I (lie) .... in bed reading.
j) When you (go) .... to the new Chinese restaurant, what (you eat) .... ?

6

Choose the correct spelling from each pair of words.

a) siting/(sitting)
b) felt/fellt
c) tryed/tried
d) crying/cring
e) wasn't/wa'snt
f) enjoyed/enjoied
g) thoght/thought
h) liveing/living
i) shopping/shoping
j) heard/heared
k) hidding/hiding
l) waited/waitted
m) plaied/played
n) whent/went
o) fitted/fited

Unit 5 Past time 2

Explanations

Past perfect
simple:
formation rules

Past perfect simple is formed with the past tense auxiliary *had* and the past participle. The past participles of irregular verbs are listed on page 246.

*I **had decided**.*   *She **had left**.*   *We **had eaten**.*

In speech and informal writing these forms are contracted to:

I'd decided.   *She'd left.*   *We'd eaten.*

Questions: *Had she left?*
Negatives: She *had not left*.   She *hadn't left*.

Meaning

● Past perfect simple is used when we need to make clear that one event in the past happened before another event in the past.

Sue left at 7.00.   *We arrived at her house at 8.30.*
*When we **arrived** at Sue's house, she **had left**.*

It may not be necessary to use past perfect simple if we use *before* or *after* to make the time clear.

*Sue **left** her house **before** we arrived.*
*We arrived at Sue's house **after she left**.*

Although both are correct, many speakers still prefer to use past perfect simple in this case.

*Sue **had left** her house **before** we arrived.*
*We arrived at Sue's house **after she had left**.*

● Note that it is not necessary to use past perfect simple just because an event happened a long time ago. We use past simple.

*The Chinese **built** the Great Wall over two thousand years ago.*

Common uses

● With *realize*.

*When I got home I **realized** I had lost my wallet.*

● With verbs of thinking:

think, know, be sure, remember, suspect, understand, etc.
*I thought **I'd seen** the film before, but I hadn't.*
*David knew he **had seen** her somewhere before.*
*Ellen was sure she **hadn't locked** the door.*
*The inspector suspected that the thief **had used** a special key.*

● See also Units 10 and 11 Reported speech.

used to

- *Used to* describes a habit or state in the past. There is not a present form. *Used to* often makes a contrast between a habit in the past and a habit we have now.
    *I **used to** have long hair when I was younger.*
    *I **used to** play tennis, but now I play football.*
  Question form: ***Did you use to**?*
  Negative: *I **didn't use to**.*

- Pronunciation
  Used is pronounced / juːst/. This is different from the past tense of the verb *use*, pronounced /juːzd/.

- Note that some grammars make *used to* an unchangeable form, and accept the written forms *Did you used to?* and *I didn't used to.*

would

- *Would* can be used to describe repeated actions in the past. It is often used in descriptive writing.
    *On winter days, we **would** all sit around the fire and tell stories.*

- Note that *would* cannot be used for states.
    *I **used to own** a motorbike.*
    *I would own a motorbike.   (Not a possible sentence.)

Past simple forms with other meanings

- Note that the forms of past simple and past perfect are used in conditional sentences. See Units 12 and 13.

- The form of past simple is also used as an unreal tense. See Unit 14.

Practice

1
Underline the error or errors in each sentence. Rewrite the sentence.

a) When we had <u>ate</u> lunch, we <u>were sitting</u> in the garden.
   ...When we had eaten lunch, we sat in the garden... .

b) While I looked for my keys, I remembered I left them at home.
   ....

c) Anna had used to play badminton when she had been at school.
   ....

d) When I got into bed, I was falling asleep immediately.
   ....

e) When I was finally finding the house, I was knocking at the door.
   ....

f) After Jill was giving Nick his books, she went home.
   ....

g) Maria would live in Sweden when she was a child.

....

h) I was using to get up early when I had gone sailing.

....

i) The Vikings had sailed to North America a thousand years ago.

....

j) Sue was sure she was seeing the tall man before.

....

2

Choose the correct word or phrase underlined in each sentence.

a) While I had waited/~~was waiting~~/waited at the bus-stop, I had noticed/was noticing/~~noticed~~ a new shop which wasn't/~~had not been~~ in the street the day before.

b) I had gone/went out into the garden to fetch my bike, but found/was finding that someone stole/had stolen it.

c) When George met/was meeting Diane for the first time, he knew/was knowing that he met/had met/was meeting her somewhere before.

d) Helen got off/was getting off the bus, and walked/was walking into the bank when she realized/had realized/was realizing that she left/had left/was leaving her handbag on the bus.

3

Put each verb given into past simple, past continuous or past perfect. More than one answer may be possible.

The police suspected that Brian (a) ...*had broken*...... (break) the window at his house because he (b) .... (want) to make them think that a burglar (c) .... (steal) his valuable stamp collection. They (d) .... (think) that Brian (e) .... (do) this because he (f) .... (need) the money. However, they (g) .... (not know) that Brian (h) .... (fly) to Brazil the week before, and (i) .... (be) abroad when the burglary (j) .... (take) place.

4
Complete each sentence, using *would* or *used to* with the verb given. More than one answer may be possible.

a) Jack (have) ...*used to have*...... a beard but he shaved it off.

b) When I was young my mother (read) .... to me every night.

c) During the holidays we (meet) .... at the beach every morning.

d) I (not like) .... spinach, but now I do.

e) Helen (write) .... to me very often, but now she phones.

f) Tina (live) .... in the house opposite.

g) I'm sure that when I was young, the summers (be) .... warmer.

h) Whenever our teacher let us leave early, we (cheer) .... !

5
Complete the second sentence so that it has a similar meaning to the first sentence and contains the word given.

a) Michael took a deep breath and dived into the water.
   After ...*Michael had taken*.................. a deep breath, he dived into the water.
   had

b) Terry was fatter.
   Terry .... to be so thin.
   didn't

c) Gary was sure his keys were in his pocket.
   Gary was .... his keys.
   forgotten

d) Last summer, Julia got up early every morning.
   Last summer, Julia .... early every morning.
   to

e) I thought the book seemed familiar.
   I thought .... the book before.
   had

f) When he was younger David played tennis.
   David .... when he was younger.
   used

g) We missed the bus so we took a taxi.
   We .... the bus.
   had

h) In those days, we spent the summer in the mountains.
   In those days, we .... the summer in the mountains.
   would

Unit 6 Present perfect 1

Explanations

Present perfect simple: formation rules

The present perfect simple is formed with the present tense of the auxiliary verb *have*, and the past participle. The past participles of regular verbs have the same form as the regular past simple. The past participles of irregular verbs are listed on page 246.

> *I **have decided** to leave tomorrow.*   (regular)
> ***Have you written** the letter yet?*   (irregular)

Meaning

Present perfect simple generally describes past events which are connected to the present. There are a number of different meanings.

- An event in the past but without a definite time.
  > *Helen **has broken** her pencil.*

  We do not know exactly when this happened, and the pencil is still broken. There is no time expression.

- A state or repeated event lasting until the present, and still happening. There is a time expression, describing how long or how often something has happened.
  > *I've **lived here** for ten years.*
  > *I've **often seen** Jim with his dog in the park.*

Common uses (no time mentioned)

- Explaining a present situation
  We often use the present perfect simple when we explain a present situation. An exact time is not mentioned.
  > *What's the matter? Why are you walking like that?*
  > *I've **hurt** my foot.*

- Experiences
  We use present perfect when we describe experiences in the past, and an exact time is not mentioned.
  > ***Have you visited** any other countries?*
  > *Yes, I've **been** to Italy and France.*

- Completion
  We often use the present perfect when we describe how many things are completed so far and an exact time is not mentioned.
  > *I've **read** a hundred pages of this book.*

Common uses
(with time
expressions)

● *ever, never*
  We use *ever* and *never* when we ask or talk about our experiences in life.
  > *Have you **ever** eaten Japanese food?*
  > *No, I've **never** eaten it.*

● *yet* and *already, so far*
  We use *yet* in questions and negative sentences. It has a similar meaning to
  so far. We use *so far* in positive sentences.
  > *Have you finished this book **yet**? No, I'm on page 56.*
  > *How many pages have you read **so far**? I've read 56 pages.*
  We use *already* to describe an action which happened before.
  > *When are you going to finish your letter?*
  > *I've **already written** it.*

● *just*
  We use *just* when we describe a very recent event.
  > *Cathy **has just phoned** from the airport.*

● Frequency adverbs: *always, often*
  We can use frequency adverbs with present perfect.
  > *He **has always loved** you.*   (a state)
  > *We **have often visited** Spain.*   (a repeated event)

● *for* and *since*
  for describes a period of time.
  > *Tom **has worked** here **for three months**.*
  since describes when the period of time started.
  > *Tom **has worked** here **since July 10th**.*

Practice

1
Use the verbs to
make a form of
the present
perfect simple.

a) What's the matter? (you cut) ...*Have you cut*.......................... yourself?
b) The ship (not sink) .... but it's in a dangerous
    condition.
c) (your sisters write) .... to you yet?
d) I (have) .... a headache ever since lunchtime.
e) Nadia (never see) .... any Chinese films.
f) Someone (steal) .... Mr Grant's bike.
g) The passengers are tired because they (not sleep)
    .... all night.
h) I'm afraid we (just break) .... your window. Sorry!
i) David (not win) .... a prize this time, I'm afraid.
j) (you ever eat) .... Spanish food? It's great!

2
Complete what
each speaker
says.

a)

We ..*have been married*................
for twenty-five wonderful years!

b)

I .... on
holiday to Australia.

c)

I ....
twenty-three letters!

d)

I .... a
snail before!

e)

I .... you
since the day we met!

f)

Oh no! I ....
my pencil!

21

3

Put a time word or phrase from the list into each space.

| yet | for | since | often | ever |
| never | already | so far | just | always |

a) Carlos has lived in the city centre ...*since*... 1996.

b) Thanks for the present! I've .... wanted a pet goldfish!

c) Have you .... drunk pineapple juice? It's fantastic!

d) I've .... heard some fantastic news! I've passed my exams!

e) Hurry up! Haven't you finished .... ? You are a slow-coach!

f) Nina has worked in this company .... five years.

g) I've .... been on a big ship before. It's an interesting experience!

h) We're very busy today. .... we've sold over a hundred bikes.

i) I've .... passed this building, but this is the first time I've been inside.

j) Can I have a different book? I've .... read this one.

4

Complete the second sentence so that it has a similar meaning to the first sentence.

a) We started working here three years ago.
We ..*have worked here for*........................ three years.

b) This is the first time I've been on a plane.
I .... before.

c) That's strange! My pen isn't here!
That's strange! .... disappeared!

d) Nicky and Jan aren't at this school any more.
Nicky and Jan .... this school.

e) I saw a friend of yours a few moments ago.
I .... a friend of yours.

f) I'm still writing my letters.
I .... my letters yet.

g) Is this your first visit to South America?
Have .... before?

h) Oh bother! My wallet is still in the car.
Oh bother! I .... my wallet in the car.

i) It's a long time since we spoke to your sister.
We .... to your sister for a long time.

j) Is Anna still asleep?
Has .... up yet?

Unit 7 Present perfect 2

Explanations

Present perfect
continuous:
formation rules

The present perfect continuous is formed with the present perfect tense of the
auxiliary verb *be*, and the present participle.
> *I've been waiting here all morning.*
> *What have you been doing lately?*

Meaning

Present perfect continuous, like present perfect simple, generally describes past
events which are connected to the present. The continuous form gives a number
of different meanings.

- It can emphasize the length of time of the action.
> *I've been waiting here all morning.*
The person speaking is not happy about this situation!

- It can emphasize that the action is recent.
> *You're very dirty! What have you been doing?*
> *I've been fixing my bike.*
This action is recent, because we can see the result.

- It can emphasize that the action is temporary.
> *I've been staying in a hotel for the past month.*
Here present perfect continuous emphasizes that this is only temporary.

Common uses

- Recent activities
> *What have you been doing lately?*
> *I've been working a lot.*
> *I've been feeling ill for weeks.*

- Continuing actions
> *How long have you been living here?*
> *Carlos has been studying English for two years.*

- Repeated actions
> *I've been phoning her for days, but she's never at home.*

- Time expressions with present perfect continuous
> *all day, all morning,* etc., *for days, for ages,* etc., *lately, recently*

Contrasts with present perfect simple	Present perfect simple often emphasizes that an action is finished, but present perfect continuous can emphasize that it is still going on.

> ***I've written*** *five letters.* (present perfect simple)

The number stresses that the action is completed.

> ***I've been writing*** *letters.* (present perfect continuous)

This suggests that the writer has not finished.

Present perfect problems	• Confusions with other tenses

Present simple
We use present simple to describe habits or states in the present, but we use present perfect to describe the time until the present.

> ***I live*** *in Prague.* (present state)

This means that I always live there. It's my home.

> ***I have lived*** *there for two years.* (time until the present)

This means that I arrived there two years ago and I live there now.

Past simple
Past simple describes a definite event in the past.

> *When **did** you **arrive** in Prague?*
> ***I arrived*** *here in September two years ago.*

Speaker attitude
The choice of present perfect simple or past simple may depend on how close to the event the speaker feels .

> *You **had** an umbrella, didn't you? Where is it?*
> *Oh bother! **I've left** it on the bus.*

This is recent, or the bus is still near.

> *I **had** an umbrella, but I **left** it on the bus.*

The event is more distant, and the speakers are probably far away from the bus.

• *have been* and *have gone*

have been

> *Mary **has been** to China.*

This means that she has visited China, but is not there at the moment.

have gone

> *Mary **has gone** to China.*

This means that Mary is not here at the moment because she is visiting China.

Practice

1
Choose the correct word or phrase underlined in each sentence.

a) I live here/I have lived here since the end of last year.

b) Someone has just stolen/has just been stealing my bicycle.

c) I'm afraid the last train left/has left an hour ago.

d) Yesterday I lost/I have lost my wallet.

e) Thank you for your offer, but I've decided/I decided not to accept.

f) Take your umbrella with you. It's started/It started raining.

g) We're enjoying our trip. We have visited/visited two countries so far.

h) I'm standing here/I've been standing here for hours and I feel tired.

i) This has been/was a busy day and it isn't over yet!

j) I feel really tired. We went/have been to a party last night.

2
Put each verb given into either present perfect simple, past simple or present simple.

a) Last week I (lose) ...*lost*.................. my scarf, and now I (just lose) ...*have just lost*...... my gloves.

b) I (work) .... for Blue Bank at the moment but I (decide) .... to change jobs.

c) We (be) .... here for hours. Are you sure we (come) .... to the right place?

d) (you see) .... my calculator? I'm sure I (leave) .... it here earlier.

e) We (have) .... some coffee after that and then (catch) .... the bus home.

f) I (never eat) .... octopus, but once on holiday I (eat) .... some squid.

g) I (hope) .... you aren't a vegetarian. I (cook) .... you some lamb chops.

h) Recently a lot of young people (take up) .... in-line skating.

i) When we (reach) .... the cinema, there (not be) .... any tickets left.

j) Please come quickly! Nick (have) .... an accident, and he (go) .... to hospital.

3

Complete each mini-dialogue, using the verbs given, in either present perfect simple or present perfect continuous.

1   A: *Terminator 2* is on at the Rex? (you see) ...*Have you seen*.................. it?

    B: No, not yet. Shall we go? I (look forward) ...*am looking forward*............ to seeing it.

2   A: What's the matter? You look really tired!

    B: I am! I (study) .... all day, and I (not finish) .... yet.

    A: Oh well, time for a break.

3   A: I (phone) .... Carol all day, but there's no reply.

    B: I expect she (go) .... swimming with her friends.

4   A: (you hear) .... the news?

    B: What news?

    A: Someone (rob) .... the bank at the end of the road.

5   A: Why is your leg in plaster?

    B: That's a silly question! I (break) .... it, of course.

    A: Someone (write) .... 'Time for a break' on the plaster!

4

Put **one** suitable word in each space.

We've had a very interesting trip (a) ...*so*........ far, and we've had some interesting adventures (b) .... the last time we wrote. We've (c) .... to some beautiful islands, and (d) .... a lot of interesting people. In fact (e) .... we've made friends with some people in a village, and they've been (f) .... us the local language. I haven't managed to learn much (g) .... , but Ann (h) .... picked up quite a lot, and can speak well. She's been (i) .... every day, and she has (j) .... me everything she knows!

5

Complete the second sentence so that it has a similar meaning to the first sentence.

a) I came to live here three months ago.
    I ...*have been living here*............ for three months.

b) Mary is out at the shops at the moment.
    Mary .... to the shops.

c) I have had French lessons since March.
    I .... French since March.

d) I'm still reading this book.
    I .... reading this book yet.

e) Paul left the room a moment ago.
    Paul has .... the room.

    f) Ten of the letters are ready.

        I .... ten letters so far.

    g) It's ages since I last went to the cinema.

        I .... to the cinema for ages.

    h) This is the first time I've eaten snails.

        I .... snails before.

    i) I don't remember Helen's phone number.

        I have .... Helen's phone number.

    j) David has a different opinion now.

        David .... his mind.

6

Underline the errors in these sentences. Rewrite each sentence.

    a) My penfriend <u>is</u> writing to me for years but has never sent me a photo.

        ...My penfriend has been writing to me for years but has never sent me a photo...

    b) We have started this course three weeks ago.

        ....

    c) 'What have you been doing all day?' 'I've been written letters.'

        ....

        ....

    d) When have you arrived in this city?

        ....

    e) You have ever been to India?

        ....

    f) Paula has been stayed in a hotel by the sea.

        ....

    g) I've been feeling ill three weeks ago.

        ....

    h) I live in this city since I was born.

        ....

    i) I wait here a long time. Where have you been?

        ....

        ....

    j) Tony has leaved his books on the bus.

        ....

Unit 8 Future 1

Explanations

Future time

We can refer to future time in English by using *will/shall*, *be going to* or by using present tenses. These forms do not all have the same meaning, and we have to choose the most suitable one.

will and *shall*

- Formation rules
  Will future is formed with the infinitive without *to*. *Shall* is used in formal situations with *I* and *we*. The negatives of *will* is *won't* and of *shall* is *shan't*. *Will* is usually shortened in speech and informal writing to *'ll*.

- Meaning
  Will generally describes a prediction or what we think will happen in the future. There is usually a time expression. We can use *perhaps* when we are uncertain, *probably* when we are almost certain, or *definitely* when we are certain.
    *United **will definitely** win tonight.*
    ***Perhaps it'll rain** tomorrow.*
    *In the next century, most people **will probably** live in big cities.*

be going to

- Formation rules
  Be going to future is formed with the verb *be* + *going* + the infinitive.
    *Jean **is going to learn** to drive.*
    *Tim and Ann **are going to travel** abroad next year.*

- Meaning
  There are two meanings which are very similar.
  Plans or intentions
  We use *going to* when we talk about plans or intentions.
    ***I'm going to do** lots of work this evening.*
  This is a plan, so it may not happen.
  Present cause
  This is a prediction based on something we can see or know about.
    *Look out! Those books **are going to fall** on your head!*

Present continuous

- Meaning
  We can use the form of the present continuous to refer to the future. We use it when we talk about events which are arranged for the future. It is often used when we talk about social arrangements.
    ***Are you doing** anything on Friday evening?*
    Not really. Why?
    ***I'm having** a party. Would you like to come?*

Problems   Choosing how to refer to the future can be difficult, as sometimes there is more than one choice.

- *going to* or present continuous?
  It is possible to use *going to* in places where present continuous is more usual, when a time is mentioned.
  > ***I'm having*** *a party on Friday.*
  > ***I'm going to have*** *a party on Friday.*
  However, we cannot use present continuous in places where *going to* is usual without changing the meaning, when no time is mentioned.
  > *Jean* ***is going to learn*** *to drive.*
  This is a plan, with no time mentioned.
  > *Jean* ***is learning*** *to drive.*
  As no time is mentioned or implied, this describes a present action.

- *will* or *going to*?
  Impersonal predictions
  Here the choice is sometimes a matter of being formal or informal.
  > *I think* ***it's going to rain*** *tomorrow.*
  This would be possible in everyday conversation.
  > *Tomorrow* ***it will rain*** *in Northern England.*
  This may be more common in a weather forecast, where the speaker is being more formal.

  Plans
  If we use *will* instead of *going to*, the meaning changes.
  > ***I'm going to do*** *lots of work this evening.*
  This is a plan or intention.
  > ***I'll do*** *lots of work this evening.*
  This sounds like a promise.

- *be*
  We usually use *will* or *going to* with *be*.
  > ***I'll be*** *back on Friday.*
  > ***I'm going to be*** *back on Friday.*

Practice

1
Choose the correct sentence, 1) or 2), in each mini-dialogue.

a) A: Can you come dancing tomorrow night?
   B: 1) Sorry, I'll play basketball.
      2) <u>Sorry, I'm playing basketball.</u>

b) A: What are your plans for the summer?
   B: 1) I'll spend a month in the mountains.
      2) I'm going to spend a month in the mountains.

c) A: What do you think about the weather?
   B: 1) It'll probably rain tomorrow.
      2) It's raining tomorrow.

d) A: What about tomorrow at about 5.30?
   B: 1) OK, I'll see you then.
      2) OK, I'm seeing you then.

e) A: Mary is buying a dog next week.
   B: 1) Really? What is she going to call it?
      2) Really? What is she calling it?

f) A: It would be nice to see you next week.
   B: 1) Are you doing anything on Wednesday?
      2) Will you do anything on Wednesday?

2
Put the verb given into a form of *will*, *going to* or present continuous. More than one answer may be possible.

a) Have you heard the news? Harry (join) ...*is joining/is going to join*.... the Army!

b) Sorry to keep you waiting. I (not be) .... long.

c) According to the weather forecast, it (snow) .... tomorrow.

d) I'm sorry I can't meet you tonight. I (go out) .... with my parents.

e) Careful! You (knock) .... that jug off the table!

f) In fifty years' time, most people (probably ride) .... bicycles to work.

g) Our teacher (give) .... us a test tomorrow.

h) I (go) .... to Manchester at the end of next week.

i) Look out! You (hit) .... that tree!

j) I think our team (probably win) ....

3
Complete the second sentence so that it has a similar meaning to the first sentence.

a) My party is on Thursday.
   I ...*am having a party*............. on Thursday.

b) Tomorrow's weather forecast is for rain.
   It's .... tomorrow.

c) I predict a victory for our team.
   I think .... win.

d) Tomorrow I'll be absent, teacher.
   I .... here tomorrow, teacher.

e) Terry intends to finish painting the kitchen this evening.
   Terry .... painting the kitchen this evening.

f) Meet me outside the station at 5.30.
   I .... outside the station at 5.30.

g) What's our arrangement for lunch?
   Where .... for lunch?

h) Everyone expects lots of tourism in this country next summer.
   Everyone thinks a large number .... this country next summer.

i) I don't plan to sell my bike after all.
   I .... my bike after all.

j) Are you free tomorrow?
   Are .... anything tomorrow?

4
Underline the sentences which are incorrect. Rewrite them.

a) <u>I go swimming next Saturday. Would you like to come?</u>
   ...*I am going swimming next Saturday. Would you like to come?*.......................

b) What are you going to discuss at the next meeting?
   ....

c) The boat is turning over! I think it will sink!
   ....

d) Sue is going to lend me her roller-skates.
   ....

e) I've read the weather forecast, and it's definitely sunny tomorrow.
   ....

f) David and Helen will be here at 9.30.
   ....

g) There is a lot to do. Is anyone going to help you?
   ....

h) Sorry I'm not seeing you tomorrow. I have to go to London.
   ....

i) Where will you be tomorrow at this time?

....

j) Bye for now. I see you later this evening.

....

5

Rewrite each sentence so that it contains *will* or *going to*.

a) I plan to study engineering in France.
   ...*I'm going to study engineering in France.*........................

b) I've arranged a party for next Friday.

....

c) I predict a score of 3–0.

....

d) We've an appointment at the doctor's, so we can't come.

....

e) Paula is likely to get the job.

....

f) Martin's wife is pregnant again.

....

g) Sarah doesn't plan to get married yet.

....

h) There's a possibility of snow tomorrow.

....

Unit 9 Future 2

Explanations

Future continuous

- Formation rules
  Future continuous is formed with *will* or *shall* + *be* + the present participle (*-ing*).
  > *This time tomorrow **I'll be eating lunch** on the plane.*
  Shall is used in formal situations with *I* and *we*.

- Meaning
  Future continuous describes a temporary situation or activity in the future. We often use it when we compare what we are doing now with what we will be doing in the future. We usually use a time expression.
  > *Where **will you be living** in five years' time?*
  We also use future continuous to describe something which will definitely happen because an arrangement has already been made.
  > ***We'll be holding** a meeting soon, so we can decide then.*
  This means that the meeting will happen anyway.

Future perfect

- Formation rules
  Future perfect is formed with *will* or *shall* + *have* + the past participle.
  > *By the time we get to the cinema, the film **will have begun**.*

- Meaning
  Future perfect describes a situation which has not happened yet. At a time in the future, it will happen.
  > *By the time we get to the cinema, the film **will have begun**.*
  This means that when we arrive at the cinema we can say, '*The film has begun.*' We often use *by* or *by the time* with future perfect.

Timetable future

- When we talk about events which are fixed and cannot be altered, we use present simple. We use this when we describe timetables.
  > *Jim's plane **leaves at 12.00**.*
  > *Our head teacher **retires next year**.*

- Future time clauses
  In a future time clause, we can refer to the future with the form of the present simple after a time word. We can also use present perfect, when we emphasize that an action is complete.
  > ***When I see** her again, I'll tell her your news.*
  > *Please wait here **until Mrs Hall comes** back.*
  > ***As soon as we're ready**, we'll phone you.*

*Let's run home **before it rains**.*
*Hand in your paper **as soon as you have finished**.*

- *in case*
  We use *in case* when we want to refer to a possible problem. We refer to the future with a form of the present simple.
  *Take an umbrella, **in case it rains**.*

Functions: *will, shall, going to*

Language functions describe the ways we use language for a purpose. Many uses of *will* and *shall* are more easily described in this way.

- Promise
  ***I'll try** as hard as I can.*

- Threat
  *Stop doing that, or **I'll tell** my dad.*

- Offer
  ***Shall I open** the door for you?*

- Parting remark
  ***I'll see** you tomorrow.*

- Decision of the moment
  *'Which one do you want?' '**I'll take** the blue silk one.'*
  This is a decision made immediately. In the example, the speaker is in a shop.

- Decision
  ***I'm going to buy** a new camera.*
  This is a general decision about buying a camera, but it is not at the same time as buying the camera. The speaker is not in the shop.

- Request
  ***Will you carry** this bag for me?*
  This is an informal request.

- Suggestion
  ***Shall we play** tennis?*
  This kind of suggestion includes the speaker.

- Other uses of *will* and *would*.   See Unit 22.

34

Practice

1
Choose the correct word or phrase underlined in each sentence.

a) This time next week Billy will lie/(will be lying) on the beach.

b) Please stay in your seats until the bell will ring/rings.

c) We will have moved /will be moving to our new house on Tuesday.

d) What time does your train leave/will your train leave?

e) Don't forget to turn off the lights before you are leaving/leave.

f) Where will you work/will you be working in ten years' time?

g) Wait for me. I'll be/I'll have been ready in a moment.

h) John won't stop/won't have stopped talking all the time!

i) Stop teasing the dog, or it's biting/it'll bite you.

2
Complete each part sentence a) to h) with one of the part sentences 1) to 8). More than one answer may be possible.

a) As soon as I hear from Helen, ..6..

b) By the time Mary arrives .....

c) Please take a seat .....

d) This time next week .....

e) The next time you see me .....

f) We'll have time to have some lunch .....

g) In a few moments .....

h) There won't be any more lessons .....

1) until the dentist is ready.

2) the match will be over.

3) I'll have had my haircut and you won't recognize me.

4) it will have stopped raining.

5) before the train leaves.

6) I'll ask her to phone you.

7) until the teachers' strike is over.

8) we'll be enjoying ourselves on holiday.

3
Rewrite each sentence with *will/shall* or *going to*, using the verb underlined.

a) How about playing tennis?

...Shall we play tennis?...

b) I've decided to study Arabic in Cairo.

....

c) I promise to be home by midnight.

....

d) I hope to meet you later.

....

e) I'd like you to go to the shops for me.

....

f) We promise not to <u>make</u> too much noise.

....

g) Would you like me to <u>help</u> you with those bags?

....

h) We could <u>come</u> back later if you like.

....

i) I've decided to <u>have</u> a lemonade.

....

j) Can you <u>take</u> the dog for a walk?

....

4
Underline the
inappropriate
verb forms.
Rewrite them.
Not all the verb
forms are
inappropriate.

a) By the time the police get here, the burglars will have vanished. ....✓........
b) When you'll grow older, you'll change your mind about this. ....
c) The bus leaves at 1.00, so we'll leave the house at 11.30. ....
d) I won't leave until you will give me the money. ....
e) As soon as the taxi will arrive, I'll be letting you know. ....
f) Will you have been using the video next lesson? ....
g) By the time we get to Helen's house, she'll leave. ....
h) 'Do you want me to carry this?' 'No that's all right, I'm doing it.' ....
i) I'll be seeing Nick tomorrow, so I can give him the message. ....
j) By the time we'll arrive, the play will have started. ....

5
Complete the
second sentence
so that it has a
similar meaning
to the first
sentence.

a) The work won't take us longer than an hour.
    We ...*will have finished*................ the work in an hour.
b) I promise to phone you before our next meeting.
    Before we .... you.
c) Would you like me to check the spelling for you?
    Shall .... for you?
d) Sheila refuses to let me share her book.
    Sheila won't .... book.
e) How about having a game of chess?
    Shall .... a game of chess?
f) Please stay here until I come back.
    Please don't .... come back.
g) After the lesson we'll meet and play tennis.
    When .... we'll meet and play tennis.
h) What job will you have in twenty years' time?
    What will .... in twenty years' time?

Problems, Errors, Consolidation 1

1

Choose the correct word or phrase underlined in each sentence.

a) When I was a child (I used to ride)/I was riding a tricycle.
b) That looks very heavy. Will I/Shall I help you?
c) I'm waiting for Sue. Have you seen her/Did you see her?
d) How long are you working/have you been working here?
e) I can't come out because I haven't finished/I didn't finish my homework yet.
f) When the phone rang I washed/I was washing my hair in the bathroom.
g) Why do you stare/are you staring at me like that?
h) I've finished my exams so I'm having/I have a party tomorrow.
i) We'd better wait here until the rain stops/will stop.
j) When did you last go/have you last been to the cinema?

2

Put each verb given into present simple or continuous, or past simple or continuous.

a) 'What (you do) ...*do you do*... ?' 'I'm an engineer.'
b) The door was open so the dog (run) .... into the living room.
c) When we arrived home Jan (sit) .... outside the door.
d) Can you help me? I (not understand) .... Spanish.
e) At the beginning of the film I (realize) .... I'd seen it before.
f) I'm sorry, I can't talk long. I (study) ....for an examination.
g) At the moment of the earthquake Pat (read) .... in bed.
h) I'll get in touch with you as soon as I (know) .... the results.
i) I (stay) .... at the Hotel Superior. Why don't you call me?
j) 'What (you do) .... when you saw the snake?' 'I ran away!'

3

Put a suitable time word or expression in each space. Each space is for one word.

Just a quick note (a) ..*before*... I leave for the airport. Sorry I haven't been in touch (b) .... Wednesday, but I've been busy getting ready (c) .... , and I haven't collected my ticket (d) .... from the travel agency. (e) .... I get to Sydney, I'll write you a letter. I've (f) .... been to Australia before but I've been reading a lot about it (g) .... It sounds great! I'll be in Sydney (h) .... the end of next week, and then I'm travelling to Melbourne. I'll be there (i) .... a month. (j) .... I get back all my friends will have forgotten me!

4

Decide which answer, a), b), c) or d), best fits the space.

Helen's homecoming

When the bus (1) ..c. in a small square, Helen (2) ..... her magazine and didn't realize that she (3) ..... at her destination. 'This is Santa Teresa,' Martin said. '(4) ..... home! I suppose your cousin (5) ..... for us. Come on. (6) ..... the bags.' Helen thought, 'all those years when I (7) ..... in New York, I (8) ..... of this moment. And now it's real, I can't believe it! Here I am, (9) ..... in the square'. Santa Teresa was Helen's birthplace, but she (10) ..... the town at the age of six. She had some memories of the town, and some photographs, but (11) ..... here still? She (12) ...... Nobody (13) ..... in the square. Perhaps her cousin Maria (14) ..... Helen's letter. 'What (15) ..... now?' asked Martin. 'There isn't even a hotel here!'

1) a) has stopped   b) stops   c) stopped   d) was stopped
2) a) was reading   b) read   c) had read   d) used to read
3) a) arrived   b) arrives   c) has arrived   d) had arrived
4) a) You arrive   b) You are arriving   c) You have been arriving
   d) You've arrived
5) a) waits   b) will be waiting   c) has waited   d) is going to wait
6) a) I'll carry   b) I carry   c) I've carried   d) I carried
7) a) live   b) have lived   c) was living   d) am living
8) a) dream   b) am dreaming   c) used to dream   d) will dream
9) a) I really stand   b) I was really standing   c) I had really stood
   d) I'm really standing
10) a) was leaving   b) had left   c) used to leave   d) has left
11) a) will she belong   b) did she belong   c) has she belonged
    d) does she belong
12) a) wasn't knowing   b) hasn't known   c) hadn't known   d) didn't know
13) a) was waiting   b) is waiting   c) waits   d) waited
14) a) wasn't receiving   b) didn't use to receive   c) had not received
    d) hasn't received
15) a) are we going to do   b) have we done   c) did we do   d) are we doing

5

Complete the second sentence so that it has a similar meaning to the first sentence.

a) Steve left before my arrival.
   When I ...*arrived Steve had*............ already left.
b) Do you need any help with your suitcase?
   Shall .... you with your suitcase?
c) What's your usual time of arrival at school?
   When .... arrive at school?
d) Alice started playing tennis six months ago.
   Alice .... six months.
e) I'll wait here until it stops raining.
   When it stops raining .... leave.

f) In the middle of my meal, the phone rang.

While I .... the phone rang.

g) I'm sorry, but Mrs Dawson isn't here.

I'm sorry but Mrs Dawson has .... out.

h) Jack has come to stay for the weekend.

Jack .... with me for the weekend.

i) I last saw David in 1990.

I .... since 1990.

j) Are you free tomorrow evening?

Are .... anything tomorrow evening?

6

Look carefully at each line. Some lines are correct but some have a word which should not be there. Tick each correct line. If a line has a word which should not be there, write the word in the space.

Dear Ann,

I'm sorry I haven't been written to you lately, but I've   1) ..*been*..

been working hard. When I received your last letter   2) ..✓......

I was acting in a play at school, and when   3) ....

I have finished that, I went on holiday with some friends.   4) ....

I meant to send you a postcard, but I had forgot to take   5) ....

your address with me. How are you getting on at   6) ....

college? You didn't say very much about this in   7) ....

your letter. I hope you are still like it, and don't   8) ....

been work all the time! Do you still want to come   9) ....

and will stay for a few days? I'm starting work in   10) ....

London after I shall leave school in July, and I want   11) ....

to see you before then. I have know you are busy,   12) ....

but by the time your term finishes, I'll have   13) ....

started my job. I've been done so many things   14) ....

lately! I've just learned to drive and my parents   15) ....

have sometimes lend me their car, so I often go out   16) ....

with friends. Maybe I'll be drive to Nottingham and   17) ....

see you one day.

Best wishes, Maria

7

Underline the error in each sentence. Correct the error.

a) By the time I got to the phone it <u>stopped</u> ringing.

...*it had stopped*..

b) I'm not very good at this game. You see, I didn't play it before.

....

c) When has Peter written to you last?

....

d) What do you do at weekends? Are you ever going to the cinema?

....

e) When I was on holiday last summer I was going to the beach every day.

....

f) Julie can't meet you tomorrow. She will play basketball.

....

g) You're always late! I'm waiting here for ages!

....

h) How long do you live in this flat? It's very tiny!

....

8

In everyday spoken English, we often leave out the subject pronoun and auxiliary. Instead of saying, *'Do you like it?'* we say, *'Like it?'* Rewrite each sentence so that the verb underlined has a subject pronoun.

a) <u>Finished</u> yet? We're all waiting!
   ...Have you finished yet?...

b) Bye for now! <u>See</u> you tomorrow!

....

c) Good holiday? <u>Had</u> a nice time?

....

d) Paul's a bit difficult. <u>Know</u> what I mean?

....

e) Hi, Tim. <u>Coming</u> out for a drink later?

....

f) <u>Been waiting</u> long? Sorry for the delay.

....

g) Good party, isn't it! <u>Enjoying</u> yourself?

....

h) <u>Heard</u> the latest? Mary's getting married!

....

Problem check

1 Check the difference between present simple and present continuous. How can you show this difference in your language?

2 Does your language have a tense with the same form as present perfect simple? Is it used in the same way? Can you show the difference in your language between present perfect simple and past simple?

3 Do you have a future tense in your language? Does it express all the meanings of *will*, *going to* and future use of present continuous?

Unit 10 Reported speech 1

Explanations

Reported speech

We often tell people what other people have told us. This is called reported or indirect speech. We usually change tenses and references to people, places and times.

Without tense changes

Statements are often repeated immediately, and the reporting verb is in a present tense. In this case, there are no tense changes.

> *'Jack is on the phone. He says **he's going** to the cinema, and do we want to go too?'*

Tense changes after a past tense reporting verb

Statements are usually reported with a past tense verb and an optional *that*. All tenses that follow move back into the past. This is sometimes called backshift.

- Present simple to past simple

  *'I **need** some help.'*
  *She said (that) **she needed** some help.*

- Present continuous to past continuous

  *'**We are having** our lunch.'*
  *She said that **they were having** their lunch.*

- Present perfect to past perfect

  *'**I have lost** my keys.'*
  *He said (that) **he had lost** his keys.*

- *will* to *would*

  *'**I will be** home at 6.00.'*
  *She said that **she would be** home at 6.00.*

- Past simple to past perfect

  *'**I wrote** two letters to her.'*
  *He said (that) **he had written** two letters to her.*

- *be going to*, to *was/ were going to*

  *'**They are going to** come back.'*
  *She said (that) **they were going to** come back.*

- *must*

  *'I **must finish** this before I **go**.'*
  *He said he **must finish** it before he **went**.*
  Note that *must* does not change.
  *He said he **had to finish** it before he **went**.*

- Note that sentences in direct speech have speech marks (inverted commas) around the spoken words. Indirect or reported speech does not use speech marks.

- Note that past perfect in reported speech can be a report of either past simple or present perfect.

  *'**I've lost** my keys!' said Joe.*   *Joe said **he had lost** his keys.*
  *'**I lost** them yesterday,' he said.*   *He said **he had lost** them the day before.*

No changes after a past tense reporting verb	If the report is about something which is always true, it may not be necessary to backshift.

> *'I like apples more than I like oranges.'*
> *She said that she **likes** apples more than she **likes** oranges.*
> *'Budapest is the capital of Hungary'.*
> *He said that Budapest **is** the capital of Hungary.*

Some speakers prefer to backshift in sentences of this kind.

Speakers in reported speech	• Speakers can be mentioned at the beginning or end of the sentence in direct speech.

Direct speech
> *Jack said, 'We're going to miss the train.'*
> *'We're going to miss the train,' said Jack.*

• Speakers are mentioned at the beginning of the sentence in reported speech.

Reported speech
> *Jack said (that) they were going to miss the train.*

Other changes	In reported speech, references to people, places and times often change, because the point of view changes.

> *'I'll see you here tomorrow,' said Sue.*
> *Sue said she would see **me there the next day**.*
> *'I bought this book yesterday,' said Martin.*
> *Martin said he had bought **the book the day before**.*

Summarizing instead of verbatim reports	• Sometimes each word is reported (verbatim reporting), but we often summarize what people say when we make reports.

> *'Look, actually, tell him I'll give him a call next week, OK?'*
> *She said **she'd call you** next week.*

• See Unit 11 for ways of reporting some kinds of statement.

Verbs easily confused: *say*, *tell*, *speak*	*Speak* describes the act of talking.

> *Simon **spoke** to me in the supermarket yesterday.*

Say describes the words used. It is followed by optional *that*.
> *'It's warm today,' she said.*
> *She **said (that)** it was warm.*

Tell describes giving information It needs an object. It is followed by optional *that*.
> *'You've won first prize,' she said.*
> *She told **me (that)** I had won first prize.*

Practice

1

Underline the errors in these sentences. Rewrite each sentence.

a) Sally <u>told</u> that she had lost her keys.

...*Sally said that she had lost her keys.*...

b) Chris said me that he must leave early.

....

c) Maria and Tony said they shall see us tomorrow.

....

d) Tom said, I'm coming to your party.

....

e) Sue said that she had wrote a letter to Lisa.

....

f) Steve said us that he was arriving at 8.00.

....

g) 'I had bought a new bike Pam told us.'

....

h) 'What's the matter? Ellen told.

....

i) Jim says that he had needed some help.

....

j) Joe said that he doesn't feel well yesterday.

....

2

Rewrite each sentence in direct speech, ending as shown.

a) Anna told us that she had finished.

'...*I've finished*.............................,' Anna told us.

b) George said that he would be back at 6.00.

'....................................,' George said.

c) Helen said she was going to go shopping.

'....................................,' said Helen.

d) Paul said that he wanted to make a phone call.

'....................................,' said Paul.

e) Tina told the teacher she had forgotten her homework.

'....................................,' Tina told the teacher.

f) David said he had to be back by 3.30.

'....................................,' David said.

g) Jan told me she would let me know.

'....................................,' Jan told me.

h) Bill said he was going to be late.

'....................................,' Bill said.

43

3

Match each sentence in direct speech with its summarized version in reported speech.

a) 'Look, sorry about this, but I'm afraid I'm going to be a bit late.' ..3.

b) 'Actually I've no idea at all where I am!' .....

c) 'The thing is, I know it's silly but I've missed the bus.' .....

d) 'Anyway, I'll be back in next to no time.' .....

e) 'I did ring, you know, earlier in the evening. .....

1) She said she would be back soon.

2) She said she had missed the bus.

3) She said she was going to be late.

4) She said she had already rung.

5) She said she didn't know where she was.

4

Complete each sentence, using *say*, *tell* or *speak* in an appropriate form.

a) Jim ...*told*.......... me that he was playing in the school basketball team.

b) I .... to Helen, and she .... she would phone you.

c) 'You're lucky,' .... Steve. 'I .... you that you would win!'

d) A translator .... the President what everyone was ....

e) 'Look,' I .... her, 'why don't you .... me what you mean?'

f) I .... my teacher that I .... Chinese, but she didn't believe me.

g) 'Please don't .... anything during the test,' our teacher .... us.

h) I .... my friends about my party, and they .... they would come.

5

Rewrite each sentence in reported speech, beginning as shown.

a) 'I won't be there because I'm having a party,'said Helen.

Helen told us that she ..*wouldn't be there because she was having a party*............... .

b) 'I've lost the map and I don't know the way,' said Jack.

Jack told me that he ....

....

c) 'When I finish the book, I'm going to watch television,' said Carol.

Carol said that when ....

....

d) 'I'm doing some homework but I won't be long,' said Mike.

Mike said that he ....

e) 'I like swimming but I don't go very often,' said Mary.

Mary told us that she ....

f) 'I got up late and I missed the bus,' said Richard.

Richard said that he ....

g) 'I'm going to visit friends in Fiji but I'm not sure when,' said Jill.

Jill told us that she ....

....

h) 'I want to buy it, but I haven't brought any money,' said Tony.

Tony said that he ....

....

Unit 11 Reported speech 2

Explanations

Commands and requests

- Commands are reported with *tell* and the infinitive.
    'Wait! Wait!'   I **told** him to stop.
    Requests are reported with *ask* and the infinitive.
    'Please wait!'   I **asked** her to wait.

yes/no questions

- Questions with the answer *yes* or *no* are reported with backshift (see Unit 10) and using *if*.
    'Does the London train stop here?' she asked.
    *She asked me **if** the London train **stopped** here.*

- Note that the question form of the direct speech is not used in reported speech, as there is no longer a direct question. There is no question mark.

whether

Whether means *if … or not.* We use *whether* when we report questions linked with *or.* The question is reported with backshift.
    'Are you staying the night, or are you going home?' he asked.
    *He asked me **whether I was staying** the night or going home.*

Wh- questions

Questions beginning *when, what, why, where, how,* etc. are reported with backshift (see Unit 10). The question forms of direct speech are not used, so the subject in bold comes before the verb. There is no question mark.
    'Where is the bus-station?' she asked.
    *She asked where **the bus-station** was.*
    'Where have you come from?' he asked.
    *He asked me where **I** had come from.*

Indirect questions

- Indirect or embedded questions are questions which have an introductory question before them. The indirect question does not have a question form. Note that there is no change of tenses (backshift).
    Introductory question: *Could you tell me … ?   Do you know … ?*

- *Wh-* questions
    Where is the post office?
    *Could you tell me **where** the post office is?*
    When does the film start?
    *Do you know **when** the film starts?*

- *Yes/no* questions
  These questions use *if*.
  > *Is this the right street?*
  > *Do you know **if** this is the right street?*

- There is a question mark, because of the introductory question.

Reporting verbs

Reporting verbs include part of the meaning of the words reported. Here are some of the most common reporting verbs.

advise	*'I wouldn't buy that car, Janos, if I were you.'*
	*I **advised** Janos not to buy the car.*
agree	*'Yes, Jill, I think you're right,' said Mike.*
	*Mike **agreed** with Jill.*
apologize	*'I'm really sorry for being so late,' said Maria.*
	*Maria **apologized** for being late.*
ask	*'Do you think you could help me, Sue?'*
	*I **asked** Sue to help me.*
congratulate	*'Well done, Tina, you've passed the exam!'*
	*I **congratulated** Tina on passing her exam.*
decide	There are two types of decision.
	'I'm going to become a doctor!' said Helen.
	This is a decision about the future, or a plan.
	*Helen **decided** to become a doctor.*
	'I'll have the fish pie, please,' said Bill.
	This is a decision of the moment.
	*Bill **decided** to have the fish pie.*
invite	*'Would you like to come to the cinema on Saturday, Pam?'*
	*I **invited** Pam to the cinema on Saturday.*
offer	*'Shall I carry your case, Dawn?' said Peter.*
	*Peter **offered** to carry Dawn's case.*
promise	*'I'll definitely be home by eight,' said Ann.*
	*Ann **promised** to be home by eight.*
	'I'll wait for you, Helen,' said Peter.
	*Peter **promised** Helen that he would wait for her.*
refuse	*'No, I won't open the door!' said Carol.*
	*Carol **refused** to open the door.*
remind	*'Don't forget to send your mother a birthday card, Joe.'*
	*I **reminded** Joe to send his mother a birthday card.*
suggest	*'How about spending the day at the beach?' said Carlos.*
	*Carlos **suggested** spending the day at the beach.*

Practice

1

Put **one** suitable word in each space.

a) Helen asked me ...*whether*.... I ...*was*......... going to school or not.

b) David asked his mother .... she .... be coming home.

c) Peter asked us .... we .... ever been to Hungary.

d) Costas asked me .... I .... many photographs.

e) Maria asked a policeman .... the museum was.

f) Dora asked her sister .... she .... fed their dog.

2

Complete each question in direct speech, ending as shown.

a) Jack asked me whether I was having lunch or going out.

'..*Are you having lunch or going out*................. ?' Jack asked me.

b) Carol asked Ann what she had done the day before.

'.. , Ann?' asked Carol.

c) John asked us if we often went sailing.

'.. ?' John asked us.

d) Kate asked me how many German books I had read.

'.. ?' Kate asked me.

e) George asked Sue if she was going to change schools.

'.. , Sue?' asked George.

f) Alice asked me who I sat next to in class.

'.. ?' Alice asked me.

g) My teacher asked me if I would be there the next day.

'.. ?' my teacher asked me.

h) Mary asked me where exactly I lived.

'.. exactly?' Mary asked me.

3

Rewrite each sentence in reported speech, beginning as shown.

a) 'Are you staying here all summer?' the little girl asked me.

The little girl asked me ...*if/whether I was staying there all summer*...................... .

b) 'What does 'procrastinate' mean?' I asked my teacher.

I asked my teacher ....

c) 'Have you done your homework, or not?' my mother asked me.

My mother asked me ....

d) 'When is your birthday?' I asked Sue.

I asked Sue ....

e) 'Did you remember to lock the door,' my father asked me.

My father asked me ....

f) 'Why have you turned off the television?' Ellen asked me.

Ellen asked me ....

g) 'Do you speak Italian?' the tourist guide asked me.

The tourist guide asked me ....

h) 'How much did you pay for your bike?' I asked Steve.

I asked Steve ....

4

Rewrite each question, beginning as shown.

a) What's the time?

Could you tell me ..*what the time is*................... ?

b) What does this mean?

Do you know .... ?

c) How much does this cost?

Could you tell me .... ?

d) What time does the museum open?

Do you know .... ?

e) Am I in the right seat?

Could you tell me .... ?

f) Where's Asham Street?

Do you know .... ?

g) Is this Trafalgar Square?

Could you tell me .... ?

h) When does this bus leave?

Do you know .... ?

5

Rewrite each sentence in reported speech, beginning as shown. Use a verb from the list.

| advised apologized congratulated invited |
| offered promised refused suggested |

a) 'I'll definitely be at your house before 8.00, Sue,' said Mike.

Mike ..*promised*.. Sue that ..*he would definitely be at her house before 8.00*................

b) 'Would you like to come to the cinema, Jean?' asked Chris.

Chris ....

c) 'I wouldn't eat too much if I were you, Dave,' said Patsy.

Patsy ....

d) 'How about going for a walk?' said George.

George ....

e) 'I'm terribly sorry for breaking the window,' said Carol.

Carol ....

f) 'Shall I do the washing-up?' said Bill.

Bill ....

g) 'Well done, you've passed your driving test,' said Tina's mother.

Tina's mother .... her ....

h) 'No, I won't go to the dentist's!' said Pat.

Pat ....

Unit 12 Conditionals: 1 and 2

Explanations

if + present simple + present simple	This type of sentence describes what always happens. *When* or *if* can introduce the sentence.
	*It's a tropical country, and so **if it rains** hard, everyone stays indoors.*
	***When it rains hard**, everyone stays indoors.*
if + imperative	This type of sentence tells people what to do in certain situations.
	***If you feel** dizzy, **stop** taking the tablets.*
	***If you change** your mind, **give** me a ring.*

Conditional 1: *if* + present simple + *will/won't*

- This type of sentence is sometimes called a real condition. It describes what someone thinks will happen in a real situation. We use real here to show the difference with the imaginary situation in Conditional 2. You believe that the things you are talking about will happen.

    *If **we walk** so slowly, **we'll be** late.*
    *If we **run**, we **won't be** late.*
    *If we **don't run**, we **will be** late.*

- Situation: You are at the supermarket with a friend. Your friend has put some eggs in one bag, and is trying to pick up lots of other bags too. You say:

    *If you **carry** too many bags, **you'll drop** the eggs.*
    *If you **drop** the eggs, **they'll break**.*
    *If the eggs **break, there will be** an awful mess on the floor!*
    *If you **are** careful, you **won't break** them.*

- It is possible to use other present tenses instead of present simple in this type of sentence.

present continuous	***If you're driving**, I'll come with you.*
present perfect	***If I've seen** the film before, I'll let you know!*

Conditional 2: *if* + past simple + *would/wouldn't*

- This type of sentence is sometimes called an imaginary condition. It refers to things that might happen in the future, or things that you can imagine happening.

    *If I **had** a helicopter, **I'd fly** to school.*
    *If I **flew** to school, I **wouldn't be** late.*

- Situation: You are watching the stars one night with a friend. You start talking about aliens. You say:

    ***If some aliens landed** on earth, **I'd make friends** with them.*
    ***If they didn't speak** English, **I'd use** sign language.*
    ***If they took** me back to their planet, **I'd learn** their language.*
    ***If anyone believed** my story, **I'd become** famous!*

- The form of the past simple is used in this type of sentence, but it does not refer to past time. See Unit 13 for Conditional 3, which refers to past time.

- We usually use *were* for all persons in Conditional 2 *if* sentences. In speech, *was* and *were* are used.
  ***If I were** an astronaut, I'd enjoy being weightless!*

- Note that *would* is usually contracted in speech.
  I'd become famous.   *I **would** become famous.*

unless   *Unless* means *only if not*. We use it to say that something will only happen in certain circumstances. Compare these sentences.
  *We'll go out for a walk **if it doesn't rain**.*
  *We'll go out for a walk **unless it rains**.*

Other uses of *would*   We also use *would* in situations which do not involve conditional sentences.

Politeness	***Would you take** a seat?*
Request	***Would you open** the window?*
Offering	***Would you like** a pot of tea?*
Refusing	*The clerk **wouldn't sell** me a student ticket.*

Practice

1
Choose the correct word or phrase underlined in each pair.

a) If (we're)/we would be late for class, our teacher (will be)/was angry.

b) If we <u>lived/would live</u> on another planet, <u>we'd see/we will see</u> the Earth in the sky.

c) If we <u>take/will take</u> a taxi, <u>we'll arrive/we arrived</u> sooner.

d) If we <u>don't hurry/won't hurry</u>, <u>we'll be/we would be</u> late.

e) If we <u>were/are</u> birds, we <u>would be able to/are able to</u> fly.

f) If you <u>don't wear/wouldn't wear</u> your pullover, <u>you'll feel/you felt</u> cold.

g) If I <u>studied/will study</u> harder, I <u>would get/get</u> better marks.

h) If I <u>had/have</u> a motorbike, <u>I'd ride/I rode</u> it to school.

i) If you <u>lend/will lend</u> me your bike, <u>I'll let/I let</u> you borrow my skateboard.

j) If I <u>had/would have</u> lots of money, <u>I'd give/I gave</u> some to all my friends.

2

Complete the sentence for each situation, using the verbs given.

a) You are standing very close to the edge of a swimming-pool. You are wearing all your clothes, not a swimming costume. A friend says:
If you (fall in) ...*fall in*........ , your clothes (get) ...*will get*...... wet!

b) You are sitting in the classroom on a hot day. You are day-dreaming about going to the beach. You think:
If today (be) .... a holiday, I (go) .... to the beach.

c) You can't answer a question in your English book. You ask a friend to help, but she doesn't know the answer. She says:
If I (know) .... the answer, I (tell) .... you.

d) You are walking towards the bus-stop with a friend. Suddenly the bus arrives. The bus-stop is far away, but you think there is a chance of catching the bus. You say:
If we (run) .... , we (catch) .... it!

e) You are planning to go to the beach tomorrow with some friends. You are not sure about the weather, because it sometimes rains at this time of the year. You arrange to meet tomorrow afternoon and say:
If it (rain) .... , we (go) .... to the cinema instead.

f) You are very busy, because you have lots of school work, and you also play in two teams. A friend ask you to join a computer club. You say:
If I (have) .... more free time, I (join) .... the club.
But it's impossible at the moment because I'm too busy!

g) You are discussing the idea of underwater cities. People are describing the advantages and disadvantages of living under the sea. You say:
If we (live) .... under the sea, we (eat) .... fish all the time!

h) You are worried about a test next week. You ask your teacher for some advice. She says:
If you (study) .... for one hour every day, you (pass) .... the test.

3

Complete each sentence, using *if*, *unless* or *would*.

a) If you had asked me to help you, I ...*would*.... .
b) We'll have lunch outside in the garden, ... it's too cold.
c) John .... win more races if he trained harder.
d) Come on! .... we hurry, we'll miss the plane!
e) .... you like to see my stamp collection?
f) The manager won't be long. .... you take a seat, please.
g) I'm sure that Carol .... go to the cinema with you, if you asked her.
h) .... you feel like a chat, phone me tonight.
i) What .... you do if you saw a snake?
j) I don't feel happy .... I swim every day.

4
Complete each sentence a) to j) with an ending from 1) to 10).

a) If you play the music too loud, ..*8*.
b) If the North Pole melted, ...
c) If we don't have enough ice-cream, ...
d) If I found someone's wallet, ...
e) If a burglar broke into this house, ...
f) If my train isn't late, ...
g) If you were famous, ...
h) If my father lends me the money, ...
i) If you took more exercise, ...
j) If you tell me what you want, ...

1) the alarm would go off.
2) I'll buy a new bike.
3) I'll be in Paris at 6.00.
4) you wouldn't see me any more!
5) you would feel better.
6) the water would flood many cities.
7) I'll buy it for you.
8) you'll wake up the neighbours.
9) we'll get some more.
10) I'd take it to the police station.

5
Complete each sentence as either a Conditional 1 or a Conditional 2 sentence using the verb given.

a) If I (have) ...*had*....... arms five metres long, I (be able) ....*would be able*..... to reach the top of that shelf!

b) Don't worry, you've just got a cold. If you (take) .... an aspirin, you (feel) .... better.

c) Vegetarians believe that if nobody (eat) .... meat, everyone (live) .... longer.

d) If I (become) .... a famous rock star, I (buy) .... my parents an enormous house.

e) It says 'No Parking'. If you (leave) .... the car here, the police (give) .... you a parking fine.

f) It's not far. If you (follow) .... this path, you (come) .... to the station.

g) If people in cities (use) .... bikes instead of cars, there (not be) .... so much pollution.

h) Actually it's a very friendly dog. If you (touch) .... it, it (not bite) .... you.

i) If you (leave) .... your books on the desk, I (give) .... them back to you at the end of the lesson.

j) If you (own) .... a pet tiger, your friends (not visit) .... you!

Unit 13 Conditionals: 2 and 3

Explanations

Conditional sentences without *if*

Conditional sentences usually begin with *if*. However, in everyday speech, we often use *imagine* or *supposing*.

>**Imagine you saw** a snake, what would you do?
>**Supposing you owned** a helicopter, what would you use it for?

If I were you

We can give advice by using a Conditional 2 sentence beginning *If I were you*.

>**If I were you**, I'd spend more time on your written work.
>**If I were you**, I wouldn't eat so much chocolate!

It is also possible to put the *if*-clause at the end.

>I'd be more careful, **if I were you**.

Conditional 3: *if* + past perfect + *would have*

- This type of sentence is sometimes called an Impossible Condition. It refers to things in the past, and it is impossible to change things that happened in the past.

- Situation: You went for a long walk, but you did not take your umbrella. It rained, and you got wet.

>**If I had taken** my umbrella, **I wouldn't have** got wet.
>**If I'd heard** the weather forecast, **I wouldn't have** gone out.

Modals in conditional sentences

- We often use *might* and *could* in conditional sentences. We use *might* or *could* when we are not certain about the results. We also use *could* to describe ability. We use *could have (done)* or *might have (done)* in Conditional 3 sentences.

Conditional 1	*If you **carry** too many bags, **you might drop** the eggs.*
	(uncertain)
Conditional 2	*If anyone **believed** my story, I **could become** famous!*
	(uncertain)
Conditional 3	*If I **had taken** some money with me, I **could have taken** a taxi.*
	(ability)

- See Units 17 and 18 for more information about modal auxiliaries.

Practice

1

Rewrite each comment, beginning as shown.

a) Supposing you had wings, what would you do?
   What ...*would you do if you had wings?*......................................

b) Why don't you leave now? That's what I'd do.
   If ....

c) Imagine you lived on Mars. How would you feel?
   How ....

d) I think you should buy a bike. That's what I'd do.
   If ....

e) Imagine you were rich. What would you do?
   What ....

f) Supposing Jim came with us, what would you say?
   What ....

g) Why don't you take the bus. That's what I'd do.
   If ....

h) Imagine you owned a robot. What would you do?
   What ....

2

Choose the correct word or phrase underlined in each sentence.

a) If you phoned/had phoned me yesterday, I had given/would have given you the news.

b) If you took/would have taken more exercise, you might feel/had felt better.

c) If Tim drove/had driven more carefully, he wouldn't have crashed/didn't crash.

d) If you had come/came to see the film, you would have enjoyed/had enjoyed it.

e) If I'd known/I would know it was your birthday, I would send/would have sent you a card.

f) If people helped/had helped one another more often, the world might be/was a better place.

g) If our team had scored/scored more goals, it had won/could have won.

h) If you would have worn/wore a coat, you wouldn't get/didn't get wet.

3

Complete the
sentence for each
situation.

a) Helen didn't leave early, and so she missed the bus.
    If Helen ...*had left early*...., she ...*wouldn't have missed*.......... the bus.

b) I didn't buy more milk, so I didn't have enough for breakfast.
    If I .... , I .... enough for
    breakfast.

c) We forgot to take a map, so we got lost in the mountains.
    If we .... , we .... in the mountains.

d) I didn't go to bed early, so I didn't wake up at 7.00.
    If I .... early, I .... at 7.00.

e) Mike didn't make a shopping list, and he forgot to buy some coffee.
    If Mike .... , he .... some coffee.

f) I didn't realize you were tired when I asked you to go for a walk.
    If I .... , I .... for a walk.

g) The Romans didn't sail across the Atlantic, so they didn't reach America.
    If the Romans .... , they ....
    America.

h) I didn't turn left at the station, and I lost my way.
    If I .... , I .... my way.

Unit 14 Wishes

Explanations

Wishes about the present

- This kind of sentence is similar to a Conditional 2 sentence.

  I wish I owned a helicopter. If I owned a helicopter, I would be happy.
  I wish I didn't have to go to school! If I didn't go to school, I would be happy.

- As in Conditional 2 sentences, the past simple form does not refer to past time.

Wishes about the past

This kind of sentence is similar to a Conditional 3 sentence.

  I wish I had lived in the eighteenth century! If I had lived in the eighteenth century, I would have been happy.
  I wish I hadn't eaten so much! I feel awful! If I had not eaten so much, it would have been better for me!

Wishes with *could*

This kind of wish is about a change you would like to make.

  I wish I could fly!
  I wish I could stay at home tomorrow.

hope

When we make wishes about the future, we use *hope*. We do not use conditional sentence rules with *hope*. It is followed by present simple or *will*.

  I hope the weather will be fine tomorrow.
  I hope you have a good time at the party.

If only

We can replace *I wish* with *If only* for emphasis. We usually stress *only* in speech.

  If only I owned a helicopter.
  If only I hadn't eaten so much!

Practice

1
Choose the correct word or phrase underlined in each sentence.

a) I am sunburnt. I wish I hadn't sunbathed/didn't sunbathe for so long.

b) I don't feel well. I wish I could stay/stayed at home tomorrow.

c) I'm not a good swimmer, but I wish I could swim/would swim well.

d) I wish I had/have a puppy or a kitten!

e) I wish I could see/saw you tomorrow, but it's impossible.

f) I wish Jim didn't sit/doesn't sit next to me. He's so annoying!

g) If only we had/would have some money we could take the bus.

h) I hope you enjoyed/enjoy yourselves at the dance tomorrow.

56

2
Choose the correct continuation for each sentence.

a) I've got lots of work to do, and I'm tired, but I can't stop. ..2..
   1) I wish I had taken a rest.   2) I wish I could take a rest.

b) I wasn't paying attention in class, and now I can't do my homework. .....
   1) I wish I listened to my teacher.   2) I wish I'd listened to my teacher.

c) Sarah painted her room green, but she doesn't like it. .....
   1) She wishes she'd painted it blue.   2) She wishes she painted it blue.

d) This is a very puzzling problem! .....
   1) I wish I'd known the answer.   2) I wish I knew the answer.

e) It's really cold and miserable here in the winter. .....
   1) I wish we lived in a warm place.   2) I hope we live in a warm place.

f) I can't repair my bike because I haven't got any tools. .....
   1) If only I would have a screwdriver.   2) If only I had a screwdriver.

g) I'm worried about my basketball team. Perhaps they won't win! .....
   1) I wish they play well.   2) I hope they play well.

h) You promised not to tell anyone my secrets but you did! .....
   1) I wish I hadn't told you.   2) I wish I didn't tell you.

3
Complete each sentence with a suitable form of the verb given.

a) I'm soaked to the skin! If only I (bring) ...*had brought*........... an umbrella!

b) This pullover was really cheap. I wish I (buy) .... two of them!

c) I like your school. I wish I (go) .... there too.

d) I must get in touch with Sue. If only I (know) .... her phone number!

e) This bus is really slow! I wish we (take) .... the train instead.

f) I'm disappointed in this camera. I wish I (not buy) .... it.

g) I answered three questions well. If only I (finish) .... the whole test!

h) I can't understand anything Marie says! I wish I (speak) .... French.

4
Complete each sentence in a suitable way.

a) I'm hungry. If only ...*I had a sandwich*.......... in my pocket.

b) Enjoy your holiday. I hope .... time.

c) This is a lovely place. I wish we .... before.

d) It's a pity you live so far away. If only you .... in my street!

e) Ellen is a fantastic dancer. I wish I .... as well as her!

57

Unit 15 Passive 1

Explanations

Transitive and intransitive

- Verbs which have objects are called transitive verbs. In this sentence, *milk* is the object.

  *Diane **drinks milk** every morning.*

- Verbs which do not have objects are called intransitive verbs.

  *Diane **walks** to college.*

- Only transitive verbs can be made passive.

Passive: formation rules

The passive is formed with the verb *be* and the past participle. The object of the verb becomes the subject in a passive sentence.

- Present simple | *We build hundreds of houses every year.*
  Passive | *Hundreds of houses **are built** every year.*

- Past simple | *The police arrested one protester.*
  Passive | *One protester **was arrested**.*

- *will* | *They will play the match on Wednesday evening.*
  Passive | *The match **will be played** on Wednesday evening.*

- Present perfect | *We have chosen Helen as the new president.*
  Passive | *Helen **has been chosen** as the new president.*

- Present continuous | *The authorities are questioning two men.*
  Passive | *Two men **are being questioned** by the authorities.*

Contexts of use

- Putting emphasis on important information.

  ***Hundreds of houses** are built every year by the Government.*

  In this sentence, it is what was done, the number of houses built, which is given emphasis. Emphasized information usually comes at the beginning of the sentence. Compare:

  ***The Government** has built hundreds of houses this year.*

  In this sentence, more emphasis is given to who did it, the Government.

- Spoken and written

  Passive tends to be used more in writing, and in formal speech.

With the agent *by*

Passive sentences often include information about who did it. This person, thing, organization, etc. is called the agent.

*Stones were thrown **by angry football fans**.*

| With the instrument *with* | Passive sentences may include information about what was used to perform an action. This is called the instrument and is introduced using *with*. |

*The windows were broken **with a baseball bat**.*

Without the agent

- It is not always necessary to mention the agent. There are several reasons for this. The passive is often used because who did it is not known or the speaker does not want us to know, it is obvious, or remains impersonal, perhaps because an authority is involved.

- Not known
  *Brenda's motorbike **was stolen** last night.*
  If we knew who had stolen it, we would mention the name of the person. It is not necessary to add by someone.

- Obvious
  *One protester **was arrested**.*
  It is not necessary to add by the police, because we know that it is always the police who do this. However, some people prefer to include this information.

- Impersonal
  Sometimes a group of people is responsible for an action, and who did it is not mentioned.
  *All school outings **have been cancelled**.*
  We assume that the school authorities have made this decision.

Practice

1
Underline phrases which are not necessary in these sentences. Not all sentences contain unnecessary phrases.

a) My wallet has been stolen <u>by someone</u>.
b) We were taught by a different teacher yesterday.
c) Nick was operated on at the hospital by a doctor.
d) The meal was served by a waiter in a red coat.
e) We were shown round the museum by a guide.
f) Two letters were delivered this morning by the postman.
g) Three men have been arrested by the police.
h) Yesterday a window was broken by someone.

2
Complete each sentence with a passive verb.

a) The police questioned George.
George ...*was questioned*............ by the police.

b) Millions of people watch this programme.
This programme .... by millions of people.

c) They will finish our new house at the end of the month.
Our new house .... at the end of the month.

d) They have elected a new president.
A new president ....

e) They are rebuilding the damaged stadium.
The damaged stadium ....

f) They have closed the mountain road.
The mountain road ....

g) Students write most of this magazine.
Most of this magazine .... by students.

h) A burglar stole my television.
My television .... by a burglar.

i) Somebody will meet you at the bus-station.
You .... at the bus-station

j) United won the cup last year.
Last year the cup .... by United.

3
Underline the errors in these sentences. Rewrite each sentence.

a) Many pet dogs <u>are losing</u> every year.
...*Many pet dogs are lost every year.*...............................

b) The ill man was been taken to hospital.
....

c) A new bridge is be built across the river.
....

d) All the food at the party was ate.
....

e) Nothing will being decided before next Saturday.
....

f) The match is playing on Friday evening.
....

g) The robber unlocked the door by a false key.
....

h) This book was writing by Sam's father.
....

4

Rewrite each sentence beginning with the words given.

a) Archaeologists have discovered a new tomb in the Valley of the Kings.
A new tomb *...has been discovered by archaeologists in the Valley of the Kings...........* .

b) The President will open the new sports stadium on Saturday.
The new sports stadium ....
....

c) One of the most famous painters in the world painted this portrait.
This portrait ....
....

d) They will announce the results of the competition tomorrow.
The results ....

e) They are redecorating our school during the summer holidays.
Our school ....

f) The police in New York have arrested three terrorists.
Three terrorists ....

g) Our company sells more than a thousand cars every week.
More than a thousand cars ....

h) They are building a new museum in the city centre.
A new museum ....

i) Alexander Fleming discovered penicillin in 1928.
Penicillin ....

j) Two million people use the London Underground system every day
The London Underground system ....
....

5

Rewrite each sentence with a passive verb, and so that the names of people are not mentioned.

a) The authorities have closed the casino.
...The casino has been closed...

b) Someone broke into the flat last week.
....

c) People all over the world speak English.
....

d) The authorities have opened the new swimming-pool.
....

e) Someone left this purse in the classroom yesterday.
....

f) The city council has banned traffic from the city centre.
....

g) People have elected a new government.
....

h) The clubs have postponed the match.
....

Unit 16 Passive 2

Explanations

Verbs with two objects

Some verbs can have two objects. These verbs include:
buy, give, lend, offer, promise, sell, take, promise, send.
> Peter gave **Karen a present**.
> Peter gave **a present to Karen**.
Sentences with these verbs can be made passive in two ways.
> **Karen was given a present** by Peter.
> **A present was given to Karen** by Peter.

Problems with passive

- *To be born* is a passive form but does not have an obvious passive meaning.
  > I **was born** in Uruguay.

- Some verbs may have a passive form in other languages, but are not translated into passive in English.

have something done

- When a professional person, e.g. a mechanic, a plumber etc. does some work for us, we can use *have something done. Have* can be used in any tense.
  > We **had our house painted** last year.
  > I'm **having my car serviced** tomorrow.
  > I've **had my room decorated**.

- We also use this for unpleasant happenings.
  > She **had her house broken into**.
  > Tim **had his arm broken** playing rugby.

Practice

1
Choose the correct word or phrase underlined in each sentence.

a) I'm having my hair cutting/cut/to have cut tomorrow.
b) The children were took/taken/taking to the seaside for the day.
c) I was sending/sent/send here by the manager.
d) Kate is having her car services/servicing/serviced tomorrow.
e) Sue had her windows breaking/broken/broke by vandals.
f) David has been offer/offering/offered a new job in Brazil.
g) Where exactly were you born/did you born/did you bear?
h) I've just had my bike repaired/repair/repairing.

2

Rewrite each sentence beginning and ending as shown.

a) Someone stole Bob's bike.

Bob ...*had his*.. bike stolen.

b) John lent me this book.

This book .... John.

c) The dentist took out one of my teeth yesterday.

Yesterday I .... out.

d) Cairo is my place of birth.

I .... in Cairo.

e) A rock concert ticket was sold to me by a friend.

I was .... by a friend.

f) Someone broke into Tom's house last week.

Tom had .... last week.

g) When is your date of birth?

When exactly .... born?

h) My parents gave me this ring.

I .... parents.

3

Rewrite each sentence so that it has a similar meaning and contains the word given.

a) They are servicing my car tomorrow.

having

...*I am having my car serviced tomorrow.*..

b) Yesterday they stole my bike.

had

....

c) Last year they painted our house.

had

....

d) They are taking out my tooth tomorrow!

having

....

e) They have just cut my hair.

had

....

f) They are fitting our new carpet tomorrow.

having

....

g) They have just painted Ann's portrait.

had

....

Unit 17 Modals 1: present and future

Explanations

Problems with form and meaning

- Modal auxiliaries do not have third person *s*, and use inversion in questions not *do/does*. They do not form tenses.

- The meaning of modal auxiliaries depends on the context. One modal can have several meanings depending on their function, or purpose.

Ability

- *can, can't, cannot*
  *I **can** swim.   **Can you** swim?*
  Cannot is generally used in writing or more formal speech.

- Pronunciation: *can* is normally unstressed /cən/ but is stressed for emphasis /cæn/.
  *Can you speak Chinese?   No, but I **can** speak Japanese.*

- *be able to*
  Be able to forms tenses and is sometimes used instead of *can*.
  *Will you **be able to help** me lift the furniture tomorrow?*

Permission

Can and *can't* are used to describe what is allowed or not allowed. See Unit 22.
  ***Can I leave** early, please?*
  *I **can't come** skating tomorrow.*

Possibility or uncertainty

- *may* and *might*
  We use *may* and *might* when we think something is possible, or we are uncertain.
  *President Jones **might win** the next election.   (It's possible.)*
  *I **may /might have** some news for you next week.   (Perhaps I will.)*
  Some speakers feel that *may* is more formal.

- Note that *may not* and *might not* describe uncertainty, not impossibility.
  *I **may not have time** to finish tonight.   (I don't know.)*

- *could*
  We use *could* when we are uncertain, especially with *be*.
  He could be stuck in the traffic.   (Perhaps he is.)

Impossibility or certainty	●	*must* and *can't*

We often know that something is impossible.

> *President Jones **can't win** the next election.*   (It's impossible.)

Sometimes we make a guess from facts, and feel almost certain about something. In this context, *must* and *can't* are very common with *be*.

> *He **must be stuck** in the traffic.*   (I'm sure he is.)
> *She **can't be in Italy**! I saw her today!*   (I'm sure she isn't.)

Obligation	●	*must* and *have to*

We can use *must* or *have to* to explain that something is necessary.

> *I **must finish** my homework before 8.00.*
> *I **have to phone** Jan at 9.00.*

● There is a difference in some contexts. We use *have to* to describe official rules: e.g. rules about school or jobs, or any other organized activity.

> *At our school, we **have to wear** a uniform.*
> *Every player in a football team **has to have** a number.*

Some speakers use *have to* to describe any rule which comes from an external authority. That means, a rule which is made by someone else.

> *When the traffic lights are red, you **have to stop**.*

● We use *must* with emphasis to show that an action is very important.

> *You **must** be here by 8.00, or the bus will leave without you.*

Note that we do not use *to* after *must*.

● In everyday speech, we use *have got to* instead of *have to*.

● *mustn't* and *don't have to*

These have different meanings.

Mustn't describes an action which is forbidden.

> *You **mustn't cross** the road when the red light is showing.*

Don't have to describes an action which is not necessary.

> *You **don't have to turn on** the central heating. It's automatic.*

Advice and opinion	●	*should* and *shouldn't*

Should and *shouldn't* give the speaker's opinion of what is a good or bad action. As this is an opinion it is often used for giving advice.

Advice   ***I think you should talk** to your teacher about it.*
Opinion   ***I think the police should arrest** hooligans.*

We can also describe what we expect *should happen*.

Expectation   *They **should arrive** here at about 6.30.*

● *ought to* and *ought not to*

Ought to and *ought not to* can be used in the same way as *should* and *shouldn't*.

> ***I think you ought to talk** to your teacher about it.*

- Note that *not* is added to *think*.
  *I don't think you **should/ought** to go.*

- Note that *should* is more frequently used than *ought to*.

- *had better*
  This has a similar meaning to *should* and *ought to*. *Had* is usually contracted.
  *I think **you'd better talk** to your teacher about it.*
  ***We'd better not forget** to turn off the computer!*

Practice

1
Choose the correct word or phrase underlined in each sentence.

a) Look at those clouds. I think it <u>can</u>/(might)/<u>must</u> rain.

b) This is impossible! It <u>can't be/ mustn't be/may not be</u> the answer.

c) Well done! You <u>may be/must be/might be</u> very pleased!

d) I've no idea where Jane is. She <u>could be/must be</u> anywhere!

e) I suppose it's possible. I <u>might/can/must</u> come to your party.

f) I'm not sure. I <u>must not/may not</u> be able to get there in time.

g) That <u>can't be/mustn't be/may not be</u> David. He hasn't got a bike.

h) Lisa isn't here yet. She <u>can be/must be</u> on her way.

i) There's someone at the door. It <u>can be/could be</u> the postman.

j) Sorry, I <u>can't come/may not</u> out. I have to do my homework.

2
Rewrite each sentence, using *can*, *can't*, *might* or *must*, and beginning and ending as shown.

a) Helen is really good at swimming.
   Helen ...*can swim really*........................... well.

b) It's possible that our team will win.
   Our team .... win.

c) I'm sure this isn't the right road.
   This .... the right road.

d) I'm sure you work very hard!
   You .... very hard.

e) Carol isn't allowed to come to our party.
   Carol .... to our party.

f) It's possible that I'll see you tomorrow, but I'm not sure.
   I .... , but I'm not sure.

g) I'm afraid that your teacher is unable to come today.
   I'm afraid that .... today.

h) I'm sure it's very hot here in summer.
   It .... here in summer.

i) Excuse me, is it all right if I open the window?

Excuse me, ... the window?

j) I suppose you are Mrs Perry. How do you do?

You .... Mrs Perry. How do you do?

3

Decide whether each pair of sentences have a similar meaning, or whether they are different. Write *S* for *same* or *D* for *different*.

a) You'd better go.	You should go.	..S..
b) You don't have to press this button.	You mustn't press this button.	.....
c) You should have a rest.	You ought to have a rest.	.....
d) You must be crazy!	You should be crazy!	.....
e) You must be here before 8.30.	You have to be here before 8.30.	.....
f) You mustn't do that!	You don't have to do that!	.....
g) You shouldn't eat so much.	You ought not to eat so much.	.....
h) We have to work harder.	We must work harder.	.....
i) I'd better write my letters.	I must write my letters.	.....
j) I ought to leave now.	I have to leave now.	.....

4

Rewrite each sentence so that it has a similar meaning and contains the word given.

a) It would be a good idea for you to see a dentist.

ought

...*You ought to see a dentist.*...................................

b) It's not necessary for us to go to school tomorrow.

have

....

c) I'm sure that isn't John, because he's in Paris.

be

....

d) Perhaps Ann is at home.

be

....

e) You ought to wear a warm coat today.

had

....

f) It's possible that I'll be late.

may

....

g) I wouldn't go skiing if I were you.

think

....

67

    h) It is forbidden to leave your bike here.
    can't

    ....

    i) Perhaps I'll see you on Thursday evening.
    might

    ....

    j) It is the rule to write this test in pencil.
    have

    ....

5

Put **one** suitable modal auxiliary in each space.

a) Soldiers ...*have*....... to obey orders.
b) I think you .... take your umbrella.
c) Sorry, I .... go now. I don't want to be late.
d) I'm not sure, but I .... be able to help you.
e) Helen isn't at home, so she .... be on her way here.
f) We .... better not leave any windows open.
g) It .... be a star, it's too bright. Perhaps it's an alien spaceship!
h) I don't .... to go to work today. It's a holiday.
i) Sorry, but I wasn't .... to finish all the work you gave me.
j) I think you .... to ask your teacher for some advice.

6

Rewrite each sentence so that it does not contain the phrase underlined.

a) <u>If I were you</u> I'd take more exercise.
   ...*I think you'd better/you should take more exercise.*................

b) <u>I expect</u> the plane will land soon.
   ....

c) You <u>are not allowed to</u> use a dictionary.
   ....

d) <u>It's impossible for that</u> to be Sue. She's abroad.
   ....

e) <u>It's possible that</u> I'll come to your party.
   ....

f) <u>It's against the law to</u> drop litter in the street.
   ....

g) <u>It's not necessary</u> for you to wait.
   ....

h) <u>You'd better</u> stay in bed today.
   ....

Unit 18 Modals 2: past

Explanations

Ability

- *could, couldn't, was able to*
  These describe ability in the past.
  > Jane **could swim/was able to swim** *when she was ten.*
  We use *was able to* when we want to show that an event was possible and also happened.
  > *When David* **fell** *in the river, Jane* **was able to** *rescue him.*

Possibility or uncertainty

might have done, may have done, could have done
The form is modal + *have* + past participle. *Have* does not change.
> *Maria* **might/may/could have taken** *the bus.* (I think perhaps she did.)

Impossibility or certainty

must have done, can't have done
The form is modal + *have* + past participle. *Have* does not change.
> *You* **must have left** *your passport on the plane.*   (I'm sure you did.)
> *Lina* **can't have written** *this.*   (I'm sure she didn't.)

Obligation

- *had to, didn't have to, didn't need to, needn't have done*
  There is no past form of *must*. We use *had to*.
  > *When I was at school, we* **had to/didn't have to wear** *a uniform.*

- There is a difference between *didn't need to* and *needn't have done*.
  > *I* **didn't need to do** *any homework yesterday.*
  > (I didn't have to do something.)
  > *I* **needn't have done** *any homework yesterday.*
  > (I made a mistake. I did something that was not necessary.)

Advice and opinion

- *should have done, ought to have done*
  The form is modal + *have* + past participle. *Have* does not change. They often describe criticism of an action.
  > *I think you* **should have worked** *harder.*   (I think you were wrong.)
  > *You* **shouldn't have eaten** *so much!*   (I think you were wrong.)

- We can use *ought to have done* and *ought not to have done* in the same way.

Practice

1
Rewrite each sentence so that it has a similar meaning and contains the word given.

a) I'm sure you dropped your wallet at the bus-stop.
must
...*You must have dropped your wallet at the bus-stop.*..............................

b) Maybe Joanna missed the last bus.
might
....

c) Peter knew how to skate when he was twelve.
able
....

d) Emma was wrong not to tell you the answer.
should
....

e) It wasn't necessary for us to pay to get in.
didn't
....

f) It wasn't necessary for me to buy any food yesterday.
need
....

g) I'm sure that Diana didn't take your books.
can't
....

h) Perhaps David didn't notice you.
might
....

i) Terry arrived early, but it wasn't necessary.
needn't
....

j) It was a bad idea for us to be rude to the policeman!
shouldn't
....

2

Rewrite each sentence beginning as shown.

a) You were wrong to study so late!
   You shouldn't ...*have studied so late*..................... .

b) Did you manage to stop him?
   Were .... ?

c) It wasn't necessary to work hard.
   I didn't ....

d) Perhaps Tim has lost his way.
   Tim might ....

e) It was possible for you to hurt yourself.
   You could ....

f) It would have been a good idea to tell me.
   You should ....

g) I'm sure the class enjoyed it.
   The class must ....

h) I helped her but it wasn't necessary.
   I needn't ....

i) It was a mistake to leave.
   You ought ....

j) I'm sure the butler didn't do it.
   The butler can't ....

3

Complete each sentence so that it contains the words given.

a) I'm completely soaked! We are silly! We ...*should have taken an umbrella*.......... .
   should/umbrella

b) I've lost my bag. I think I ....
   must/bus

c) I tried to phone Sam, but I ....
   couldn't/get through

d) I forgot Kate's birthday. I ....
   should/present

e) The cat doesn't like fruit! It ....
   can't/orange

f) Jo hasn't turned up yet. I suppose she ....
   might/address

g) I did badly in the test. I ....
   ought/harder

h) It's a shame we didn't go on holiday. We ....
   could/good time

Problems, Errors, Consolidation 2

1

Choose the correct word or phrase underlined in each sentence.

a) Jim (asked)/told the teacher if the book was his.

b) I have had/had two teeth taken out last week.

c) I can't do these sums. I wish I have/had a calculator with me.

d) Ann refused/said she didn't want me to borrow her bike.

e) Helen can't have stolen/must have stolen the money from the office. She didn't come in to the office on the day it was stolen.

f) If I have/had more money, I'd pay for you too.

g) It's getting very late, so I think you'd better/you could leave.

h) Ann phoned earlier and said that she had been/would be late.

i) The next two lessons were been/have been cancelled.

j) If we'd remembered/we remembered to bring the map, we wouldn't have got lost.

2

Look carefully at each line. Some lines are correct but some have a word which should not be there. Tick each correct line. If a line has a word which should not be there, write the word in the space.

Do-It-Yourself

Last week my brother and I decided to paint our	1) ..✓..
bedrooms if while our parents were out for the	2) ..if..
day. Our parents usually they have the painting done	3) ......
by a local firm, but we thought we could to save some	4) ......
money if we did paint it ourselves. We had watched the	5) ......
painters the last time the house had to been painted,	6) ......
so we thought we would be able to do the job.	7) ......
'First all the surfaces must have to be washed,' my	8) ......
brother said. 'That can't have be very difficult,' I	9) ......
replied. 'We'd better if put some newspapers on	10) ......
the carpet. If we can make a mess, we'll get into	11) ......
trouble.' After that had been have done, we looked	12) ......
for some paint in the garden shed. 'We could use	13) ......
this red paint,' I was suggested. My brother said that	14) ......
he preferred green paint. Just as if we were going to	15) ......
start, our parents arrived home. 'You should have been	16) ......
asked us first,' my mother said us. 'You can paint the	17) ......
rest of the house too!'	18) ......

3

Decide which answer, a), b), c) or d), best fits the space.

Making arrangements with Paul

A few days ago Paul phoned me and (1) ..c.. whether I (2) ..... looking after his dog when he (3) ..... away. I (4) ..... that I didn't really like dogs, but he said that he (5) ..... all his other friends, and that I (6) ..... his only hope. He invited me round to his house (7) ..... to meet the dog, and he told me that he (8) ..... dinner for me. An hour later he phoned again and said that he (9) ..... after all, so I (10) ..... meeting the following day for lunch. The next morning he cancelled this appointment and, after he (11) ..... , said that he (12) ..... the dog to my house at 6.00. 'I don't know exactly (13) ..... ,' he said. 'Could you tell me how (14) ..... there?' I quickly said I (15) ..... out and put the phone down. Luckily I haven't heard from him since.

1) a) told   b) said me   c) asked me   d) spoke
2) a) would mind   b) want   c) like   d) will help
3) a) has gone   b) went   c) would go   d) will go
4) a) told him   b) said him   c) asked him   d) replied him
5) a) asks   b) would ask   c) will ask   d) had already asked
6) a) am   b) will be   c) had been   d) was
7) a) this evening   b) that evening   c) the evening   d) in evening
8) a) is cooking   b) will cook   c) would cook   d) had cooked
9) a) had to go out   b) went out   c) goes out   d) has to go out
10) a) had suggested   b) would suggest   c) suggested   d) suggest
11) a) has done   b) told me sorry   c) asked   d) had apologized
12) a) would bring   b) had brought   c) brought   d) brings
13) a) where is it   b) if it is   c) where it is   d) how was it
14) a) do I get   b) I get   c) I will get   d) I'm getting
15) a) went   b) go   c) will go   d) was going

4

Complete the second sentence so that it has a similar meaning to the first sentence.

a) I don't know the answer, so I can't help you.
   If I ...*knew the answer, I would help you*..................... .
b) Don't run fast, or you'll feel tired.
   If ....
c) An off-duty policewoman arrested the robber.
   The robber ....
d) We didn't leave early, so we missed the train.
   If we ....
e) I ate all the ice-cream, and now I regret it.
   I wish ....
f) Where is the bus station?
   Could you .... ?

g) The local council is building a new sports centre.

A new sports centre ....

h) I think you should go to the doctor's.

If I ....

i) Someone used a hammer to break the window.

The window ....

j) 'Don't forget to buy some milk, Sue,' I said.

I reminded ....

5

Rewrite each sentence so that it has a similar meaning and contains the word given.

a) It wasn't necessary for me to go to work yesterday.

have

...*I didn't have to go to work yesterday.*..

b) I'd like to be rich!

wish

....

c) I'm going to the hairdresser's tomorrow.

having

....

d) Perhaps David missed the bus.

might

....

e) Marconi was the inventor of radio.

by

....

f) I think you were wrong to forget the keys!

shouldn't

....

g) It would be a good idea for us to take an umbrella.

better

....

h) I'm sure that Maria worked very hard.

must

....

i) Helen gave a camera to Richard.

by

....

j) It was unnecessary for us to buy so much food.

bought

....

6

Put **one** of the words or phrases from the list in each space. Words can be used more than once.

| could didn't have to don't have to might have must
mustn't must have should had to have to |

a) We ...*don't have to*.... wear a uniform at my school. We can wear whatever we like.

b) You .... play with matches! It's very dangerous!

c) I'm not sure, but I think I .... left my wallet in the bank.

d) I'm getting up early, because I .... go running before school.

e) Sorry I can't stay any longer, but I really .... go home.

f) If you want to, we .... go swimming this afternoon.

g) Sorry I'm late, but I .... take my dog to the vet's.

h) Tim usually wears clothes like that, so I think it .... been him.

i) I think you .... go to bed earlier, and stop drinking coffee.

j) Luckily, I .... do any homework last night, so I went to the cinema.

7

Complete the second sentence so that it has a similar meaning to the first sentence.

a) The painters are coming to our house tomorrow.
...*We are having our house*........................ painted tomorrow.

b) Someone stole Peter's car last week.
.... stolen last week.

c) 'I've lost my ticket, Kate,' said George.
.... lost his ticket.

d) Paul advised Diane not to take the job.
'.. were you, Diane,' said Paul.

e) When does the play start?
.... starts?

f) Let's go for a picnic if the weather's good.
.... the weather's bad.

g) I stayed up late because I didn't feel tired.
.... stayed up late.

h) Jim lived in Italy then, so it was impossible that you met him here.
You .... Jim here, because he lived in Italy then.

i) 'Do you have to leave early tomorrow, Ann?' asked Mary.
.... early the next day.

j) 'Do you think you could pass me the salt, Peter?' I said.
.... to pass the salt.

8
Underline the error in each sentence. Correct the error.

a) *War and Peace* was <u>writing</u> by Leo Tolstoy.   ...*written*...............

b) That mustn't be David! He's on holiday in Bermuda.   ....

c) David asked a passer-by where was the railway station.   ....

d) If I had lived in Ancient Greece, I might be a slave!   ....

e) In the army, you'd better wear a uniform.   ....

f) Kate told me that she must to finish her homework.   ....

g) I think someone must open your bag. That's the only explanation.

   ....

h) I wish I am taller!   ....

i) I repair my car by a qualified mechanic.   ....

j) If I saw a snake, I'll scream and run away!   ....

Problem check

1   Do you change tenses when you use reported speech in your language? Check the punctuation of direct speech in Unit 44.

2   Check the difference between Conditional 2 and 3. Remember that the past tense verb in Conditional 2 does not refer to past time.

3   When do we use the passive? Does your language use verbs with a passive form in situations where English uses an active verb?

4   How do we use *must*, *have to* and *should*? Are they all the same? When might you say:
   a) Jim has to get up early every day.
   b) Jim must get up early every day.
   c) Jim should get up early every day.

5   Explain the difference between each pair of sentences.
   a) I'm cutting my hair.
      I'm having my hair cut.
   b) I must have lost my keys.
      I can't have lost my keys.
   c) I didn't need to buy any food yesterday.
      I needn't have bought any food yesterday.
   d) If you came by bus, you'd get here faster.
      If you had come by bus, you would have got here faster.

Unit 19 Purpose

Explanations

for

For followed by a noun can be used to describe purpose, especially with verbs of motion.

> *I went to the shops **for some milk**.*

Infinitive

We can use the infinitive to describe the purpose of the person mentioned in the opening of the sentence.

> *Jim went to the station **to meet** his parents.*

so (that) + present simple

We can use *so (that)* and present simple to describe a habitual purpose.

> *Bill wears thick socks in bed **so (that)** his feet **don't get** cold.*

so (that) + will and *would*

- We can use *so (that)* and *will/won't* to describe a future purpose.
  > *We'll take an umbrella **so (that)** we **won't get** wet.*

- We can also use present simple.
  > *We'll take an umbrella **so (that)** we **don't get** wet.*

- When we describe in the past a future event, *will* becomes *would*.
  > *We took an umbrella **so (that)** we **wouldn't get** wet.*

- We can also use past simple.
  > *We took an umbrella **so (that)** we **didn't get** wet.*

so (that) + *can/could*

- We can use *so (that) + can* for present time and *so (that) + could* for past time when we describe purpose.
  > *I leave the window open **so (that)** the cat **can get** in and out.*
  > *Dora left class early **so (that)** she **could go** to the dentist.*

- If the person mentioned in the opening of the sentence and the action in the second part of the sentence are different, we can't use Infinitive of Purpose. We have to use *so (that) + can/could*.
  > *Helen played the piano to entertain her friends.*
  > *Helen played the piano **so (that) everyone else could dance**.*

in order to

- In formal speech and writing we can use *in order to*. Both verbs must have the same subject.
  *The President **made** a speech **in order to explain** the policy.*
  This means:
  The President wanted to make a speech because the President wanted to explain the policy.

- Note that Infinitive of Purpose is more often used than *in order to*.

- See Unit 20 Result and reason and Unit 43 Text organizers.

Practice

1

Put **one** suitable word in each space. Contractions count as one word.

a) I wrote the date in my diary ...*so*........ ..*that*.... I wouldn't forget it.

b) Most tourists come here .... visit the ancient temples.

c) Mary called a meeting .... announce the team.

d) The thief .... in black so that nobody .... see him.

e) Jack came to me .... advice.

f) Our teacher made us sit far apart so that we .... cheat!

g) I'll leave the box open so that you .... help yourself.

h) Lisa got up early so that she .... finish her homework.

i) We went into town by bike so that we .... have parking problems.

j) The school sent everyone a letter .... explain the new rules.

2

Rewrite each sentence so that it contains the word given.

a) I went to the shops to get some eggs.
   for
   ...*I went to the shops for some eggs.*..

b) Ann came here for a meeting with the director.
   to
   ....

c) We went on holiday to have a rest.
   for
   ....

d) Peter plays chess for relaxation.
   to
   ....

e) I opened the window to let in some air.
   for
   ....

f) Helen went shopping to buy some new clothes.
    for

    ....

g) I went to a private school for English lessons.
    to

    ....

h) Sam went to a specialist to get treatment.
    for

    ....

3
Complete the second sentence so that it has a similar meaning to the first sentence.

a) Paul had to go to the doctor's, and left work early.
    Paul ...*left work early*.... so that ...*he could go*....... to the doctor's.

b) The school was rebuilt because it wasn't large enough.
    The school .... in order to .... larger.

c) Tina wanted Jack to call her, and gave him her phone number.
    Tina .... so that .... her.

d) I might get sunburnt, so I'll put on some suntan oil.
    I'll .... so that .... sunburnt.

e) Cathy hid the presents and nobody saw them.
    Cathy .... so that .... them.

f) We wanted people to dance, so we had the party in a large hall.
    We .... so that .... dance.

g) Dick wanted to get a good seat, so he arrived early.
    Dick .... so that .... a good seat.

h) I couldn't see well in the cinema, and changed seats.
    I .... so that .... better.

i) Harry wanted his friends to notice him so he wore a funny hat.
    Harry .... so that .... him.

j) We didn't want to feel hungry, so we took some sandwiches.
    We took .... so that we ....

Unit 20 Result and reason

Explanations

so, because

- We can link results and reasons with *so* and *because*.
  > *Tim had eaten fifteen ice-creams, (and) **so** he didn't feel very well.*
  > *Tim didn't feel well, **because** he had eaten fifteen ice-creams.*

- Normally we do not begin sentences with *because*, but this is possible in informal writing and speech.
  > ***Because** Tim had eaten fifteen ice-creams, he didn't feel very well.*

as, since

We can use *as* and *since* in formal speech and writing. They have the same meaning as *because*.
> ***As/since** Tim had eaten fifteen ice-creams, he didn't feel very well.*
> *Tim didn't feel well, **as/since** he had eaten fifteen ice-creams.*

so much, so many, so few, so little

These expressions can be used with *that*, but *that* is often left out in speech and informal writing.

- Countable.
  > *I bought **so many books (that)** I couldn't carry them all.*
  > *There were **so few people** in the theatre **(that)** the actors didn't perform well.*

- Uncountable
  > *There is **so much rain** at the moment **(that)** we hardly ever go out.*
  > *We have **so little free time (that)** we don't watch television.*

so + adjective + *that*

That is often left out in speech and informal writing.
> *Last night was **so hot (that)** I couldn't sleep.*

such + adjective + noun + *that*

That is often left out in speech and informal writing.
> *It was **such a lovely day (that)** we went for a walk in the country.*

too + adjective + infinitive with *to*

Too always suggests difficulty, and that something cannot be done.
> *It was **too far to walk** so we took a taxi.*
> *The mountain was **too difficult (for us) to climb**.*

not + adjective + *enough* + infinitive with *to*

Compare the use of *too* + adjective and *not* + adjective + *enough*.
> *Little Gerry is **too young to walk** to school.*
> *Little Gerry is **not old enough to walk** to school.*

not + enough + noun, *too many +* noun, *too much +* noun,
too little + noun,
too few + noun

These sentences suggest a result, even when it is not stated.

● Countable

*We **haven't** got **enough** books, (so you'll have to share).*
*There are **too few** books.*
*There are **too many** people in the class.*

● Uncountable

*We **haven't got enough** time, (so we'll have to hurry).*
*There's **too little** time.*
*There are **too many** things to do.*

as a result, in the end, eventually

We can also introduce the result of a situation by using a result phrase, such as *as a result*, or time expressions such as *in the end* and *eventually*. We usually use these in formal speech or writing.

*Two metres of snow fell during the night. **As a result**, several main roads were blocked.*
*It started raining while we were having our picnic, and **eventually** we decided to go home.*
*Kate and Tim waited for the bus for a long time, and **in the end** they took a taxi.*

Practice

1
Choose the correct word or phrase underlined in each sentence.

a) It was such/so a delicious drink, that I had to have another glass.
b) Jack ate so much/so many cakes that he could hardly walk!
c) Kate's offer sounded so/too good to be true!
d) There are so few/so little good programmes on TV that I rarely watch it.
e) I felt so/too weak that I couldn't stand up.
f) We had so much/so many free time, that we got bored.
g) I waited for Mary for ages, and as a result/in the end I gave up.
h) There was so much/so many rain last night, that the roads were flooded.
i) David was too tall/tall enough/enough tall/very tall to reach the shelf.
j) I had so few/so little knowledge of the subject that I got zero in the test.

2
Put **one** suitable word in each space.

a) My tea is ...*too*.. hot to drink at the moment.

b) I had to stand at the back, ... there weren't any seats left.

c) Tom had .... homework, that he had to stay up until midnight.

d) There were .... people in front of us that we couldn't see.

e) Helen missed the bus, ... she took a taxi.

f) There were .... customers that the shop closed down.

g) The room wasn't large .... for so many guests.

h) Sue was .... tired that she fell asleep on the train.

i) We had .... money that we couldn't even buy a sandwich.

j) .... it was raining, the school picnic was postponed.

3
Rewrite each sentence so that it has a similar meaning and contains the word given.

a) I felt really tired, so I stayed at home and had a rest.
because
...*I stayed at home and had a rest because I felt really tired*...............................

b) I didn't use that piece of string, because it was too short.
enough
....

c) The question was so difficult that I had to ask for help.
such
....

d) There weren't enough seats for all the guests.
few
....

e) There weren't enough seats for all the guests.
many
....

f) I couldn't take any more clothes as there wasn't any space in my suitcase.
little
....

g) It was such a good play that the audience cheered.
so
....

h) I've got such a lot of work that I can't go out.
so
....

i) She had lots of children and didn't know what to do.
many
....

j) I haven't got enough time to do all my work.

too

....

4
Underline the errors in these sentences. Rewrite each sentence.

a) Sorry, but I haven't got <u>little</u> time.

...*Sorry, but I haven't got enough time.*...........................

b) Helen is not enough old to drive a car.

....

c) Paul has so much friends that he is always busy.

....

d) We had too few time to go sight-seeing.

....

e) It's too hot that I can't think!

....

f) There was too much snow that we couldn't travel.

....

g) It was so a long way that we decided to drive there.

....

h) So that I had run a long way, I felt exhausted.

....

5
Complete the second sentence so that it has a similar meaning to the first sentence.

a) I'm afraid you're not fast enough to be in the running team.

I'm afraid you're too ...*slow to be in the running team*................. .

b) It's not very far to the house, so we can walk.

We can walk ....

c) The film was so long that we missed our last bus.

It was ....

d) Tina felt unhappy and she cried.

Tina felt so ....

e) Some millionaires have lots of money, and don't know what to do with it.

Some millionaires have so ....

f) Jim is too young to get married.

Jim isn't ....

g) I can't afford to buy this bike.

I haven't got ....

h) There are too few plates I'm afraid.

There aren't ....

Unit 21 Contrast

Explanations

although, *though* and *even though*

- *Although* is used to introduce a contrasting clause. This is a second statement which contrasts with the first statement.
    *Maria went to school **although** she was ill.*
    ***Although** she was ill, Maria went to school.*

- *Although* is often emphasized by expressions such as *still*, *anyway* and *all the same*.
    *Maria **still** went to school, **although** she was ill.*
    ***Although** she was ill, Maria went to school **anyway/all the same**.*

- *Even though* is used to emphasize the contrast.
    ***Even though** she felt very ill, Maria went to school.*

- *Though* is used in speech and informal writing. In these contexts, the two clauses are often made into two sentences, and *though* is put at the end.
    *Maria went to school. She was ill, **though**.*

while and *whereas*

While and *whereas* can often be used in formal speech and writing instead of *although*.
    ***While/Whereas** some experts expect the Government to win the election, most believe that the opposition will win.*

despite

- *Despite* is used to introduce a contrasting clause. It is always followed by a noun phrase, or the verbal form of the noun (*-ing*). It cannot be followed by a main verb.
    ***Despite her illness**, Maria went to school.*
    ***Despite being ill**, Maria went to school.*

- Note that we cannot say:
    * *Despite she felt ill, Maria went to school.*
    (incorrect sentence)

in spite of

- *In spite of* is used to introduce a contrasting clause. It is always followed by a noun phrase, or the verbal form of the noun (*-ing*). It cannot be followed by a main verb.
    ***In spite of her illness**, Maria went to school.*
    ***In spite of being ill**, Maria went to school.*

- Note that we cannot say:
    * *In spite of she felt ill, Maria went to school.*
    (incorrect sentence)

however

- *However* introduces or completes a contrasting sentence. *However* always has punctuation before and after. *However* is more common in formal speech and writing.
  > *Maria was ill.* **However**, *she went to school.*
  > *Maria went to school. She was ill,* **however**.

- Note that we cannot say:
  > **However she was ill, Maria went to school.*
  > (Incorrect sentence)

but and *yet*

- The most common kind of contrast is made with *but*.
  > *Maria felt ill,* **but** *she went to school.*

- *But* is often emphasized by expressions such as *still*, *anyway* and *all the same*.
  > *Maria felt ill,* **but** *she went to school* **anyway/all the same**.
  > *Maria felt ill,* **but** *she* **still** *went to school.*

- *Yet* can be used instead of *but* in formal speech and writing.
  > *Maria felt ill,* **yet** *she went to school.*

on the other hand

- *On the other hand* introduces a contrasting opinion. It is usually used in formal speech and writing.
  > *Television has many advantages. It keeps us informed about the latest news, and also provides entertainment in the home.*
  > **On the other hand**, *television has been blamed for the violent behaviour of some young people, and for encouraging children to sit indoors, instead of taking exercise.*

- See also Unit 43 Text organizers.

Practice

1

Choose the correct word or phrase underlined in each sentence.

a) I read the book you suggested. I didn't enjoy it, although/(however)

b) <u>In spite of/Although</u> we warned him, Harry still got lost.

c) <u>Although/However</u> I like it here, I won't stay here long.

d) Cars are fast and convenient. <u>On the other hand/Whereas</u>, they cause traffic problems in cities.

e) I didn't have much time, <u>but/however</u> I managed to visit lots of places.

f) Kate won the race, <u>although/despite</u> falling over.

g) <u>Although/In spite of</u> the delay, the train arrived on time.

h) I didn't manage to jump over the wall, <u>although/yet</u> I tried twice.

2

Put **one** suitable word in each space.

a) ..*Although*..... Tim felt tired, he stayed up to finish his homework.

b) Alan didn't enjoy skating, ... he went with his friends all the same.

c) I found French hard at first. .... , I soon started to enjoy it.

d) Jane kept running, ... though she knew she couldn't win.

e) Mike was lost, but he .... refused to look at the map.

f) Carol went to see the film, ... she had seen it before.

g) .... the rain, the school sports were a great success.

h) Helen won the swimming competition, in .... of her cold.

i) I'm not sure I agree with you. .... , your ideas are worth discussing.

j) Tony was short of money, but he .... lent some to his sister.

3

Complete the second sentence beginning as shown, so that it has a similar meaning to the first sentence.

a) Although it was snowing, we went out for a walk.
Despite ..*the snow, we went out for a walk*.............................. .

b) Some experts think the world is growing warmer, but others disagree.
While ....

c) I don't enjoy rock music, but I went to the concert anyway.
Although ....

d) Even though they were losing at half-time, City won in the end.
Despite ....

e) Despite the heat, Diana wore her winter clothes.
Although ....

f) Whereas prices rose last year, this year they have gone down.
Prices rose last year ....

g) Jim had a headache, but he still read until late.
In spite of ....

h) Although Sam hadn't studied, he did well in the test.
Sam hadn't studied ....

Unit 22 Functions

Explanations

What is a function?

- A function is a way of describing language according to its purpose. This section gives examples of some of the most commonly used functions.

- Most functions have several different ways of expressing the purpose. The language we use often depends on:
The situation we are in.
  Is it in private or public?
The person we are talking to.
  Is the person our own age, do we know them well, etc?
What we are talking about.
  Are we borrowing a pen, or a large amount of money?

- The functions below are classed as formal, neutral or informal, but remember that you might be informal with a friend if you want to borrow a pen, but formal if you want to borrow a large amount of money.

Advising

Asking for and giving advice or making recommendations.
  I think you should stay at home.   (formal)
  If I were you, I'd stay at home.   (formal)

Asking, accepting and refusing

  Can you help me?   Sorry, I can't/Of course I can.   (neutral)
  Will you wait here, please?   (formal)
  Would you wait here, please?   (formal)

Asking for information

The order is from neutral, to most polite.
  Can you tell me what time the bus from Glasgow arrives?
Note the indirect question, and the present simple for timetable times.
  Could you tell me ... ?
  Would you mind telling me ... ?

Making offers

Making an offer to do something.
  Shall I carry this suitcase for you?   (neutral)
  Thank you very much./Thanks, but I can manage.

Offering

Offering something.
  Would you like a soft drink?   (neutral)

Permission	Asking for, giving and refusing permission.
	The order is from neutral, to most polite.
	  Is it all right *if I leave early please?*
	  Can I *leave early, please?* *Yes, of course.*
	  Could I *leave early, please?* *Sorry, but you can't.*
	  Note that we do not say *'Sorry but you couldn't'.
	  May I leave *early, please?* *Yes, you may.*

Offers and
preferences
	When we offer people things, we often ask them what they would prefer, would
	 like or would rather have.
	All these are neutral.
	  Would you like *tea or coffee?*
	  I'd rather have *coffee, please.*
	  I'd prefer *tea, please.*
	  I don't mind.
	When we ask people what they prefer, we do not use *would.*
	  Do you prefer *rock or folk music?*

Promising	All these are neutral.
	  I'll be back at 11.30.
	  I won't do anything silly!

Requesting	Making and responding to requests
	The order is from neutral, to most polite.
	  Can you *open the window, please?* *Sure.*
	  Could you *open the window please?* *Of course.*
	  Would you mind *helping me?* *Sure, no problem.*
	Note that it is best to avoid answering *Would you mind … ?* questions with *yes*
	or *no.* Often requests are not answered, but an action is performed instead.

Suggesting	Making suggestions.
	All these are neutral.
	  Let's go *to the cinema.*
	  Why don't we go *to the cinema?*
	  How about going *to the cinema?*
	  We could go *to the cinema.*
	
	● See also Unit 9.

Practice

1

Match the utterances a) to j) with the functional descriptions 1) to 10).

a) Would you like a cup of tea? ..4..

b) Excuse me, do you know what time the museum opens? .....

c) Actually, I think I'd rather have a Chinese meal. .....

d) I know, we could walk along the river. How about that? .....

e) Sorry, but I won't do it. .....

f) That looks difficult. Shall I help you? .....

g) Excuse me, but do you think you could turn your music down a bit? .....

h) Well, to be honest, I think you should go to the police. .....

i) Is it all right if I pop out to the shops for a moment? .....

j) I'll definitely be there at 6.00. I won't be late! .....

1) Giving advice.
2) Asking for information.
3) Making an offer.
4) Offering something.
5) Asking permission.
6) Refusing to do something.
7) Expressing a preference.
8) Making a promise.
9) Making a request.
10) Making a suggestion.

2

Choose the correct word or phrase underlined in each sentence.

a) I'm very busy. Would you mind/Let's giving me a hand?

b) If I were you, I'd write/How about you write the letter again.

c) Why don't we go/going to the theatre tomorrow?

d) Could you/Would you mind close the door please?

e) Do you like/Would you like some more water?

f) I promise. I don't do it/I won't do it again.

g) I'm quite good at cooking too. Would I help/Shall I help you?

h) I have a suggestion. Why don't you go/Could you go to the beach?

i) Would I borrow/Could I borrow your ruler?

j) Are you tired? I think you should go/you can go to bed early.

3

Replace the underlined parts with a more appropriate or accurate expression.

a) Look, don't worry about me, there's a bus at 12.30. So <u>I'm back</u> by 2.00, I promise!
...*I'll be back*...

b) A: Would you like an ice-cream? Or some cake perhaps?
   B: <u>I choose ice-cream</u>, please.
....

c) A: I'm having problems at school. What do you think I should do?
   B: <u>I talk it over with your parents.</u>
....

d) A: This suitcase is really heavy, and my back is killing me!
   B: <u>Do I carry it?</u>
....

e) A: I'm not sure what to do this evening. Any ideas?
   B: <u>You will go to the cinema, perhaps?</u>
....

f) A: I've got an appointment at the dentist's. <u>Shall I leave school early?</u>
   B: Have you brought a note from your parents?
....

g) Excuse me, I want to catch a bus from here to London. <u>Tell me how much does it cost.</u>
....

h) A: I feel really hungry. Have you got anything to eat?
   B: <u>Do you like some lemonade?</u>
....

i) A: It's very hot in here. <u>Are you opening the window?</u>
   B: Of course.
....

j) A: Come on, hurry up! Tidy your room and make your bed!
   B: <u>No, I don't!</u> It's not fair!
....

4

Complete the second sentence so that it has a similar meaning to the first sentence.

a) Please take a seat.
   Would ..*you mind taking a seat*............... ?

b) Fruit juice would be better for me.
   I'd rather ....

c) I'd like you to wait for me.
   Can .... ?

d) Will you allow me to leave the room?
   May .... ?

e) I'd like you to turn off the television.
   Could .... ?

f) Let's go for a walk.
   How .... ?

g) I promise not to talk to Richard again.
   I ....

h) Would you like me to help you?
   Shall .... ?

i) When does the plane arrive?
   Would .... ?

j) My advice is to see a doctor.
   If I ....

5

Put **one** suitable word in each space. More than one answer may be possible.

a) I think you ...*should*.. spend more time on your homework.

b) .... you help me carry these bags?

c) Excuse me. .... you tell me what street this is?

d) What a terrible noise! .... you please be quiet!

e) .... go skating tomorrow.

f) Would you .... telling me what time it is?

g) Thanks for the offer, but I'd .... stay at home.

h) .... you sign your name here, please, sir?

i) .... you like another slice of pizza?

j) Please .... I leave the table?

Unit 23 Relative clauses 1

Explanations

Relative clauses

Relative clauses are normally joined by relative pronouns, but these pronouns can sometimes be left out. Some types of relative clauses are more common in formal speech and writing. It is important to know whether a relative clause is Defining or Non-defining, and whether it is a subject or object clause. See below.

Defining and Non-defining clauses

- Defining clauses give information which cannot be left out because it gives important information about the subject.
    *The doctor **who treated me** told me not to worry.*
  This describes which doctor we are talking about.

- Non-defining clauses give extra information. This is separated from the main sentence by commas.
    *Pablo Picasso, **who died in 1973**, was a painter and sculptor.*

Defining clauses

- *which, that*
  Which and *that* refer to things. *That* is less formal than *which*, and some speakers prefer to use *which*. *That* is also used to refer to people in speech and informal writing in defining clauses.
    *The bus **which** goes to Cairo leaves from here.*
    *The road **that** we took led to an ancient temple.*
    *The woman **that** we spoke to gave us directions.*

- *who* and *whom*
  Who and *whom* refer to people. We use *whom* in formal speech and writing to introduce an object clause. (See page 93). *Whom* is used after a preposition in formal language. In informal language, many people prefer to use *who*, or *that*, instead of *whom*. Many speakers never use *whom*. (See also Leaving out relative pronouns.)
    *The woman **who** teaches us music also plays in an orchestra.*
    *It was the same boy **whom** I met yesterday.*   (formal)
    *No one knows by **whom** the victim was shot.*   (formal)
    *No one knows **who** the victim was shot by.*   (informal)
    *The people **that** live next door make a lot of noise.*

- *whose*
  Whose means 'of whom'.
    *The girl **whose** case had been stolen went to the police station.*

Subject and object clauses	● Subject clauses refer to the subject of the sentence.
	    The doctor who treated me *told me not to worry.*
	    The doctor (subject) *treated* *me* (object).

	● Object clauses refer to the object.
	    The doctor that/who/whom I spoke to *told me not to worry.*
	    I (subject) *spoke to* *the doctor* (object).

Leaving out relative pronouns	● We cannot leave out the relative pronoun in non-defining clauses. *Pablo Picasso,* ***who died in 1973,*** *was a painter and sculptor.*
	● We can leave out the relative pronoun in defining clauses which are object clauses. ***The doctor I spoke to*** *told me not to worry.*
	● We cannot leave out the relative pronoun in defining clauses which are subject clauses. *The doctor* ***who*** *treated me told me not to worry.*
	● We can also leave out the relative pronoun after a superlative. *That was the* ***best meal*** *I've ever eaten!*

Practice

1
Choose the correct word underlined in each sentence.

a) An old man, (who)/which was carrying a suitcase, knocked at the door.
b) The girl who/whom lives here knows my sister.
c) The box that/whom Jean picked up had a hole in it.
d) The winner, whom/whose bike was an unusual design, won a medal.
e) The girl who/whom spoke to me turned out to be in my class.
f) The museum, which/whose was in a beautiful building, was closed.
g) A policewoman that/which we asked told us how to get there.
h) The boy whose/whom house I was staying at was an old friend.
i) The last person which/whose pen I borrowed didn't get it back!
j) The train which/who leaves at 8.00 stops at every station.

2
Put either *who* or *whom* in each space.

a) The waiter by ..*whom*... we were served expected a large tip.
b) The teacher .... taught us yesterday also teaches my brother.
c) The friend to .... I lent my basketball managed to lose it.
d) The boy .... opened the door looked familiar.
e) The man to .... I spoke told me to wait outside the office.
f) The people with .... I travelled were good company.
g) The assistant .... sold me the computer made a mistake with the bill.

h) The player .... had the ball was tripped by the goalkeeper.

i) The girl from .... I received the card was someone I met on holiday.

j) A strange man .... said he knew you phoned while you were out.

3
Put *who*, *whose*
or *that* in each
space.

a) The friend ...*whose*... house I stayed in is coming to stay with us.

b) The guidebook .... we bought explained everything.

c) It's difficult to say .... this portrait was painted by.

d) The couple .... house I bought both worked in my office.

e) I'd like you to tell me .... you were talking to.

f) The girl .... ruler I had borrowed wanted it back.

g) The game .... we played was difficult to understand.

h) I can't remember .... I lent my bike to.

i) Do you know .... Catherine works for?

j) The places .... we visited were all very interesting.

4
Decide whether
the clause
underlined is
Defining or
Non-defining.
Write D or N
next to each
sentence.

a) The girl <u>who was waiting</u> was becoming impatient. .D.

b) The room, <u>which was enormous</u>, was filled with lines of chairs. .....

c) The students, <u>who were late</u>, waited in the playground. .....

d) The food <u>which was left</u> was eaten the following day. .....

e) A tall girl, <u>who was wearing a hat</u>, came into the room. .....

f) The dog, <u>which was lying on the sofa</u>, had long pointed ears. .....

g) The train <u>which leaves at 8.00</u> doesn't stop at Bath. .....

h) Two boys, <u>who were playing football</u>, saw the robbery. .....

5
Underline
relative
pronouns which
can be left out in
these sentences.

a) The book <u>that</u> John was reading was a bit frightening.

b) The travel agency which sold me the ticket was near my office.

c) The name of the girl who lived next door was Ellen.

d) In the end, our holiday was the best that we had ever had.

e) The dentist who I go to isn't very expensive.

f) The film which we saw last week was much better than this one.

g) The people who were leaving couldn't find their coats.

h) The garden, which wasn't very large, was full of flowers.

i) The car which David bought was not in good condition.

j) The girl who I sit next to in class is my best friend.

6

Rewrite each formal sentence as an informal one, ending with the word given.

a) These are the boys with whom I went on holiday.
...*These are the boys I went on holiday*........................... with.

b) This is the letter for which I have been waiting.
.... for.

c) That is the shop from which Sue bought her bike.
.... from.

d) That is the bed-and-breakfast at which I stayed.
.... at.

e) Tim is someone to whom I hardly ever write.
.... to.

f) Do you know by whom this book was written?
.... by?

g) Ravenna was the most interesting town in which we stayed.
.... in.

h) United were the best team against which we played.
.... against.

7

Add a relative pronoun to each sentence.

a) Friday was the last time I saw Jim.
...*Friday was the last time that I saw Jim*...........................

b) The island we visited was extremely beautiful.
....

c) The girl I met was a friend of Harry's.
....

d) The meal we ate was not very tasty.
....

e) Mary was the first person I asked.
....

f) The book I read didn't explain the problem.
....

g) The teacher we usually have was away ill.
....

h) The friends I met last night send you their love.
....

i) Unfortunately I've lost the pen I always use.
....

j) The bus I catch stops outside the university.
....

Unit 24 Relative clauses 2

Explanations

Combining
sentences

- Note the changes made when sentences are combined using a relative clause.
  A bus goes to Cairo. It leaves from here.
  *The bus **that/which** goes to Cairo leaves from here.*

  We took a road. It led to an ancient temple.
  *The road **(that)** we took led to an ancient temple.*

  We spoke to a woman. She gave us directions.
  *The woman **(that)** we spoke to gave us directions.*

  A woman teaches us music. She also plays in an orchestra.
  *The woman **who** teaches us music also plays in an orchestra.*

- Note that articles are often changed e.g. from *a/an* to *the* when sentences are combined.
  A girl's case was stolen. She went to the police station.
  ***The** girl whose case was stolen went to the police station.*

  A doctor treated me. She told me not to worry.
  ***The** doctor who treated me told me not to worry.*

  *I spoke to **a** doctor. She told me not to worry.*
  ***The** doctor I spoke to told me not to worry.*

- Note this common error.
  The bus that/which goes to Cairo **it leaves from here.*
  The subject is not repeated (*The bus ... it*) in a relative clause.

Non-finite
clauses

These are clauses with an *-ing* form verb.
  *I sent a card to the girl **living** across the street.*
  (I sent a card to the girl who was living across the street.)

Nominal relative
clauses

These can be used as subject or object. They are common with *what* which here
means *the things which*.
  *We didn't understand **what** she said.*
  ***What** I want now is a cup of tea.*

96

Practice

1
Choose the correct word underlined in each sentence.

a) The train (which)/who goes to Brighton leaves from here.
b) That/What I like best is an afternoon at the beach.
c) I didn't know who/which to ask about my timetable.
d) The people which/whose luggage was lost had to wait a long time.
e) Where's the ruler whose/that I left on this desk?
f) The shop what/that I went to didn't have any milk.
g) Do you know whom/whose bag this is?
h) Everyone who/which was there will remember the day forever.
i) The second bus, which/whose was full, didn't stop either.
j) Jim was helped by someone who/whom told him the answer.

2
Some sentences have a word which should not be there. Write the word at the end, or put a tick ✓ if the sentence is correct.

a) The woman whom I asked didn't know the way.   ..✓..
b) The man whose his car had been damaged was very angry.   .....
c) That was the longest film I've ever seen.   .....
d) The train which it goes to London leaves from here.   .....
e) The policewoman who she stopped me asked me my name.   .....
f) The Eiffel Tower, which it was completed in 1889, is made of iron. .....
g) Everyone that Helen spoke to advised her to try again.   .....
h) The children that they live next door are my friends.   .....

3
Rewrite each pair of sentences as one sentence, and include the word given. Begin as shown, and make any necessary changes.

a) We want to visit a museum. It opens at 12.00.
that
The ...*museum that we want to visit opens at 12.00*...................................
b) A boy's bike was taken. He visited the police station.
whose
The ....
c) A friend met me at the airport. He carried my suitcase.
who
The ....
d) Tom cooked a meal. It was delicious.
that
The ....
e) A friend is staying with me. She comes from Paris.
who
The ....

f) I found a man's wallet. He gave me a reward.

whose

The ....

g) I go to a shop in the centre. It is cheaper.

that

The ....

h) I went to a girl's party. She phoned me.

whose

The ....

i) I know someone. This person likes you.

who

I ....

4

Put **one** word in each space, or tick the space if the sentence is correct.

a) We sent a present to the children .....✓......... living next door.

b) Mike doesn't really know .... he wants.

c) I started talking to some boys .... sitting by the side of the road.

d) I asked Mary .... she was thinking, but she wouldn't tell me.

e) There were lots of people at the party .... we went to.

f) I don't really know .... you are talking about.

g) We saw two rabbits .... playing in the garden.

h) .... we need now is a map and a compass.

Unit 25 Questions 1

Explanations

yes/no questions | These are questions with the answer *yes* or *no*.

Present simple | ***Do you live*** *in Prague?*
Present continuous | ***Are you sitting*** *comfortably?*
Present perfect | ***Have you ever eaten*** *octopus?*
Past simple | ***Did you phone*** *Sue?*
Past continuous | ***Were you having*** *a bath?*
Past perfect | ***Had you*** *already* ***left?***
can/could | ***Can*** *you swim?* ***Could*** *you see?*
must | ***Must*** *you go? Do you have to go?*

Wh- questions | These are questions with *what, why, when, who, whose, which* and *how.*

Present simple | ***When*** *do you usually leave?*
Present continuous | ***What*** *are you doing?*
Present perfect | ***Why*** *have you stopped?*
Past simple | ***How*** *did you feel?*
Past continuous | ***Where*** *were you living?*
Past perfect | ***Who*** *had told you?*
can/could | ***What*** *can I do?* ***Where*** *could he go?*
must | ***What*** *must I do?* ***What*** *do I have to do?*

Subject or object questions | Questions about the subject do not use *do/does/did.*

Cats (s) *eat fish* (o).

What *do cats eat?* | *Cats eat* ***fish.*** | (object question)
Who *eats fish?* | *Cats eats fish.* | (subject question)

Positive and negative questions | A positive question could have a *yes* or *no* answer.

Do you like dogs? | *Yes, I do./No, I don't.*

A negative question supposes that the answer will be *no.* A *yes* answer means that the questioner has supposed wrongly.

Don't you like *dogs?* | *No, I don't.*
Don't you like *dogs?* | ***Yes, of course I do.*** *What made you think that?*

Short answers | Auxiliary verbs, and modal auxiliaries, are used for short answers.

Do *you speak French?* | *Yes,* ***I do.***
Have *you seen this film?* | *No, I* ***haven't.***
Did *you stay long?* | *No, I* ***didn't.***
Will *you be late?* | *No, I* ***won't.***
Have *you got a pen?* | *Yes, I* ***have.***
Can *you drive?* | *No, I* ***can't.***

Practice

1

Write a question for each answer.

a) ...*What time do you usually get up?*...   Get up? At about 7.30 usually.

b) ....   I was reading *War and Peace*.

c) ....   I went there to buy some food.

d) ....   So far I've only eaten breakfast.

e) ....   Now you have to put it in the oven!

f) ....   Yesterday? I felt absolutely awful.

g) ....   I'm washing my hair. I can't talk, sorry.

h) ....   Because I haven't paid the electricity bill!

i) ....   My bike? I left it outside the school.

j) ....   My party? All my friends are coming.

2

Write a *who* or *what* question for each answer.

a) ...*Who lives next door?*.................   A family of three lives next door.

b) ....   I play with my little brother.

c) ....   Mrs Dawson teaches me maths.

d) ....   I usually eat a sandwich for lunch.

e) ....   Horror films frighten me.

f) ....   I talk most to my friend Dina.

g) ....   I sit next to Maria in English.

h) ....   I take my dog for a walk every evening.

i) ....   My friend Tim makes me laugh.

j) ....   Music helps me study.

3

Write a short answer for each question, beginning as shown.

a) Have you been ill long?   No, ...*I haven't*............ .

b) Are you waiting for me?   Yes, ...

c) Did you go to the cinema?   Yes, ...

d) Will you be here tomorrow?   Yes, ...

e) Did you have to pay a lot?   No, ...

f) Can you help me with this problem?   No, ...

g) Do you know where the theatre is?   Yes, ...

h) Is George going to be there?   No, ...

Unit 26 Questions 2

Explanations

Reply questions

Reply questions are a way of replying to a statement, when you do not agree or are not sure, or are surprised.

We're leaving at 6.00.	***Are we?***	(not sure)
I've never eaten spaghetti.	***Haven't you?***	(surprise)

Tag questions

Tag questions add a question to the end of a statement. The meaning depends on whether the question is positive or negative, and on the intonation.

Formation

Tag questions are formed using the auxiliaries. When the main verb is positive, then the tag is negative. When the main verb is negative, then the tag is positive.

*You **speak** French, **don't you**?* (negative tag)
*You **don't speak** French, **do you**?* (positive tag)

Meaning and intonation

- There are two possible questions, each with two intonations. Negative tags generally suppose the answer will be *yes*. The rising tone is like a real question because the speaker is not really sure and needs information. The level/falling tone is used to check information.

  You speak French, don't you? (rising)
  I'm not sure, so tell me if I'm right.
  You speak French, don't you? (level/falling)
  I'm sure that you do, but I'm checking.
  Positive tags generally suppose the answer will be *no*.
  You don't speak French, do you? (rising)
  I'm sure you don't./I'm surprised that you do.
  You don't speak French, do you? (level/falling)
  I'm sure that you don't, but I'm checking.

- Tenses
  This is a selection of examples, with explanations of meaning. Not all types are included.

Present simple	*You don't know the answer, **do you**?*	(L/F)
	You've been pretending to know.	
Present continuous	*We're enjoying ourselves, **aren't we**?*	(L/F)
	You want someone to agree with you.	
Present perfect	*He's moved house, **hasn't he**?*	(R)
	You're not sure about this.	
Past simple	*You didn't tell her, **did you**?*	(R)
	You're angry because it's true!	

Past continuous	*I wasn't driving fast, **was I**?*	(L/F)
	You need a witness to prove this.	
Past perfect	*She hadn't met him then, **had she**?*	(R)
	You're surprised by what was said.	

- Modals

can	*They can't be here yet, **can they**?*	(R)
	You're surprised.	
could	*You couldn't jump over it, **could you**?*	(L/F)
	I didn't suppose that you could!	
should	*You shouldn't do that, **should you**?*	(L/F)
	I think it's wrong.	

let's

Let's uses shall as a tag.
    *Let's go to the cinema, **shall we**?*

Problems

Imperative, *be* and *have*
Polite instructions use *will* or *won't* as a tag for the imperative.
    *Sit down, **will you**?*   *Sit down, **won't you**?*
There is no difference in meaning in this context.
Be also uses *will* or *won't* as a tag for the imperative.
    *Be quiet, **will you**?*   *Be quiet, **won't you**? This is an order!*
Have in a polite instruction uses *will* or *won't* with the imperative.
    *Have a seat, **won't you**?*

Practice

This unit also includes further practice for Unit 25.

1

Add a short
answer to each
sentence.

a)	Have you ever been to Brazil?	No, ...*I haven't*.......
b)	Do you like sausages?	Yes, ...
c)	Are you coming to the match tomorrow?	Yes, ...
d)	Did Helen phone you today?	No, ...
e)	Has Jack done his homework?	Yes, ...
f)	Can George and Sue skate?	Yes, ...
g)	Will you be late?	No, ...
h)	Has Tina got a brother?	No, ...
i)	Is that your house?	Yes, ...
j)	Did Jane give you that book?	No, ...

2

Add a reply question to each sentence.

a) We've got a test tomorrow.   ...*Have we*...... ?
b) I don't understand this sentence.   .... ?
c) Sue phoned me last night.   .... ?
d) I don't like ice-cream.   .... ?
e) Tom is leaving tomorrow.   .... ?
f) There's a policeman at the door.   .... ?
g) Lisa has just had a baby.   .... ?
h) I haven't eaten Chinese food.   .... ?
i) There isn't any milk in the fridge.   .... ?
j) I met David in France.   .... ?

3

Add a tag question to each sentence.

a) We're nearly there, ...*aren't we*....... ?
b) You haven't got a spare pen, ... ?
c) You're coming to my party, ... ?
d) You won't be late, ... ?
e) Harry's fifteen, ... ?
f) Kate and Pat live in Leeds, ... ?
g) You don't feel well, ... ?
h) You like fish, ... ?
i) Richard's bought a new bike, ... ?
j) I shouldn't tell you this, ... ?

4

Make a new sentence with a tag question which has the same meaning as the first sentence, and begins as shown. Make any necessary changes.

a) I'm sure that Paul doesn't like football.
   Paul ...*doesn't like football*............ , ...*does he*............ ?
b) I'm checking that you've got a sister.
   You .... , ... ?
c) I don't think that you've done your homework!
   You .... , ... ?
d) I'm angry that you sat next to Ellen!
   You .... , ... ?
e) I'm surprised that the guests have arrived.
   The guests .... , ... ?
f) I'm checking that your name is John.
   Your name .... , ... ?
g) I'm surprised to meet you and think that your name might be John.
   Your name .... , ... ?
h) You are certain that you didn't leave your wallet on the desk.
   I .... , ... ?

i) You're surprised that William has got married.

William .... , ... ?

j) You're checking that this book is by Martin Aimless.

This book .... , ... ?

5

Choose the best sentence in each context.

a) Why did you forget your keys! You are silly!

1) I didn't tell you to forget them, did I?

2) <u>I told you not to forget them, didn't I?</u>

b) Ugh! I can't believe it! I'm sure they must taste horrible!

1) You like eating snails, don't you?

2) You don't like eating snails, do you?

c) If we go to Italy, we might have problems with the language.

1) You speak Italian, don't you?

2) You don't speak Italian, do you?

d) I told you to keep the party a secret. It's supposed to be a surprise for Stella. So, I just want to make sure.

1) You didn't tell her, did you?

2) You told her, didn't you?

e) Well, Mr Robinson, I think it's time you told the police the truth. You see, we've found your fingerprints on the murder weapon.

1) You didn't murder Lord Chumley, did you?

2) You murdered Lord Chumley, didn't you?

f) Only two minutes to the end of the match and United are still 5–1 in the lead. It looks certain now.

1) United aren't going to win, are they?

2) United are going to win, aren't they?

g) I haven't see Ann for ages. She's working abroad I think.

1) She's got a job in France, hasn't she?

2) She hasn't got a job in France, has she?

h) I just can't answer this question. It would be nice to have some help.

1) You could help me, couldn't you?

2) You couldn't help me, could you?

Unit 27 *it* and *there*

Explanations

its and *it's*

Its is the possessive form of *it*. *It's* is a contraction of *it is* or *it has*.

    I like this hotel. ***It's*** *comfortable and* ***its*** *restaurant is good.*

    It's *got a lovely swimming-pool, too.*

Verb forms with *it*.

- Impersonal verbs

  Some verbs which describe impersonal activities are normally only found in third person with *it*.

      It's *raining.*   ***It's*** *snowing.*

- *be* with adjectives

  The verb *be* is often used in this way with adjectives and *that*.

      It's interesting that *you like jazz too.*

      It's strange that *we've never spoken before.*

- *look, seem, appear*

  Look is usually followed by *as if* with verbs and *like* with nouns. *Seem* and *appear* can be followed by *that*.

      It looks as if *Carol has won. She looks like a real champion.*

      It seems that *the Brazilians are going to win.*

      It appears that *one of the customers called the police.*

there, they're and *their*

There can refer to place, or is used when a subject is needed for *be* or some other verbs.

    A famous writer used to live ***there***.

    There *is a shop at the end of the street.*

They're is a contraction for *they are*.

    Nancy and Jim have arrived. ***They're*** *both wearing fancy dress.*

Their is the possessive form of *they*.

    Ask them to leave ***their*** *coats in the hall.*

Verb forms with *there*

There is used with *seem* and *appear*.

    There seems/appears *to be a problem. She seems unhappy.*

it and *there*

It and *there* are used as subjects for *be*. *It* refers to something already mentioned.

    There is *a shop at the end of the street.*

    It is *open every day.*

Practice

1
Choose the correct word underlined in each sentence.

a) Are their/(there) any eggs in the fridge?

b) It's/Its really cold this morning.

c) Peter says they're/there arriving at about 5.00.

d) I like this bike but its/it's wheels are too small.

e) Is there/they're anybody their/there?

f) It's/Its a pity we missed the opening of the film.

g) Kate and Sue have sold their/they're house.

h) What a lovely dog. What's it's/its name?

2
Put *it* or *there* in each space.

a) ...*There*.... is a tree in the garden. ...*It*......... is an apple tree.

b) .... looks as if .... is going to rain.

c) .... is strange that .... are no restaurants in this town.

d) 'Who's that at the door?' '............. is only me!'

e) 'Which house is yours?' '............. is the one at the end of the street.'

f) .... seems to be something under the cupboard, but what is .... ?

g) .... appears that .... was nobody .... when I phoned.

h) Near the park .... is a swimming-pool. .... is only open in summer.

3
Rewrite each sentence ending as shown so that it has a similar meaning to the first sentence, and so that it contains *it* or *there*.

a) Near the hotel is a small restaurant.
...*There is a small restaurant*................ near the hotel.

b) You went to Spain for your holiday too, which is strange.
.... to Spain for your holiday too.

c) My road has a big tree at the end of it.
.... road.

d) The plane apparently had engine trouble.
.... engine trouble.

e) Brian seems to have left.
.... has left.

f) Today is really cold!
.... today.

g) Budapest is a long way from here.
.... to Budapest.

h) Your torch hasn't got any batteries in it.
.... torch.

i) We appear to be lost again!
.... lost again!

j) The police haven't arrived, which is strange.
.... haven't arrived.

Unit 28 Place and position

Explanations

in, out, inside, on

- *in* and *inside*

  In generally describes things contained by something else.

  > *There are some cups **in** that cupboard.*

  We use *inside* to emphasize the idea of containing.

  > *Luckily there was nobody **inside** the blazing house.*

  Compare:

  > *Kate is **in**.*   (she's at home)
  >
  > *Kate is **out**.*   (she's not at home)
  >
  > *Kate is **inside**.*   (in the house, not out here in the garden)

  There are many expressions with *in*. This is a selection.

a country	*My parents are **in Canada** at the moment.*
a city	*My sister lives **in Madrid**.*
street	*Jack lives **in Garden Avenue**.*
road	*She was walking **in the road**, not on the pavement.*
mirror	*Tony could see his face **in the mirror**.*
hole/crack	*There was a hole **in my shoe**.*
hand	*Ellen had a bunch of flowers **in one hand**.*
armchair	*She sat **in an armchair**.*
country	*Paul and Mary live **in the country**, not in the city.*
hospital	*Sally is ill, and is **in hospital**.*
prison	*Keith stole some money and ended up **in prison**.*

- *on*

  On generally describes a thing on the surface of another thing.

  > *Don't leave your bag **on the floor**.*

  Expressions with *on*.

transport	*There were few passengers **on the plane/bus/train**.*
chair	*She sat **on a chair**.*
television	*What's **on television/the radio** this evening?*
wall	*Let's hang this picture **on that wall**.*
injuries	*Tim cut his foot **on a piece** of glass.*
left/right	*There's a cinema **on the left**.*
side	*There are small houses **on this side** of the street.*
pavement	*She was walking in the road, not **on the pavement**.*

at, *to* and *in*	● *At* and *in* are used to describe a person's position. *At* describes position at a point or place.
	In describes position in a place which has walls (like a building). It is also used with cities and towns, etc. The difference between *at* and *in* is clear in examples.

> *We met **at the airport**.* (the place in general)
> *We met **in the airport building**.* (inside the building)
> *I'll see you **at the cinema**.* (the place in general)
> *I'll see you **in the cinema**.* (inside the building)

At and *in* are used with *arrive*.

> *We arrived **in Prague**.* (the city) *We arrived **at Prague Airport**.* (the place)

● *To* is used with verbs of motion.

> *Last night we **went to the cinema**.*

Expressions with *at* and *to*	● *At*

> *There's a café **at the end** of the street.*
> *Do you sit at the front or **at the back** of the class?*
> *John isn't **at school**. He's **at home**.*
> *Mr King wasn't **at work** yesterday.*

● *To*

> *Could you take this letter **to the post office**?*
> *I sent a parcel **to my sister**.*

above, *over*, *below*, *under*	● *above* and *over*

Above means *higher than*.

> *You can see the top of the tower **above the trees**.*

Over means *higher than*, but in the same position.

> *The alien spaceship **hovered over** the building.*

It also means *across* or *covering*.

> *There was a plastic sheet **over the hole** in the roof.*
> *There is a footbridge **over the motorway**.*

● *below* and *under*

below means *lower than*.

> *From the mountain, I could see the lake **below**.*

Under means *lower than*, but in the same position.

> *I keep my suitcase **under my bed**.*

next to, *near*, *by*, *beside*	● *next to* and *near*

Next to means *exactly at the side of*.

> *Maria sits **next to** Paula.*

Near means *close to*.

> *Tom's house is **near** the sports centre.*

- *beside* and *by*

  beside means the same as *next to*. Some speakers feel it is more formal.

  > *Come and sit **beside me** on the sofa.*

  By means the same as *near*. It is often used in descriptions of rooms.

  > *There was a table **by** the window. He was standing **by** the door.*

opposite

Opposite means exactly on the other side of a space.

> *There is a baker's **opposite** our house.*

- See Units 31 and 32 Articles.

Practice

1

Choose the correct word underlined in each sentence.

a) There's a small shop (at)/by the end of the road.

b) Paula was standing on/with one foot.

c) Helen has moved at/to Barcelona.

d) Don't walk at/in the road! It's dangerous!

e) From the plane we could see the mountains below/under.

f) Brian spent his holiday at/in Hungary.

g) When the horse came to a small stream it jumped above/over it.

h) Julia's house is at/on the other side of the street.

i) Lisa cut her foot at/on some broken glass.

j) Tim was sitting in/on an armchair.

2

If the word underlined is not appropriate, write a new word in the space. Tick if the word is correct.

a) Jane's sister has a job at Manchester Airport.   ....✓.....

b) I met David yesterday by the city centre.   ....

c) Ellen had a large hole at her left boot.   ....

d) Jack sits in the back of the class.   ....

e) There was a small table at the bed.   ....

f) The robber was holding a gun in one hand.   ....

g) There was a beautiful portrait hanging at the wall.   ....

h) Bill didn't feel well and his doctor sent him to hospital.   ....

i) The children usually sit at the back seat of the car.   ....

j) To reach our village we take a road above the mountains.   ....

3

Put **one** suitable word in each space.

a) Maria lives ...*in*..... Bellingham Road.

b) Can you put the plates back .... the shelf please?

c) Please don't stand .... your desks!

d) I'd really like to live .... the country.

e) Go down this street, and you'll see the cinema .... the right.

f) The police searched the building but there was no one ....

g) I met Ann .... the bus yesterday.

h) Sorry, George isn't here at the moment. He's ....

i) Alice wants to know what's .... television this evening.

j) Just as Tom arrived .... the bus-stop, the bus left.

4

Put **one** suitable word in each space.

a) The statue was holding a sword ...*in*.... one hand.

b) What's on .... the cinema this week?

c) When I look .... the mirror, I don't recognize myself!

d) What have you got .... your bag?

e) Peter found someone's wallet .... the pavement.

f) My family moved from the country .... the city.

g) You've got a small hole .... your pullover.

h) The burglar climbed .... the fence and into the garden.

5

Choose the correct word or phrase underlined in each sentence.

a) Karen is living at/(in) London Street.

b) Mary sits by/next to Sally in the physics class.

c) I want to send this letter at/to Brazil.

d) When I opened the box, there was nothing in/inside.

e) Exactly by/opposite the cinema, there's a fast-food restaurant.

f) We had a holiday in a small village by/near Monte Carlo.

g) Paula lay down at/on the floor to do her exercises.

h) We had a lovely meal in/on the plane.

6

Put **one** suitable word in each space.

a) I decided to visit my grandmother ...*in*.... hospital.

b) We put a blanket .... the injured man to keep him warm.

c) It's not far. We're getting ....

d) We found our cat hiding .... a car.

e) Jim hung his coat .... the back of a chair.

f) I decided to go the shops .... my bike.

g) What time is the news .... the radio?

h) Bye for now. I'll see you .... school tomorrow.

Problems, Errors, Consolidation 3

1
Choose the correct word or phrase underlined in each sentence.

a) We arrived early, <u>so that we/in order to</u> get tickets.
b) It was <u>too/enough</u> long to wait, so we went home.
c) Tim and Helen have arrived, and <u>they're/there</u> waiting outside.
d) The boy <u>of which/whose</u> bike I borrowed had forgotten about it.
e) We went to the beach <u>for/so that</u> a swim.
f) Ann felt lonely <u>because/so</u> no one had invited her to the party.
g) <u>Despite/Although</u> I felt tired, I worked until late.
h) We spent a lovely holiday <u>in/into</u> the country.
i) Yesterday was <u>so/such</u> cold that I stayed at home.
j) <u>However/In spite of</u> the rain, we went for a walk.

2
Complete the second sentence so that it has a similar meaning to the first sentence.

a) Although it was late, we decided to go for a walk.
It was late *but we decided to go for a walk* .
b) John is someone with whom I used to work.
.... with.
c) The exam was so difficult that I couldn't finish it.
It was ....
d) Although it was raining, we worked in the garden
Despite ....
e) Let's spend the afternoon at the beach.
How .... ?
f) Ann's house has got four large bedrooms.
.... in Ann's house.
g) We might feel hungry, so we'll take some sandwiches.
We'll .... so that
.... hungry.
h) The cat hasn't come home, which is strange.
.... home.
i) Harry can't afford to go on holiday.
Harry hasn't got ....
j) Where's the National Museum?
Would .... ?

3

Decide which answer, a), b), c) or d), best fits the space.

A case of mistaken identity

When Diana got off the train, (1) ..*b*.. was a woman waiting for her (2) ..... the platform. '(3) ..... ?' she asked. '(4) ..... a car waiting for you (5) .....' Diana was not very surprised, (6) ..... she thought that her aunt must have been (7) ..... busy to meet her (8) ..... the station. (9) ..... she did not recognize the woman, (10) ..... was dressed very formally, and had an attaché case (11) ..... her arm, she was (12) ..... tired after the journey that she was happy to get (13) ..... the car. The woman, (14) ..... , just said a few words to the driver, and then walked away. Diana wondered (15) ..... she was. 'It's strange that she didn't even introduce herself,' she thought.

1) a) who   b) there   c) whose   d) it
2) a) below   b) to   c) on   d) in
3) a) You Diana, are you   b) You're Diana, isn't it   c) Are you Diana
   d) You aren't Diana
4) a) There's   b) Theirs   c) Its   d) It's
5) a) out   b) In   c) inside   d) outside
6) a) so   b) despite   c) too   d) as
7) a) so   b) too   c) enough   d) very
8) a) at   b) to   c) in   d) for
9) a) However   b) Since   c) In spite of   d) Although
10) a) she   b) who   c) and   d) whose
11) a) at   b) in   c) under   d) by
12) a) enough   b) so   c) too   d) very
13) a) with   b) by   c) at   d) into
14) a) however   b) despite   c) although   d) in spite of
15) a) whether   b) there   c) who   d) however

4

Put one suitable preposition in each space.

There was another woman (a) ...*on*... the bus, and Kate sat (b) .... her and started chatting. She said she was going (c) .... Forbes Road too. 'I've got an interview (d) .... a place called Murcott House,' said Kate. 'Is it (e) .... the bus-stop?' 'It's not far. It's (f) .... the right (g) .... the end of the street,' the woman replied. 'In fact, I live (h) .... When I look out of my window, I can see people working (i) ....' When they arrived (j) .... the stop, they got off and walked up the street together.

5

Look carefully at each line. Some lines are correct but some have a word which should not be there. Tick each correct line. If a line has a word which should not be there, write the word in the space.

A case of mistaken identity

After a few minutes, the car stopped in front of   1) ..✓..

a large hotel. The driver who opened the door, and   2) *who*

said, 'Please follow me.' They went up in to a lift.   3) ......

Then there was a long corridor with two or three   4) ......

doors. Although it seemed strange so that the car hadn't   5) ......

taken her to her aunt's house, Diana who wasn't surprised.   6) ......

Her aunt, who she was very rich, owned several large   7) ......

hotels, which she often stayed in them. I suppose she felt   8) ......

so much bored at home that she decided to stay here.   9) ......

'Please you wait here, will you?' said the driver, and   10) ......

disappeared into a room at the end of the corridor.   11) ......

There seemed to be a lot of people that in one of the   12) ......

rooms. Then the driver, who he hadn't been gone long,   13) ......

came back at and asked Diana to follow him. They went   14) ......

into a large room full of people, who all started clapping.   15) ......

There was a poster that it said, 'Diana Harris, Supermodel.'   16) ......

'Oh dear,' said Diana, 'I think so there's been a mistake!'   17) ......

6

Rewrite each pair of sentences as one sentence with a similar meaning, completing it as shown.

a) Sue read a book. She really enjoyed it.

which

Sue ..*read a book which she really*.................. enjoyed.

b) Some friends visited me. They brought me a present.

who

The friends .... present.

c) I stayed in a hotel. It was cheaper than this one.

that

The hotel .... this one.

d) I borrowed a friend's bike. He wanted it back.

whose

The .... back.

e) I saw the vase in the shop. I wanted to buy it.

that

I wanted .... shop.

f) A girl sings in the group. She's got green hair.

who

The girl .... green hair.

g) I met a girl. Her brother is in my class.
   whose
   .... class.
h) We are taking the train. It leaves at 4.30.
   that
   The train .... at 4.30.
i) A man knocked at the door. He was selling brushes.
   who
   The man .... brushes.
j) I saw a film with Tom. It was interesting.
   which
   The film .... interesting.

7
Complete each space, using the verb given where necessary.

a) '...*You have got*..... (have got) a book, haven't you?'   'Yes, thanks.'
b) 'They'll be back by 6.00, ... ?'   'I expect so.'
c) '........................ (go) for a walk, shall we? It's a lovely day!'   'Good idea!'
d) 'You .... (leave) now, are you? Stay a bit longer.'   'Sorry, I can't, I have to catch the bus.'
e) 'Jim and Ellen have seen this film, ... ?'   'Yes, I think so.'
f) 'You can meet Helen at the station, ... ?'   'Yes, of course I can.'
g) '........................ (be) here yesterday, were you?'   'No, I wasn't.'
h) 'You don't happen to know the time, ... ?'   'Sorry, I don't.'
i) 'Both drivers were driving too fast, ... ?'   'Yes, that's right.'
j) 'You .... (forget) the milk, did you?'   'No, I bought two cartons.'

Problem check

1 Check the different uses of *so*, *too* and *enough* in Unit 20. When do we use *so* and *such*?

2 Check the differences between *although*, *however* and *despite/in spite of*.

3 Can you add any more expressions to the list of functions in Unit 22? How important is your intonation and tone of voice? What do you say in similar situations in your language?

4 Check when you can leave out relative pronouns.

5 Check the meaning of *they're*, *their* and *there*.

6 Check the differences between *at*, *in* and *to*.

Unit 29 Time expressions

Explanations

in, *on* and *at*

- *in*

Years	*in* 1999	Morning	*in* the morning
Months	*in* January	Afternoon	*in* the afternoon
Seasons	*in* the summer	Evening	*in* the evening

- *on*

  Days   *on* Wednesday   *on* my birthday

- *at*

  Times   *at* 4.00   *at* midday   *at* midnight

  Night   *at* night

during

During is used about periods of time.

> I didn't feel nervous *during* the performance.

Calendar references

We say: *the seventh of September*   *September the seventh*

We write: *7 September*   *7th September*   *September 7th*

Dates are written Day/Month/Year in British English: *7/9/99*

Day references

If today is 7 September:

tomorrow	*8 September*
the day after tomorrow	*9 September*
yesterday	*6 September*
the day before yesterday	*5 September*

Periods of the day

this morning	*this afternoon*	*tonight*
yesterday morning	*yesterday afternoon*	*last night*
tomorrow morning	*tomorrow afternoon*	*tomorrow night*

for, *since* and *ago*

For refers to a period of time.

> I have lived here *for six years*.   I studied French *for two years*.

Since refers to a point at the beginning of a period of time.

> I have lived here *since 1995*.   I've been waiting *since 3.30*.

Ago refers to a point in the past.

> We arrived *five hours ago*.   I knew that *ages ago*!

once and *one day*

- *Once* refers to a state in the past.

  > *Once I owned* a motorbike.

- *One day* can refer to past or future.
  One day I was walking through the town centre when I met Jill.
  One day I'll be famous!

now and
nowadays

- *Now* refers to an exact moment, or a general state.
  *You have to finish ... **Now**!*
  *Peter used to live in Rome, but **now he's living** in Florence.*

- *Nowadays* is used when we generalize about the present.
  ***Nowadays** people are not as polite as they used to be.*

then, afterwards,
after and *later*

- *Then* refers in the past to the following moment.
  *We went to the cinema, and **then** we had a pizza.*

- *Afterwards* can be used in the same way.
  *We went to the cinema, and **afterwards** we had a pizza.*

- When *after* is used, there is an object.
  ***After the film** we had a pizza. **After that** we went home.*

- *Later* means at a later time.
  *Mrs James isn't here at the moment. Can you come back **later**?*

until and *by*

- *Until* refers to the latest point in a period of time.
  *I waited for Alex **until 6.00**, and then I left.*
  *I'll be here **until** the end of March.*

- *By* means at a time before. We use it when we do not know exactly when
  something happened or will happen.
  *We'll be there **by 5.30**.*   (not at 5.30, but not later)
  *Helen worked all day, and **by 6.30** she felt exhausted.*

at last, in the end
and *at the end*

- We use *at last* when we are pleased that a long wait has ended.
  ***At last** we can be together!*

- *In the end* describes the final result.
  *We waited for Tim for ages, and **in the end** we left.*

- *At the end* describes a point at the end of something.
  ***At the end** of the film we all cried.*

on time and *in*
time

- *On time* means at the hour which was arranged.
  *The plane took off exactly **on time**.*

- *In time* means with enough time to do something.
  *We arrived **in time** to have a meal before the plane left.*

116

Practice

1

Choose the correct word or phrase underlined in each sentence.

a) I met Tina a day/(one day) last week.

b) In these days/Nowadays everyone seems to watch too much television.

c) This morning/The morning I was busy in the garden.

d) We have to finish this project by/until the end of the week.

e) Bye. I'll see you the day after tomorrow/the next day.

f) During/While the film I remembered where I'd left my keys.

g) John played tennis, and after/afterwards had a shower.

h) Helen's birthday is in/on January 10th.

2

Complete the second sentence so that it has a similar meaning to the first sentence.

a) We had lunch, and afterwards we went for a coffee.

After *...we had/had had lunch, we went for a coffee....* .

b) Jill is never late for lessons.

Jill is always ....

c) I won't leave before 8.00.

I'll be here ....

d) I've been living here for three months.

I started living here ....

e) When we met for lunch it was 12.00.

We met for lunch ....

f) What do you do in your country on January 1st?

What do you do in your country on the .... ?

g) I'll see you not tomorrow but the next day.

I'll see you the ....

h) It's 10.00 and I've been waiting here since 7.00.

I've been waiting here .... hours.

3

Put **one** suitable word in each space.

a) Would you like to go out ...*on*.... my birthday?

b) Rita moved to this town four years ....

c) I won't phone Jim now. I'll phone him ....

d) I woke up twice .... the night.

e) .... midnight the frog turned into a prince.

f) People in cities used to take the bus, but .... most use their cars.

g) Luckily Kate arrived just .... time to catch the train.

h) We felt fine in the restaurant, but we both felt ill ....

i) I've been waiting here .... half an hour!

j) Don't wait for me any longer. I'll see you ....

4

Rewrite each sentence so that it has a similar meaning and contains the word given.

a) I spend the summer at the seaside.
   in
   ...*I go to the seaside in summer.*...

b) I'll see you in a few hours.
   later
   ....

c) I started at this school in 1997.
   since
   ....

d) George had a bath and after that washed his hair.
   then
   ....

e) Diane left my house at 10.00.
   until
   ....

f) The train arrived exactly when it was supposed to.
   on time
   ....

g) I won't arrive later than 2.00.
   by
   ....

h) Paul tried hard but finally gave up.
   end
   ....

i) I was too late to say goodbye to Lisa.
   time
   ....

j) I've been learning English for two years.
   ago
   ....

5

Put **one** suitable word in each space.

a) Did you sleep well ...*last*......... night?
b) .... the hot weather, we have our meals in the garden.
c) .... the lesson, Mike and Tina decided to play basketball.
d) Sam hasn't seen Lisa .... three weeks.
e) I know that .... day you will be a star!
f) It's very important to arrive .... time for the examination.
g) The robber ran out of the bank and was arrested shortly ....
h) There is a lot of noise in our street .... night.

Unit 30 Countable and uncountable

Explanations

a/an, zero article, *some*, *any*

- Nouns are either countable or uncountable. Uncountable nouns are sometimes called mass nouns. Countable nouns have plural in *s* or an irregular plural. Some countable words do not have *s* plural e.g. *people*.

- *A/an* the indefinite article is used with singular nouns. See Unit 31.
  *Sue has got **a motorbike.***

- Zero article is used with countables and uncountables. See Unit 31.
  *I don't like fizzy drinks. I prefer **still mineral water.***

- *Some* is used with countables and uncountables. *Any* is used for questions and negatives.
  *We've got **some** lemonade, but we haven't got **any glasses.***
  *Have you got **any cups**?*

- *Some* is used in questions when we ask about something we have a definite idea about. This is necessary in requests beginning *Can/Could … ?*
  *Have you got **some letters** for me?*
  (I think this is probable.)
  Have you got any letters for me?
  (I don't know the answer.)
  ***Can/Could I have some** more tea, please?*

much and *many*

Much is used for uncountables and *many* is used for countables. They are used mainly in questions and negatives.
  *How **much money** have we got?*   *There isn't **much water** here.*
  *How **many chairs** are there?*   *There aren't **many cushions**.*

Materials

- Materials are uncountable.
  ***Wood** burns easily.*

- Words for materials often have a countable meaning. See page 120.

Problem uncountables

- Some words are uncountable grammatically, although we might not expect this. Examples are:

advice	*hair*	*knowledge*	*spaghetti*
English (language)	*health*	*luggage*	*travel*
furniture	*information*	*machinery*	*weather*

● A singular verb is used:

*His **advice was** very useful.*   ***French is** difficult.*

● *A/an* cannot be used.

*Could I have **some information**?*   *Do you **any luggage**?*

Alternatives:
a/some

Some uncountable words have a different meaning with *a/an* or *some*.

a fish (the animal)	*some fish* (a portion of food)
a loaf	*some bread* (the material)
a coffee (a cup of coffee)	*some coffee* (the material)
a paper (a newspaper)	*some paper* (the material)
a wood (a small forest)	*some wood* (the material)
an iron (for pressing clothes)	*some iron* (the material)
a glass (for drinking)	*some glass* (the material)

Alternatives:
with *a/an* or *s*
plural

● Some uncountable words usually with zero article have a different meaning with *a/an* or *s* plural.

*I can't stand **noise**.*   (in general)

*I heard **a strange noise**.*   *I keep hearing **noises**.*   (specific)

● Nouns ending *-ing* usually have a general meaning and are uncountable, but some also have countable meanings.

Do you like drawing/painting?   (in general)

I bought a painting/a drawing last week.   (specific)

● Some nouns change meaning with *a/an* but cannot have *s* plural.

Education is very important.   (in general)

*Diana had **a very good education**.*   (her time at school)

Knowledge can be dangerous!   (in general)

***A knowledge** of boats is useful.*   (knowing about a subject)

Other problems

news   singular verb

*The **news is** on.*

money   singular verb

*There **isn't any** money.*

police   plural verb

*The police **are** coming.*

Government/Army   singular or plural verb

*The Government **has/have** decided to resign.*

scissors/trousers   always plural

*Where **are** my scissors?*   *I bought some new trousers.*

Practice

1

Choose the correct word or phrase underlined in each sentence.

a) (How much)/How many spaghetti have we got?

b) Where is/are my new trousers?

c) I put some/any chocolate somewhere, but where is it?

d) Peter went to buy a/some glass so he could fix the broken windows.

e) I'm afraid we haven't got much/many time.

f) The news is/are on at 9.00.

g) How much/How many furniture shops are there?

h) I've found the milk but I can't find a/some glass.

i) Could you give me some/any orange juice, please?

j) Mary's advice was/were not very useful.

2

Put **one** word in each space. Put a dash (–) if the space should be blank.

a) My trousers need ironing. Have you got ...*an*...... iron?

b) Could you go to the baker's and buy .... loaf, please?

c) I'd like .... information about trains to Paris.

d) Tina has .... very good health.

e) The war ended .... years ago.

f) Jane isn't very good at .... drawing.

g) Harry didn't have .... very good education.

h) Vanessa bought .... paper and read it on the bus.

i) Could you give me .... advice, please?

j) Do you know .... people in this village?

3

Complete the second sentence so that it has a similar meaning to the first sentence and contains the word given.

a) Let me tell you what I think you should do.

advice

Let me ...*give you some advice*................. .

b) I need a clean pair of trousers.

any

I haven't got ....

c) There isn't a lot of water in the pool.

much

.... water in the pool.

d) I have to wash my hair.

washing

My hair ....

e) I can't find my scissors.

where

.... scissors?

121

f) The book did not contain any information.

in

The information ....

g) What did your new bike cost?

how

.... your new bike cost?

h) All the sandwiches have been eaten.

left

There ....

4

Choose the best alternative, 1) or 2), to complete each sentence.

a) The fire is going to go out. Can you go and get ...*some wood*.... .

   1) a wood   2) some wood

b) .... money all over the floor!

   1) There was   2) There were

c) Let me give you ....

   1) an advice   2) some advice

d) Lemonade? Sorry, no, we haven't got ....

   1) some   2) any

e) Peter keeps .... at the bottom of his garden.

   1) a chicken   2) some chicken

f) The information we were given ....

   1) were very useful   2) was very useful

g) .... people were there on the bus?

   1) How many   2) How much

h) Look at Rita's hair! ....

   1) It's green!   2) They're green!

i) I've called the police and ....

   1) they're on their way   2) it's on its way

j) The assembly hall was full of ....

   1) a noise   2) noise

5

Put **one** suitable word in each space.

a) I wanted to have a bath but there wasn't any hot ...*water*..... .

b) When is the .... on? I haven't heard any today.

c) Tim's eyesight was bad and he had to have new ....

d) Helen had to pay extra at the airport because she had too much ....

e) If you want to make an omelette there are some .... in the fridge.

f) You can't cut that with a knife. You need some ....

g) We need some bread. Could you go and buy a large ....

h) When the burglar ran out of the house he was arrested by a ....

Unit 31 Articles 1

Explanations

Zero article

Zero article is used when a general statement is made.

- Plurals
    ***Dogs are not allowed** in this shop.*
    Compare   *The dogs next door bark all night.*
    Here we are referring to some particular dogs, not to dogs in general.

- Uncountables
    ***Milk is** good for you.*
    Compare   *The milk on the top shelf is fat-free.*
    This group includes:
Abstract ideas	***War** is a terrible thing.*
Food and drink	*I love **chocolate**. I don't like **orange juice**.*
Languages	***Spanish** is spoken by about 300 million people.*
Materials	*This chair is made of **plastic** and **leather**.*
Verbal Nouns	***Speaking** is not permitted during the examination.*

    See Unit 30 for other uncountables.

- Buildings and purpose
    Zero article is used with certain buildings when their purpose is important.
        *Jim is **in prison***   (He committed a crime.)
    Compare   *My company is repairing **the prison**.*
    Words of this type are:
be in or *go to*	*hospital, prison, bed, class, court*
be at or *go to*	*work, school, university, sea*
others	*be at home, go home*

- Countries, states and cities
    Zero article is used with most countries.
        *Marie comes **from France**.*
    Countries which are a group or plural have a definite article.
        *We left **the Netherlands** and crossed to **the United Kingdom**.*
    Note that *Great Britain* has zero article.
    Zero article is used with most states and cities.
        ***Los Angeles** is in **California**.*

- Streets
    Zero article is used with most streets.
        *I bought this dress from a shop **in Bond Street**.*
    Definite article *the* is used in ***the High Street**.*

- Buildings
  Zero article is used with names of buildings preceded by place names.
  > *We visited **Blenheim Palace** and **Coventry Cathedral**.*
  The is generally used when there is a phrase after the noun, often with *of*, which adds more information.
  > *We visited **the Palace of Westminster**.*

- Names of people
  Zero article is used with names, but *the* is used with titles.
  > *Carol Parker is **the Minister of Communications**.*

- Meals
  Zero article is used with meals when we refer to them in general.
  > ***Dinner** is at 7.30.*
  > Compare   *At the end of the conference there was **a dinner**.*
  >   ***The dinner** they serve here is really fantastic.*

- Geographical features
  Zero article is used with geographical areas, lakes, mountains and islands.
  > *We visited **Lake Victoria**. It's in **East Africa**.*
  > *They climbed **Mt. Everest** in record time.*
  > *Helen spent her holidays on **Crete**.*

- General historical references
  > *I'd like to have lived in **Prehistoric Europe/Ancient Rome**.*

- Transport
  Zero article is used with *by* for general forms of transport.
  > *We went there **by car**.*
  Compare *We went there in **a really old car**.*
  Note that we say *on foot*.

a/an

- *A/an* refers to one thing, or to something indefinite or not described. See Unit 30 for *a/an* and *some*.
  > *I've got **a brother and a sister**.*   (not two)
  > *Tim works in **a factory**.*   (not described)
  Compare *Tim works in **the factory** down the road.*
  Note that *a/an* are unstressed, and are pronounced /ə/ and /ən/.

- General descriptions
  > *An ocelot is **a wild animal**, similar to **a leopard**.*
  Descriptions often use plurals.
  > *Ocelots are **wild animals**, similar to **leopards**.*

- *A/an* are used when we describe the job or the character of a person.
  > *Peter is **a fool**!*   *Mary is **an engineer**.*

Practice (See Unit 32 for activities including *the*)

1

Underline the errors in these sentences. Rewrite each sentence.

a) Have you ever <u>visited United Kingdom</u>?
   ...*Have you ever visited the United Kingdom?*...............................

b) On our trip, we visited the Canterbury Cathedral.
   ....

c) Love is wonderful thing.
   ....

d) The pets are not permitted in this hotel.
   ....

e) Rabbit is small wild furry animal with long ears.
   ....

f) The New York is in United States of the America.
   ....

g) The judge sent David to the prison for a month.
   ....

2

Put *a/an* or leave the space blank.

a) ...—... love makes the world go round.
b) Sheila has got .... German car.
c) Rita works in .... office in .... West Street.
d) I've got .... friend who is .... electrician.
e) Paul goes to .... special school for .... musicians.
f) You are .... silly boy! This is .... cat not .... dog!
g) Jack is in .... hospital and can't go to .... school.
h) Carol wants to go to .... university and study to be .... doctor.

3

Complete the second sentence so that it has a similar meaning to the first sentence.

a) Mary teaches English.
   Mary ...*is an*......... English teacher.
b) Charles has a factory job.
   Charles works .... factory.
c) You are not allowed to park here.
   .... is not allowed here.
d) Jim is on a ship at the moment.
   At the moment .... sea.
e) Susan conducts the orchestra.
   Susan .... of the orchestra.
f) We walked to the station.
   We went .... foot.
g) Frogs are small amphibious animals.
   .... animal.

Unit 32 Articles 2

Explanations

Definite article: *the*

- *The* refers to something definite or described.
  The is usually pronounced /ðə/ before consonants and /ði:/ before vowels.
    The beginning.   The end.

- We often use *the* when we refer to something already mentioned.
    *We saw a good film last night. It was **the new film** by Berghini.*

- Reference with *of*
    *The film was about **the love of a girl** for her cat.*
  Compare   *Love is a wonderful thing!*

- Other references
    ***The war between the two countries** lasted for six weeks.*
  Compare   *War is a terrible thing.*

- Unique objects and known references
  Definite article *the* is used with objects which are unique.
    *How many astronauts have landed on **the moon**?*
  The is used when the context is known, and we understand what is meant.
    *Where's **the newspaper**?*

- Groups
  Definite article *the* is used with nationalities and other groups.
    *I really admire **the Italians**.*

- Classes
  Definite article *the* is used with adjectives to describe groups.
    ***The old, the sick** and **the unemployed** need our special care.*

- Other uses

Playing musical instruments	*Do you play **the guitar**?*
Time	*In **the past** /in **the future***
	But: *at present*
Superlatives (See Unit 35)	*This is **the biggest** one.*
Fixed phrases	***The** sooner **the** better.*
Names of ships	*We sailed on **the Neptune**.*
Rivers	***The Amazon, the Danube***
Oceans	***The Pacific, the Atlantic***

Practice

1
Choose the correct word underlined in each sentence.

a) Where's an/(the) electric heater? I can't find it.
b) What happened at an/the end of a/the film?
c) David has an/the appointment at a/the optician's.
d) An/The old person sometimes feels lonely.
e) Peter owns a/the largest model plane in a/the world.
f) Luckily a/the fire brigade soon came and put out a/the fire.
g) Harry's mother bought him a/the guitar for his birthday present.
h) I'm thinking of buying a/the new pair of trousers.
i) In the end there was a/the war between the two countries.
j) I didn't know an/the answer to a/the question, so I left it out.

2
Complete the second sentence so that it has a similar meaning to the first sentence.

a) Jim is a very good pianist.
Jim ..*plays the piano*.......................... very well.
b) Poor people need help from the Government.
The Government should .... poor.
c) Helen's bike is faster than everyone else's.
Helen's .... fastest.
d) Tom has a doctor's appointment.
Tom .... doctor's.
e) The film was about an artist's life.
The film .... of an artist.
f) The only goal of the match was scored by Italy.
The .... Italians.
g) The school term finishes today.
This is .... school term.
h) No one in the class is taller than Jane.
Jane is .... class.

3
Put *a/an* or *the* in each space or leave the space blank.

a) *.The. President* is *.the.* largest cruise ship in *.the.* world.
b) Everyone in .... class agreed that .... happiness was important.
c) There's .... strange person at .... door.
d) Someone who saw .... robbery called .... police.
e) At .... beginning of .... film, ... very tall man sat down in front of me.
f) When I arrived at .... station, I ate .... sandwich and waited for .... train.
g) .... person with .... good education usually gets .... good job.
h) Have you seen .... new film at .... Embassy cinema?
i) In .... past, most of .... population lived in .... country.
j) I needed .... new pair of trousers so my mother gave me .... money.

Practice (Units 31 and 32 mixed activities)

1

Put *a/an/the* in each space, or leave the space blank.

a) *.The.* Italians eat *..a...* lot of *..—..* spaghetti.

b) .... most people thought that .... *Beatles* were .... very good group.

c) I usually drink .... glass of .... milk in .... morning.

d) What's .... difference between .... rabbit and .... hare?

e) .... first person who crosses .... finishing line is .... winner.

f) .... playing .... guitar is .... interesting .... hobby.

g) .... Helen got on .... bus and bought .... ticket.

h) There's .... newspaper shop at .... end of .... street.

2

Correct the errors in these sentences by adding or removing *a/an/the*.

a) Could you get loaf of bread from baker's?

...*Could you get a loaf of bread from the baker's?*...............

b) The milk is good for the children.

....

c) The John is at a work at moment.

....

d) We travelled to the Italy by a car.

....

e) Have you got a brother or the sister?

....

f) War between two countries was longest in the history.

....

g) Who was first astronaut who landed on moon?

....

h) Nile is longest river in world.

....

3

Rewrite each sentence so that it has a similar meaning and contains the word given.

a) We travelled there by train.

on

...*We travelled there on the train.*...............

b) There isn't a larger size than this one.

largest

....

c) Clara sings for her living.

singer

....

d) People who are unemployed often feel depressed.

the

....

e) Anna is learning to be a guitarist.

play

....

f) Mike is an office-worker.

works

....

g) Marie is a Frenchwoman.

France

....

h) David is still working.

at

....

4

Complete each sentence so that it has a similar meaning to the first sentence.

a) I didn't expect to see George.

...*George was the*........................ last person I expected to see.

b) Do you have a dog in your house?

Do .... home?

c) Nick teaches chemistry.

Nick is .... teacher.

d) My friends gave me a wonderful present.

.... gave me was wonderful.

e) The Australian capital is Canberra.

Canberra .... Australia.

f) The French lesson is the first tomorrow.

.... French.

g) Someone is phoning you.

There's someone on ....

h) We saw a very entertaining film last night.

.... was very entertaining.

5

Put *a/an/the* in each space, or leave the space blank.

..*A*.. (1) friend of mine, Sally Milton, wanted to become .... (2) dancer when she was .... (3) girl. .... (4) every morning before .... (5) school she used to practise in .... (6) living room at .... (7) home. .... (8) dancers need .... (9) lot of .... (10) exercise, so Sally used to go to .... (11) gym two or three times .... 12) week. In .... (13) end she got .... (14) job in .... (15) theatre company and became .... (16) actress. In .... (17) fact, ... (18) last week I saw her in .... (19) programme on .... (20) television!

Unit 33 Determiners and pronouns

Explanations

all, some, no

- *all*

  All is usually followed by a plural noun and verb.

  > **All students are expected** to arrive on time.

  In the expressions *all day, all night, all the time*, the noun is singular.

  All can be followed by *the* and a noun. *All of* is also used when *all* is followed by *the* or a possessive adjective (*my* etc.).

  > **All (of) the tickets** for the match had been sold.

  Not is also used with *all*.

  > **Not all students** have bikes.   **Not all (of) my friends** have bikes.

  All is also used as a pronoun at the beginning of a sentence.

  > **All I want** is some peace and quiet!

  > **All I need** is £400!   **All I have** is £50!

  All is not normally used as an object. See Unit 41 Pronouns: *everything*.

- *some*

  Some is used in the same way. *Some* is not used with *not*.

  > **Some students** are expected to help.

- *no*

  No is used as the opposite of *all*.

  > **No students** actually arrive on time!

  No cannot be followed by *the*. See *none* on page 131.

each, both, every

- *each*

  Each refers to the separate things in a group.

  > The name of a person was written on **each box**.

  Each is used with a singular noun and verb.

  > **Each person** in the room was wearing a hat.

  Each is often used with *one*.

  > There were ten people in the room. **Each one** was wearing a hat.

  Each of is used when *each* is followed by *the* or a possessive adjective.

  > **Each of you** can carry one parcel.

  Each is also used after the subject.

  > My sisters **each have** their own room.

  Each can also be used at the end of a sentence.

  > My uncle gave my brother and I £5 **each**. (Gave £5 to each of us.)

- *both*
  Both refers to two things and is used with a plural verb. Note the position.
  > **Both people** in the room were wearing hats.
  > The people in the room **were both wearing** hats.
  > There were two people in the room. **Both** (of them) were wearing hats.
  > **Both of you** can help me.   **You can both** help me.

- *every*
  Every has a similar meaning to *each* in some contexts. It refers to all the things together, while *each* refers to them separately.
  > **Every box** was wrapped in coloured paper.
  > **Every person** in the room was wearing a hat.
  We cannot say *every of you*. See Unit 41 Pronouns: *everyone*

either, neither

- *Either* means 'this one or the other one'. It is followed by a singular noun/verb.
  > We can paint it green or blue. **Either colour** matches the walls.
  It is often used with *end/side* and here means *both*.
  > There are trees on **either side** of the street.

- *Either of* is also used when *either* is followed by *the* or a possessive adjective.
  > **Either of the books** will be very useful.

- *Neither* means 'not this one nor the other one'.
  > We can't paint it green or blue. **Neither colour** matches the walls.
  > There are trees on **neither side** of the street.
  > **Neither of these books** will be very useful.

none of

- *None of* means 'not one of'. It is followed by a singular verb, but many speakers use a plural verb.
  > **None of the guests is/are** here yet.

- *None* can be used alone. It means *not one*. It is often used with *at all*.
  > 'Were there any letters for me?'   Sorry, **none** for you.'
  > 'How many people turned up?'   '**None at all!**'

Expressions with
not a, *not one*

- *Not a* and *Not one* are used to emphasize the idea of *none*.
  > 'How many people turned up?'   '**Not one!**'
  > '**Not a** single one!'

- Other examples:
  > **Not one person** has done any homework!
  > I haven't had **a single** phone-call today.

Practice

1
Choose the correct word or phrase underlined in each sentence.

a) There were <u>none/no</u> people at the bus-stop.

b) My two brothers <u>each/every</u> have their own car.

c) <u>Not one/Not no</u> student has come late this week!

d) <u>Some of/Some</u> restaurants charge extra for bread.

e) Sorry, but I can't hear <u>either/neither</u> of you properly.

f) When I got on my bike I noticed that <u>both tyres/every tyre</u> were flat.

g) According to the song, <u>all/each</u> you need is love.

h) I looked for the books, but <u>none of/no</u> them was there.

2
Put **one** suitable word in each space.

a) I sent letters to ten people, but ...*not*...... ...*one*...... replied!

b) I'm sorry, but there are .... tickets left for the concert.

c) There are only two rooms, and .... of them is large enough.

d) .... I ate for breakfast was a banana.

e) I've tried .... medicine I can find, but nothing works.

f) .... desk had a name label stuck on it.

g) I tried .... the supermarkets, but .... one was closed.

h) I had two phone calls, but there were .... for you, I'm afraid.

i) You two are always quarrelling! Stop it, ... of you!

j) Both roads lead to the city centre. You can take .... one.

3
Rewrite each sentence so that it has a similar meaning and contains the word given.

a) All the dogs in the garden were barking.
every
...*Every dog in the garden was barking.*...

b) Nobody at all came to the meeting.
single
....

c) Not all the members of the class were on time.
some
....

d) Not one of my friends has got a car.
none
....

e) This chair is not comfortable, and nor is this other one.
neither
....

f) There weren't any boys in the class.
no
....

g) We only want to listen to a few cassettes.

all

....

h) The two books are interesting.

both

....

4

Complete the second sentence so that it has a similar meaning to the first sentence.

a) These books aren't interesting.

None ...*of these books is interesting*...

b) You have only ten minutes left.

All ....

c) The hotels were both unsuitable.

Neither ....

d) No one replied to my letter.

Not a ....

e) Paul and his brother David are ill.

Both ....

f) Nobody in the team played badly.

All ....

g) The police searched all the houses in the street.

Every ....

h) Not all the questions in the test were easy.

Some ....

5

Choose the correct continuation for each sentence.

a) We looked at two different houses but ..*1*..

1) both of them were too small.   2) either of them was too small.

b) Liz invited a dozen guests to her party but .....

1) no turned up.   2) none turned up.

c) Helen and Mark are well behaved, but please let me know if .....

1) both of them misbehave.   2) either of them misbehaves.

d) Mary feels so tired because she .....

1) didn't sleep for a single moment.   2) slept all for a moment.

e) Write down the number of the car on this list .....

1) each time one passes.   2) all the time one passes.

f) How many presents did you get on your birthday? .....

1) One at all.   2) None at all.

g) There were ten people standing at the bus-stop and .....

1) all people had umbrellas.   2) each one had an umbrella.

h) We wrote all our answers on the blackboard but .....

1) no one of us was right.   2) none of us was right.

Unit 34 Adjectives and adverbs

Explanations

Adjectives

Adjectives have the same form for singular and plural. They do not change for male and female. Most adjectives are used in front of nouns.

Order of adjectives

- When more than one adjective is used, the order is important. It is not advisable to put more than three adjectives together.
  There are four main groups of adjectives, numbered here Position 1 to Posititon 4. The order inside the opinion group is also important.

- Position 1   One or more of these types of adjective

	a opinion	**b** size	**c** age	**d** shape	**e** temperature
	lovely	*large*	*old*	*round*	*hot*

  Position 2   Colours   *green, blue*, etc.
  Position 3   Material   what it is made of: *wooden, plastic*, etc.
  Position 4   Purpose   what it is for: *a swimming-pool*
  Position 5   Noun   *a swimming-**pool***
  An old leather football boot.
  old = age   *leather* = material   *football* = purpose
  Note that a word usually a noun (*football*) can be used as an adjective.
  A lovely green silk shirt.
  lovely = opinion   *green* = colour   *silk* = material

Problems with adjectives

- Gradeable adjectives
  Some adjectives describe similar qualities. For example, there are many adjectives which describe hot and cold:
  boiling   hot   warm   cool   cold   freezing
  Which one you use depends on your opinion.

- Adjectives ending -*ed* and -*ing*
  It is easy to confuse these adjectives.
  *My work was **tiring**.*   *It made me **tired**.*
  *This film is **interesting**.*   *I am **interested** in the film.*
  Others of the same kind are: *excited/exciting, embarrassed/embarrassing, worried/worrying, bored/boring.*

- Adjectives with *be, become, feel, look*
  Adjectives can be used on their own after these verbs.
      *This beach is **fantastic!***   *Sue has **become happy**.*
      *I **feel terrible!***   *You **look ill!***
  If we use more than one adjective, we can separate them like this.
      Sue has become happy and rich.
      Sue has become happy, rich and famous.

- *one*
  We can use *one* instead of repeating a noun.
      *I like your new coat. It's a really **lovely one!***

Adverbs

- Adverbs describe actions. Most adverbs are formed from adjectives by adding *-ly*.
      slow – slowly   *quick – quickly*   *careful – carefully*

- Some adverbs have the same form as adjectives.
      *This train is very **fast**.* (adj)   *This train goes **fast**.* (adv)

- Some adverbs have the same form as adjectives and a different meaning for the *-ly* form
      *It was a very **hard** question.* (adj)   *We worked **hard**.* (adv)
      *I could **hardly** stand up.* (adv: meaning *almost not*)
      *I don't feel **well**.* (adj)   *Everyone acted **well**.* (adv)

- See Unit 3 for Frequency adverbs. Note their position with *be* and auxiliaries.
      *Katherine **is never** late.*   *She **has never arrived** late.*

Intensifiers

- These are used to describe *how much* with adjectives. The adjective has to be gradeable, i.e. an adjective which can have more or less of a quality.
      *Peter is **happy** at his new school.*   *Happy* is gradeable.
  We can say   ***very** happy*   ***really** happy*   ***extremely** happy*

- When an adjective has an extreme meaning, a strong intensifier is not used.
  We cannot say   **The film was extremely excellent.*
  We can say   *The film was **terribly/awfully/really** good.*

Practice

1
Put each group
of words into the
best order.

a) old a plastic large bag green
   ...*a large old green plastic bag*..

b) wooden square two tables
   ....

c) red a dress silk beautiful
   ....

d) silver a of jugs antique pair
   ....

e) bowl small a plastic
   ....

f) winding road country long a
   ....

g) boots some old football dirty
   ....

h) cotton long a skirt yellow
   ....

i) of trousers old pair a blue
   ....

j) squeezed cold juice a freshly glass orange of
   ....

2
Choose the
correct adjective
underlined in
each sentence.

a) I can't drink this tea! It's boiling/warm!
b) Look at that skyscraper! It's gigantic/large.
c) Jill couldn't drive any further that day as she was so tired/tiring.
d) I love summer evenings when at last it feels cool/freezing.
e) The first part of the film was really excited/exciting.
f) That was the best play I've ever seen. It was fantastic/good.
g) You look worried/worrying. Is anything the matter?
h) We won't go camping until the weather is more boiling/warmer.
i) If you feel bored/boring, why don't we go to the cinema?
j) I didn't think you were interested/interesting in ancient history.

3

Rewrite each sentence so that it has a similar meaning and contains the word given.

a) The old couple lived together and were happy.

happily

...*The old couple lived happily together.*...

b) This has been hard work for you.

worked

....

c) Chris and Paul are slow walkers.

walk

....

d) George is a good pianist.

plays

....

e) Sue is a graceful dancer.

dances

....

f) Kate is ill.

well

....

g) Michael's skating was wonderful.

skated

....

h) Mary is a careful writer.

writes

....

i) David didn't sleep well.

slept

....

j) Ann completed the course with success.

successfully

....

4
Complete each sentence with one of the words from the list. Use each word once only.

> extremely   fast   good   happy   hard
> hardly   ill   quite   terrible   well

a) When I heard that Kate had passed her driving test I was really ..*happy*........ .

b) Jack dances very .... and never steps on people's feet.

c) Alan was so tired that he could .... keep his eyes open.

d) The hotel was .... , but we didn't like the food in the restaurant.

e) Clara was extremely .... and spent a month in hospital.

f) George was driving too .... and was stopped by the police.

g) It's not a wonderful film, but it's .... good.

h) Helen worked very .... and was given an extra holiday.

i) When I realized I hadn't paid for the coat, I felt ....

j) I can't afford to buy that bike because it's .... expensive.

5
Underline the errors in these sentences. Rewrite each sentence.

a) Peter has been working very <u>hardly</u>.
...*Peter has been working very hard.*...................

b) My sister bought me a blue lovely woollen sweater.
....

c) This book I'm reading is extremely excellent.
....

d) David felt badly because he was tall, thin.
....

e) Everyone in the team played good.
....

f) Too much exercise can make you feel tiring.
....

g) Paula felt happily when her exams were over.
....

h) Harry has arrived late at school never.
....

i) One boxer hit the other really hardly right on the chin.
....

j) I'm not really interesting in this car.
....

Unit 35 Making comparisons

Explanations

Formation of comparatives and superlatives

- Adjectives
  Comparative adjectives with one syllable are normally formed by adding *-er* to the adjective. In one syllable words ending with one consonant, the final consonant is doubled. Words ending in consonant + *-y* change *-y* to *-i*. Superlative adjectives are normally formed by adding *-est* to the adjective.

*long – long**er***	*big – big**ger***	*dry – dri**er***
*long – long**est***	*big – big**gest***	*dry – dri**est***

- Comparative adjectives with two or more syllables are normally formed with *more*. Superlative adjectives with two or more syllables are normally formed with *most*. There are some exceptions.

modern – **more modern**	*interesting –* **more interesting**
modern – **most modern**	*interesting –* **most interesting**

- Some adjectives with two syllables can form in either way.
  *common   common**er**/common**est**   **more/most** common*
  Others include: *quiet, tired* and words ending *-ow, -le* and *-er*.

- Adverbs
  Comparative adverbs are normally formed with *more*. Superlative adverbs are normally formed with *most*.
  *Can you work **more quickly**?*
  *The film ended **most happily**.*

Irregular forms

- Adjectives
  Irregular comparatives and superlatives:

good	*better*	*best*
bad	*worse*	*worst*
far	*farther/further*	*farthest/furthest*
little	*less*	*least*
much/many	*more*	*most*

  When we describe family members we can use:
  old   elder   eldest
  *This is my **elder** brother.   Jane is their **eldest** daughter.*

- Adverbs
  Many commonly used adverbs have comparative and superlative forms in
  -*er* and -*est*. These include: *early, far, fast, hard, late*. In informal speech
  loud, quick, slow are also formed in this way.
  > *Could you drive **more slowly**, please?*
  > *Could you drive **slower**, please?*   (informal)

Meaning of comparatives and superlatives

Comparatives are used to compare two separate things. Superlatives compare
one thing in a group with all the other things in that group.
Comparative   *Mary is a **better player** than Monica.*
Superlative   *Sarah is **the best player** in the team.*
Note that *the* comes before a superlative if a noun follows.
Superlatives can be used without nouns. *The* is still used.
> *Sarah is **the greatest**!*

Making comparisons

- *Than* is used with comparatives.
  > *Mary is **better than** Monica.*
  > *Mary is **a better player than** Monica.*

- Note that when we compare actions, we use an auxiliary instead of repeating
  the verb.
  > *Mary plays better than Monica **does**.*
  > *You've done more work than **I have**.*
  We can also say:
  > *Mary plays **better than** Monica.*
  > *You've done more work **than** me.*

- *just as … as* is used when the things compared are equal.
  > *Mary is **just as good as** Cathy.*
  > *Mary is **just as good** a player **as** Cathy.*

- *not as … as* is used when we compare things negatively.
  > *Cathy is **not as good as** Mary.*
  > *Cathy is **not as good** a player **as** Mary.*

- *more* and *less than* is used for longer adjectives.
  > *This game is **more interesting** than the last one.*
  > *I think this game is **less interesting** than that one.*

Intensifiers

When we make comparisons the adjective is often strengthened with an
intensifier.
> *This house is **much/a lot/far bigger** than that one.*
We can also use intensifiers with *more/less*
> *The Italian film was **much more interesting** than this one.*
> *That film was **far less frightening** than this one.*

Practice

1

Choose the correct word or phrase underlined in each sentence.

a) The fish was <u>so tasty as</u>/(<u>as tasty as</u>) the meat.

b) This book is <u>the most interesting/the more interesting</u> I've ever read.

c) This temple is the <u>eldest/oldest</u> in Europe.

d) That dress is a lot longer <u>than/that</u> the other one.

e) Nothing is <u>worse/worst</u> than being stuck in a traffic jam.

f) That skyscraper is one of the <u>taller/tallest</u> buildings in the world.

g) The test wasn't <u>as hard as/hard as</u> I thought.

h) Actually, today I feel <u>more bad/worse</u> than I did yesterday.

i) Our journey took <u>longer than/the longest</u> we expected.

j) Could you work <u>more quietly/more quieter</u> please?

2

Complete each sentence with a comparative or superlative form of the adjective given. Include any other necessary words.

a) The Nile is ...*the longest*.... river in the world.
   long

b) I was disappointed as the film was .... than I expected.
   entertaining

c) Most planes go a lot .... trains.
   fast

d) Yesterday was one of .... days of the year.
   hot

e) I think this book is much .... the other one.
   good

f) The twins are the same height. Tim is .... Sue.
   tall

g) The first exercise was easy but this one is ....
   difficult

h) The Mediterranean is not .... the Pacific Ocean.
   large

i) This classroom is .... the one next door.
   big

j) This is .... television programme I've ever watched.
   bad

3

Rewrite each sentence beginning as shown so that it has a similar meaning to the first sentence.

a) David is a better runner than Paul.

Paul is not ...*as good a runner as David (is)*................ .

b) Nobody in the class is taller than Carol.

Carol is the ....

c) I haven't written as much as you.

You've written ....

d) We expected the play to be better.

The play wasn't ....

e) Jane's hair isn't as long as Helen's.

Helen's hair is ....

f) No student in the school is noisier than I am!

I am the ....

g) This exhibition is much more interesting than the last one.

The last exhibition was not ....

h) This is as fast as the car can go.

The car can't ....

i) This bike is not as expensive as the green one.

The green bike is ....

j) Kate ate much less than George did.

Kate didn't ....

4

Put **one** suitable word in each space.

a) Our team is ..*just*... ..*as*..... good ..*as*..... your team. They are both the same.

b) This is one of .... famous paintings in the world.

c) Everyone did .... work .... Harry ....

d) You're not a safe driver! You should drive .... slowly.

e) Ann is taller .... Mike but their son Dave is .... tallest in the family.

f) What an awful book. It's one of .... interesting I've ever read.

g) It makes no difference, because this road is .... bad .... that one.

h) Today is .... cold .... yesterday, so I'm wearing my shorts.

i) Nobody knows .... about electronics .... Tina ....

j) I don't think that pet cats are .... friendly .... pet dogs.

5

Rewrite each sentence so that it has a similar meaning and contains the word given.

a) Could you not talk so fast, please?

slowly

...*Could you talk more slowly, please?*...

b) The last film we saw was more frightening than this one.

as

....

c) Nobody in the class cooks better than Sam.

best

....

d) I haven't eaten as much as you.

more

....

e) Supermarkets are more convenient than small shops.

as

....

f) Skating isn't as exciting as skiing.

more

....

g) Richard doesn't work harder than Alan.

just

....

h) Jack isn't as interested in football as his brother is.

more

....

i) Bill is the youngest in the family.

older

....

j) You ran a lot faster than I did.

fast

....

6

Correct the spelling of these words where necessary.

a) bigest   ...*biggest*....
b) greattest ....
c) shorter   ....
d) likeliest ....
e) tallest   ....

f) fater   ....
g) smalest   ....
h) longest   ....
i) hardder   ....
j) wettest   ....

k) fitter   ....
l) tighter   ....
m) newest   ....
n) heavier   ....
o) widder   ....

Unit 36 Phrasal or multi-word verbs 1

Explanations

Phrasal verbs:
use

- The term phrasal verb is used here for verbs followed by one or more prepositions. They are also called multi-word verbs. The meaning cannot usually be guessed from the meaning of the verb on its own.
These verbs are common in informal writing and speech, but many are used in formal speech and writing. There are many verbs of this type, and the ones listed here are those which are common, or which occur elsewhere in this book.

- Verbs are divided here into different types. Verbs can belong to different types with a different meaning for each type. It is advisable to study the context of use, and check the meaning in a dictionary.

Verbs with three
parts

These verbs are followed by an object. The object cannot be put after the first or second word.
Verbs marked * can be used without the final part, but with no object.

*catch up with** (reach someone by going faster)
> *You can rest now and **catch up with** us later.*
> *You're going too fast! I can't **catch up**!*

*cut down on** (reduce or reduce the amount spent on)
> *Sheila has decided to **cut down on** holidays this year.*
> *You're eating too many sweets. You should **cut down**.*

*drop in on** (visit, perhaps unexpectedly)
> *Let's **drop in on** David while we are in Paris.*
> *The next time you are nearby, please do **drop in**!*

*get along/on with** (have a friendly relationship with)
> *James doesn't **get on** well **with** his maths teacher.*
> *We work in the same office, but we don't **get on**.*

*keep up with** (move at the same speed as)
> *You're going too fast! I can't **keep up with** you.*
> *Patty finds this class difficult, and can't **keep up**.*

live up to (be as good as was expected - usually used with promise or
> expectation)
> *The film didn't **live up** to our expectations.*

look forward to   (want to happen, as you think you will enjoy it)
  *I'm **looking forward** to going on holiday this year.*
Note that *to* is a preposition so is followed by the verbal noun *-ing.*

look out onto/over   (have a view of)
  *Our hotel room **looks out onto** the garden.*

put up with   (tolerate)
  *I can't **put up with** all this noise!*

run out of*   (have none left)
  *I think the car is about to **run out of** petrol!*
  *There isn't any more milk. We've **run out.***

Verbs with two parts: transitive inseparable

These verbs are followed by an object. The object cannot be put between the verb and the preposition.

call for   (come to your house and collect)
  *We'll **call for** you about 8.00 so please be ready.*

call on   (pay a short visit: usually formal)
  *I **called on** Professor Jones and wished her a Happy Birthday.*

deal with   (take action over, handle)
  *Could you **deal with** this customer's problem please?*

get at   (try to say)
  *Helen couldn't understand what her boss was **getting at.***

get over   (recover from)
  *Peter was ill with flu, but he's **getting over** it now.*

join in   (take part in, contribute to)
  *When Alex started singing, everyone **joined in.***

make for   (go in the direction of)
  *The escaped prisoner is thought to be **making for** London.*

see to   (pay attention to, often meaning 'repair')
  *The brakes on your car need **seeing to.***

stand for   (tolerate)
  *I will not **stand for** so much talking!*

take after   (be similar in appearance or character)
  *Karen **takes after** her mother. They're very similar.*

Practice

1
Complete each sentence a) to h) with an ending from 1) to 8).

a) If you have any kind of problem, just call me and I'll deal ..3..

b) I've been so busy lately that I've decided to cut .....

c) Ann and Sue are really looking .....

d) Our teacher told us that she would not stand .....

e) Nearly everybody says that George takes .....

f) Clara is very friendly and generally gets .....

g) Half-way through the race, Martin found that he couldn't keep .....

h) We were told that the concert was going to be good but it didn't live .....

1) for cheating in our end-of-term test.

2) on well with the people she works with.

3) with it as soon as I can.

4) after his father's side of the family.

5) down on the amount of time I spend watching television.

6) up with the others any more.

7) up to our expectations at all.

8) forward to seeing you both again in July.

2
Rewrite each sentence so that it has a similar meaning and contains the word given.

a) Someone needs to look at the central heating system.
seeing
...The central heating system needs seeing to...

b) Let's pay a surprise visit to Julia while we are here.
drop
....

c) We're going in the direction of Paris.
heading
....

d) Our hotel room has a view of the main road!
looks
....

e) Two children started playing, and then the others played too.
joined
....

f) We paid a visit to my aunt on her birthday.
called
....

g) I'm afraid that we haven't got any eggs left.
run
....

h) Kate will come and collect you at 6.30.
   call

   ....

i) Nobody understood what I was trying to say.
   getting

   ....

j) I can't bear so much air pollution!
   put

   ....

3
Rewrite each sentence so that it does not contain the words underlined, and so that it contains a phrasal verb.

a) Brian <u>and</u> his mother <u>are very similar</u>.
   ...Brian takes after his mother...

b) <u>There isn't any</u> food <u>left</u>!

   ....

c) Mike and Tom <u>are not very good friends</u>.

   ....

d) Jean is very good at <u>handling</u> people's <u>problems</u>.

   ....

e) The handlebars on my bike need <u>fixing</u>.

   ....

f) Julia was very ill, but she's <u>recovered</u> now.

   ....

g) What exactly are you <u>suggesting</u>?

   ....

h) Paul's new school <u>wasn't as good as he expected it to be</u>.

   ....

4
Complete each sentence with a suitable form of one of the phrasal verbs in the list. Use each one once only.

| catch up with   cut down on   drop in on   get on with |
| keep up with   (not) live up to   look forward to   run out of |

a) The book you lent me ...*didn't live up to*....... my expectations.
b) Any time you're in the area, feel free to .... us.
c) Sorry, we have .... orangeade. Would you like some water?
d) Unfortunately Susie doesn't .... her new neighbours.
e) Bill left before I did, but I ran and .... him.
f) I'm really .... my holiday in Italy next week.
g) It was a difficult class, and I couldn't .... the other students.
h) You should .... smoking if you can't stop completely.

Unit 37 Phrasal or multi-word verbs 2

Explanations

Changes of meaning

Verbs are divided here into different types. Verbs can belong to different types with a different meaning for each type. It is advisable to study the context of use, and check the meaning in a dictionary.

Verbs with two parts: transitive separable

These verbs are followed by an object, or the object is put between the verb and preposition. Pronouns such as *you*, *it*, *him*, *her*, *us*, *them* are always put between the verb and the preposition. Verb and preposition are not usually separated by long phrases. These are put after the preposition.

bring up   (educate, look after a child)
> *Tom's aunt **brought him up** after his parents died.*

call off   (cancel)
> *The school **called off** the match because of bad weather.*

clear up   (make clean and tidy)
> *Could you help me **clear up** the room after the party?*

cut off   (be disconnected during a phone-call)
> *I'd just got through to Delhi when I was **cut off**.*
This is usually used in the passive.

fill in   (complete a form)
> *Could you **fill this form in** with all your details, please?*

give up   (choose to stop doing something)
> *Paul had to **give up** gymnastics because of injury.*

knock out   (hit and make unconscious)
> *Bryson **knocked his opponent out** in the second round.*

let down   (disappoint, fail to keep a promise)
> *Ann said she would help, but she **let me down**.*

look up   (search for information in a reference book)
> *I **looked this word up** in a dictionary and in an encyclopedia.*

pick up   (collect in a car)
> *The taxi will **pick you up** at 6.30.*

put off   (postpone)
> *The weather was bad, so they **put off** the match for a week.*

put up   (stay in someone's house)
　　　　*A friend in Prague **put me up** for a couple of nights.*

take up   (start doing a hobby or activity)
　　　　*Sam has just **taken up** parachuting.*

try on   (put on clothes to see if they are suitable)
　　　　*I **tried the coat on**, but it was too big and the wrong colour.*

turn on/off   (begin or stop operating electrical equipment)
　　　　*Don't forget to **turn off** the light before you go to bed.*

wash up   (clean plates, knives and forks, etc.)
　　　　*After the party, Martin **washed up** all the glasses.*

Verbs with two parts: intransitive

These verbs do not have an object.

break down   (stop working, especially cars)
　　　　*The car **broke down** when we were on the motorway.*

drop out   (leave without finishing)
　　　　*Two of the runners **dropped out** half-way through the race.*

get on   (make progress)
　　　　*Nina likes her new college, and is **getting on** well.*

get away   (escape)
　　　　*One of the burglars was caught, but the other **got away**.*

grow up   (change from a child to an adult)
　　　　*I **grew up** in a small town in Peru.*

set off/out   (begin a journey)
　　　　*We **set off** early to avoid the traffic.*

take off   (when a plane leaves the ground)
　　　　*Our plane **took off** more than three hours late.*

turn up   (arrive, or arrive unexpectedly)
　　　　*We invited twenty people, but only five **turned up**.*

Practice

1
Put **one** suitable word in each space.

a) Sue asked if she could help me ...*wash*..... up the dirty dishes.

b) I need a dictionary, so I can .... up this word.

c) If I were you I'd .... off early because Edinburgh is a long way.

d) Our meeting tomorrow has been .... off, I'm afraid.

e) I'm not sure about the size of this coat, so can I .... it on?

f) Jim had to .... in a form, giving all his personal details.

g) You'll never guess who .... up at our school party last week!

h) Six people applied for the job, but one of them .... out.

2
Complete each sentence a) to h) with an ending from 1) to 8).

a) It's very cold and wet at the moment so we have put ..*3*.

b) Mary's parents were quite strict and brought her .....

c) Your room is very untidy! Could you clear .....

d) I was talking to Helen when suddenly we were cut .....

e) Tina tried to persuade her mother to give .....

f) Tim started painting his room this morning and he's getting .....

g) The branch of a tree fell and knocked .....

h) If you like, we could come and pick .....

1) it up please, and put everything away.

2) Peter out for a few moments.

3) off our garden party until next week.

4) up smoking, but she didn't have much success.

5) on very well so far.

6) off and I couldn't get her number after that.

7) you up in our car at about 7.00.

8) up to be very polite and obedient.

3
Rewrite each sentence so that it contains a form of the phrasal verb given.

a) Don't leave the lights on when you leave the school.
turn off
...*Turn the lights off when you leave the school.*...................................

b) You should use a dictionary to find this word.
look up

....

c) The athletics meeting was postponed for a week.
put off

....

d) The doctor told David to stop playing football.
give up

....

e) Could you write all the details on this form?
fill in

....

f) Jack arrived half-way through the lesson.
turn up

....

g) You can stay with us for a week.
put up

....

h) Helen is doing well in her English class.
get on

....

4
Rewrite each sentence so that it has a similar meaning and contains the word given.

a) Paula spent her childhood in Uruguay.
grew
...Paula grew up in Uruguay...

b) As soon as it was dawn, we started our journey.
set

....

c) Parachuting is dangerous so you should stop doing it.
give

....

d) Martin tidies his room every morning.
clear

....

e) How do you start the computer?
turn

....

f) Can I see if these shoes are the right size?
try

....

g) Carol checked the dates in an encyclopedia.
look

....

h) Skating is a great sport. When did you start doing it?
take

....

Problems, Errors, Consolidation 4

1

Choose the correct words underlined in each sentence.

a) I think my school is <u>just as good</u>/(better) than yours.

b) There are enough apples for one <u>each/every</u>.

c) Paula has been working very <u>hard/hardly</u>.

d) Could you give me <u>an/some</u> information, please?

e) This is the <u>best/better</u> ice-cream in the world!

f) I have been working in this company <u>for/since</u> three months.

g) There are <u>no/none</u> eggs left in the fridge.

h) The news <u>is/are</u> on in a few minutes.

2

Decide which answer, a), b), c) or d), best fits the space.

Life on the farm

I was (1) ..d.. by my uncle and aunt and (2) ..... on a small farm in the West of England. I think it was better (3) ..... living in a city, because (4) ..... day I ran about in the open air. (5) ..... I went to school, (6) ..... I did was play on the farm all day. (7) ..... my aunt and uncle worked with the animals, and although they worked very (8) ....., they always explained (9) ..... things to me. They didn't have (10) ..... money, but they (11) ..... well with everyone, and we didn't have (12) ..... of the problems of living in the city. I always felt (13) ..... on the farm. There was (14) ..... noise or pollution, and it was (15) ..... peaceful. That's probably why I became a farmer when I was older.

1) a) lived up to b) taken after c) grown up d) brought up
2) a) grew up b) joined in c) turned up d) put off
3) a) as b) more c) than d) the
4) a) every b) in c) for d) both
5) a) by b) nowadays c) in time d) until
6) a) every b) each c) none d) all
7) a) either b) both c) neither d) all
8) a) hardly b) harder c) hard d) hardest
9) a) interests b) interesting c) interest d) interested
10) a) much b) lots c) many d) too
11) a) dropped in b) got along c) kept up d) dealt with
12) a) much b) none c) no d) any
13) a) happily b) a happy c) happy d) the happy
14) a) any b) no c) none of d) not
15) a) too b) much c) really d) as

3

Complete the second sentence so that it has a similar meaning to the first sentence.

a) These classrooms aren't very large.
   None ...*of these classrooms is very large*............... .

b) George won't leave here before the end of April.
   George will be here ....

c) We don't allow smoking in this cinema.
   No ....

d) Can you tell me what you think I should do?
   Can you give me .... ?

e) You have waited longer than I have.
   I haven't ....

f) It's 4.00 now, and I started waiting here two hours ago.
   I've been waiting here since ....

g) All classrooms must be kept clean.
   Each ....

h) Most of the class walks to school.
   Most of the class comes to school ....

i) This is as far as we can go along this road.
   We can't ....

j) The fire brigade arrived too late to save the burning house.
   The fire brigade didn't arrive ....

4

Rewrite each sentence so that it contains a form of a phrasal verb using the word given. Make any other necessary changes.

a) You can come and stay with me.
   put
   ...*I can put you up*...

b) Harry can't stand loud music.
   put
   ....

c) Peter is making good progress at university.
   get
   ....

d) I'll tidy up the room if you do the washing-up.
   clear
   ....

e) We're going in the direction of Madrid.
   make
   ....

f) Why don't you search for this word in the dictionary?
   look
   ....

g) Jane is very similar to her father.
take

....

h) Sue's father is trying to stop smoking.
give

....

5
Look carefully at each line. Some lines are correct but some have a word which should not be there. Tick each correct line. If a line has a word which should not be there, write the word in the space.

Holiday problems

Last month we decided to drive to Scotland for a	1) ....✓.......
few days, for a short holiday. We were the really	2) ..*the*....
looking it forward to a quiet rest in the country.	3) ....
Unfortunately, a lots of things went wrong. First	4) ....
of all, the car was broke down just after we had left	5) ....
home, and we had to phone a garage and then	6) ....
wait by the side of the road for hours ago. By the	7) ....
time the car had been repaired, it was too much late	8) ....
to go on, so we went the home. The next day we set	9) ....
off more early to avoid the traffic, but we had forgotten	10) ....
that it was a public holiday. Every one single person	11) ....
in the country must have had the same idea, so we	12) ....
found ourselves in a long traffic jam. We after decided	13) ....
that the best thing to do was to take after a different	14) ....
road, and look up for a hotel. First we got lost on	15) ....
a narrow country road, and then the car once ran	16) ....
out of the petrol. Finally, we gave up and went home	17) ....
for the second time.	

6
Put **one** suitable word in each space, or leave the space blank.

While Helen was visiting (a) ...*the*.. United States, she decided to go by (b) .... plane from (c) .... New York to (d) .... West Coast. She had already stayed with her friends (e) .... two weeks, and they had told her that (f) .... California was a (g) .... more exciting. 'It's (h) .... warmer for a start, and you'll be able to swim in (i) .... Pacific Ocean!', they said. Helen didn't have (j) .... information about flights or fares, so she went to (k) .... travel agent's next door to (l) .... block of flats where she was staying. She discovered that there were two flights (m) .... following morning, but she couldn't get (n) .... seat on (o) .... of them.

7
Rewrite each sentence so that it has a similar meaning and contains the word given.

a) Nobody at all picked up the litter.
    single
    ...*Not a single person picked up the litter.*...

b) Paul started learning Hungarian in 1997.
    since
    ....

c) There isn't any cheese in the fridge.
    is
    ....

d) People who are rich aren't necessarily happy.
    the
    ....

e) Jane's drawing is beautiful.
    draws
    ....

f) I haven't seen a worse film than this one.
    ever
    ....

g) Helen left Paris in July.
    stayed
    ....

h) Do you find opera interesting?
    are
    ....

8
Put **one** suitable word in each space.

a) You work ...*much*.. harder ...*than*... I do.
b) In .... future, people will live longer .... they do now.
c) Alex plays .... guitar in .... rock band.
d) I think the film was terrible! It was .... interesting than the one we saw last week.
e) There is .... hot water left, but there isn't ....
f) These three bedrooms .... have windows on .... sides of the house.
g) .... Bill and Mary studied hard, and .... the end they passed the exam.
h) Jogging isn't .... interesting .... playing tennis.
i) I'll wait here .... 6.00, so try and be here .... then.
j) That was great! It was the .... meal you have .... cooked!

155

9
Underline the error or errors in each sentence. Rewrite each sentence.

a) I'm really <u>interesting</u> in <u>the</u> travel.
...*I'm really interested in travel.*.......................

b) Kate's brother is doctor.
....

c) I ate a food with Jack, and after I went home.
....

d) The milk is good for you.
....

e) Can you give me an advice?
....

f) I've looked in the box. All is broken, I'm afraid.
....

g) They will have finished the new hospital until the end of March.
....

h) There's a police waiting outside.
....

i) I come to class with the feet.
....

j) Your hair are very beautiful.
....

Problem check

1 Time words like *for*, *since* and *ago* are linked to the use of tenses. Check Units 4, 5, 6 and 7.

2 The same word can be countable and uncountable with a change of meaning. Which words of this kind do you know?

3 Compare the uses of articles with articles in your language, if it has articles. Keep a checklist of common differences. Note that the choice of article can depend on meaning and context.

4 Avoid using more than three adjectives together. Note the difference between *hard* and *hardly*.

5 What is the difference between comparative and superlatives? Are they used in the same ways in your language?

6 Phrasal verbs can have many meanings, so check in a dictionary.

Unit 38 Verbs followed by verbal noun or infinitive 1

Explanations

When you learn a new verb, it is advisable to check in a dictionary whether it is followed by a verbal noun (this is also called the *-ing* form, and the gerund) or infinitive (with *to*, or without *to*, also called bare infinitive). Units 38 and 39 include some of the most common verbs, but these are only a selection. See also Unit 40 Verbs followed by prepositions.

Verbs followed by verbal noun *-ing* or infinitive: with little or no change of meaning

- These include:

    begin, continue, not bear, hate , intend, like, love, prefer, start

    *When she stood up, the President **began to speak**.*
    *When she stood up, the President **began speaking**.*
    *Some people at the back **continued chatting/to chat**.*
    *I can't **bear listening/to listen** for a long time.*
    *What do you **intend doing/to do** about it?*
    *I don't **like watching** television. I **prefer reading/to read**.*
    *I think you should **start practising/to practise** now!*

- When we use *prefer*, we **prefer** one thing **to** another thing. If the things are activities, gerund is used.

    *Tom **prefers reading to watching** television.*

- For some speakers there is a difference between *like to do* and *like doing*.

    *I **like to** listen to the radio every morning while I'm in the bath.*
    (a habitual action)
    *I **like listening** to the radio.*
    (likes and dislikes)

- *Hate to do* is more usual than *hate doing* in some idiomatic contexts.

    *I **hate doing** the washing-up!*
    *I **hate to tell** you this, but we've missed the last train!*

- *Love to do* is more common than *love doing* in some idiomatic contexts.

    *Sue really **loves swimming**.*
    *He's the man they **love to hate**!*

- Note that when *would* is used with *like*, *love* and *prefer*, they are followed by infinitive with *to*.

    *I'**d like to go** to Portugal this summer.*

Verbs followed by infinitive + *to*	These include: *afford, ask, choose, happen, help, manage, offer, refuse, wait, want* *I can't **afford to go** to the cinema twice in one week.* *In the end, Laura **chose to study** Economics.* *Do you **happen to know** the time?* *Could someone **help me to carry** this?** (*Help* is also used without *to*. *Could you **help me carry** this?*) *Jim can't manage **to come** this evening.* *I **offered to give** her a lift, but she said she'd ordered a taxi.* *The manager **refused to see** me.* *There are some people **waiting to see** you.* *What do you **want to do** this evening?*

Verbs followed by infinitive + *to*, or *that*-clause

- These include:

    agree, decide, expect, hope, learn, pretend, promise, seem, wish

- It is possible to leave out *that* in everyday speech.

- Note that *that*-clauses often follow sequence of tense rules, as in reported speech. See Units 10 and 11. The main verbs of this type are:

    *Sarah **agrees to meet** you after school.*
    *Sarah **agrees that she will meet** you after school.*
    *Sarah **agreed to meet** me after school.*
    *Sarah **agreed (that) she would meet** me after school.*

*We **decided to go** home.*	*We **decided (that) we would** go home.*
*Mike **expects to win**.*	*Mike **expects (that) he will** win.*
*I **hope to see** you later.*	*I **hope (that) I'll see** you later.*
*Helen **pretended to be** ill.*	*Helen **pretended that she was ill**.*

- There is a small difference in the meanings of *learn*.
    *At school Graham **learned to speak** French.*
    (learn a skill)
    *At school we **learned that** the Earth goes round the Sun.*
    (learn information)

- Note the uses of *seem*. *It + seem + that*-clause is very common.
    *You **seem to know** the answer!*   ***It seems that you know** the answer.*

- *Wish* followed by infinitive with *to* has a similar meaning to *want*.
    *I **wish to leave** early today.*
    Wish followed by a *that*-clause usually includes *would* or *could*.
    *I **wish (that) I could** leave early.*
    *I **wish (that) my teacher would** let me leave early.*

Practice

1
Correct the errors. Some sentences do not have errors.

a) Jim can't afford going to the cinema twice a week.

...*Jim can't afford to go to the cinema twice a week*...................................

b) David wishes leaving the room.

....

c) Are you waiting to use the phone?

....

d) I'd really like going swimming on Saturday.

....

e) Everyone decided to put off the football match.

....

f) Emma pretended leaving, but waited outside.

....

g) Jack agreed to meet me at the beach.

....

h) My bike seems having something wrong with it.

....

i) The director refused answering Helen's phone call.

....

j) What exactly do you intend to say to Mrs Dawson?

....

2
Complete each sentence with a form of one of the verbs from the list. Use each verb once only.

| afford   bear   continue   expect   happen |
| learn   love   offer   prefer   pretend |

a) John really ...*loves*............ spending all day at the beach.
b) I'm completely broke, so I can't .... to go on holiday.
c) Excuse me, but do you .... to know the way to Old Street?
d) We .... our team to win, but they were badly beaten.
e) Kate .... to speak French and German when she was at school.
f) Even when the examiner told him to stop, Bill .... speaking.
g) I'm sorry, but I can't .... to listen to this awful music!
h) Last week George .... to help me paint my bike.
i) Paul .... to have a bad leg so he didn't have to go to the gym.
j) Sam usually .... playing football to doing homework.

3
Complete the second sentence so that it has a similar meaning to the first sentence.

a) My teacher wouldn't let me leave early.
My teacher refused ...*to let me leave early*............................. .

b) Jill sang without stopping for an hour.
Jill continued ....

c) Apparently you have passed the exam.
It seems ....

d) Richard thinks he is going to do well.
Richard expects ....

e) What are your plans for the summer?
What do you intend .... ?

f) Clearing up my room is something I dislike!
I hate ....

g) Helen said she'd go to the cinema with me.
Helen agreed ....

h) Tina and Brian are getting married.
Tina and Brian have decided ....

i) See you later, I hope.
I hope ....

j) What do you fancy doing this evening?
What do you want ....

4
Complete each sentence with one of the words from the list.

| agreed | asked | chose | decides | hate |
| hopes | like | refused | seems | want |

a) Jack often ...*seems*...... to be worried.

b) I .... to tell you this, but we've lost all our money.

c) I .... Ann to wait for me, but she didn't.

d) Do you .... to go for a walk this afternoon?

e) Carol .... to become a champion skater.

f) The police officer .... to listen to my explanation.

g) Peter .... to work on Saturday instead of on Friday.

h) I'd .... to see you again some time.

i) Jim often .... to stay at home and go to bed early.

j) I asked my teacher for help, and she .... to give me extra lessons.

5

Rewrite each sentence so that it has a similar meaning and contains the word given.

a) What are you thinking of doing?

intend

...*What do you intend to do?*..

b) I find getting up early unbearable!

bear

....

c) I'll see you in the morning, I expect.

to

....

d) 'I won't help!' said Tom.

refused

....

e) Pat was taught to drive when he was young.

learned

....

f) 'Would you like me to help you?' I asked Joe.

offered

....

g) Ellen didn't have enough money for the ticket.

afford

....

h) 'I'll be back at 6.00,' said Susan.

promised

....

Unit 39 Verbs followed by verbal noun or infinitive 2

Explanations

When you learn a new verb, it is advisable to check in a dictionary whether it is followed by a verbal noun (-*ing* form, or gerund) or infinitive (with *to*, or without *to*, also called bare infinitive). Units 38 and 39 include some of the most common verbs, but these are only a selection. See also Unit 40 Verbs followed by prepositions.

Verbs followed by verbal noun -*ing* or infinitive + *to* or *that*-clause: with change of meaning

These include: *forget, mean, remember, stop, try*

forget

*Sorry, I **forgot to post** your letter.*   (I didn't remember)
*I'll never **forget learning** to drive!*   (I'll always remember)
*I forgot that I'd promised **to phone you.***

mean

*Jan meant to **watch** the programme, but she forgot.*   (intended)
*Keeping fit **means taking** exercise every day!*   (involve)
*When I miss the bus, it **means that I have to** walk to school.*

remember

Remember to take your keys!   (don't forget a future action)
I remember telling you!   (remember a past action)
Then I remembered that you were out.

stop

*Jo has **stopped learning** French.*   (give up)
*We **stopped to look** at the view.*   (purpose infinitive)
*Stop is not followed by a *that*-clause.*

try

*Peter **tried to lift** the table, but it was too heavy.*   (try/fail)
*If you have a headache, **try taking** two of these pills.*   (suggesting an action)

*Try is not followed by a *that*-clause.*

Verbs followed by verbal noun -*ing* or bare infinitive: with change of meaning

● These include: *feel, hear, see, watch*
*I could **feel my hands shaking** with fear!*   (continuing action)
*I **felt the building move**!*   (completed action)
*We **watched Joe eating** his lunch.*   (not completed)
*We **watched Joe eat** his lunch.*   (completed)

● *Feel, hear* and *see* are also used with a *that*-clause, with change of meaning.
*I **feel that** this is the time to resign.*   (an opinion)

We **heard that** you were ill.	(receive news)
I **saw that** it was too late.	(realize)

Verbs followed by verbal noun -ing or noun

These include: *dislike, enjoy, fancy, *can't help, *keep, mind, practise, can't stand*
Those marked * have a change of meaning.

> I **dislike going out** in the rain.
> I really **dislike my new boss.**
> Everyone **enjoys going** to parties.
> I **enjoyed this lesson.**
> Do you **fancy going** to the cinema?
> I **fancy a swim!**
> I **can't help feeling hungry.**
> I **can't help myself!**   (I can't stop)
> Sue **keeps phoning** me late at night.   (a bad habit)
> **Keep this.** Don't throw it away.
> Do you **mind waiting?**
> Do you **mind cold weather?**
> I must **practise speaking** French more often.
> Julia **practises the violin** every day.
> I **can't stand waking up** early.
> I **can't stand hot and spicy food.**

Verbs followed by verbal noun -ing, noun or that-clause

- These include: *admit, deny, imagine, suggest*
  > The Minister **admitted taking** a bribe.
  > Paul **admitted that** he was wrong.
  > Tina **denied stealing the money.**
  > Both men **denied that** they had done anything wrong.
  > **Imagine travelling** to another planet!
  > Do you really **imagine that** I want to see you again?
  > I **suggest going** for a pizza.
  > I **suggest that** we go for a pizza.

- *Suggest* is also followed by *should*.
  > I **suggest that we should** go for a pizza.

Practice (Contrasts with verbs from Unit 38 are included here.)

1

Choose the correct word or phrase underlined in each sentence.

a) Tom suddenly realized he had forgotten (to lock)/locking his door.

b) On the way back we stopped <u>to have/having</u> some tea.

c) Could you stop <u>to talk/talking</u>, please.

d) Learning a language means <u>to be/being</u> interested in another culture.

e) Ann tried <u>to open/opening</u> the window, but it was too high to reach.

f) Please remember <u>to take/taking</u> the dog for a walk.

g) Cathy says she will never forget <u>to sky-dive/sky-diving</u> for the first time.

h) I don't really remember <u>to start/starting</u> school when I was five.

2

Complete each sentence so that it has a similar meaning to the first sentence.

a) Would you like to go to the beach?

...*Do you fancy*................................... going to the beach?

b) The boy admitted stealing the bike.

.... stolen the bike.

c) In my opinion, you are wrong.

I feel ....

d) Why don't we wait for the bus?

.... waiting for the bus.

e) David often interrupts me.

.... interrupting me.

f) Is it all right if you come back later?

.... coming back later?

g) Think what being a millionaire would be like!

.... being a millionaire!

h) Paula said that she hadn't written the letter.

.... writing the letter.

i) It's not my fault if I eat a lot.

.... eating a lot.

j) The building collapsed and we saw it.

.... collapse.

3

Choose the correct verb underlined in each sentence.

a) Helen (chose)/enjoyed to learn French.

b) I really can't <u>afford/stand</u> to travel by plane.

c) Do you <u>mind/want</u> coming back in half an hour?

d) Tina <u>meant/suggested</u> to buy some potatoes, but she forgot.

e) Kate <u>denied/refused</u> opening the office safe.

f) Bill <u>admitted/agreed</u> making a serious mistake.

g) My parents <u>decided/disliked</u> to send me to a different school.

h) I really <u>fancy/like</u> a trip to the country.

4

Complete each sentence with a form of one of the verbs in the list.

deny   enjoy   expect   imagine   manage
mean   try   practise   pretend   refuse

a) If you ...*try*.......... to work a bit harder, I'm sure you'll pass the exam.

b) Harry .... to have toothache, and left school early.

c) The builders are not sure of the exact date, but .... to start work soon.

d) Ann .... to call you last week, but she forgot.

e) The woman arrested by the police .... robbing the bank.

f) You should .... speaking to an audience, to gain confidence.

g) It's interesting to .... myself living on a desert island.

h) I phoned the director six times, but she .... to speak to me.

5

Put **one** suitable word in each space.

a) Don't ...*forget*...... to buy some milk on your way home.

b) If I'm late, it .... I have to wait until the next lesson begins.

c) I .... throwing the ball, but I didn't break the window.

d) Paul can't .... thinking about his favourite team.

e) Lisa .... leaving her books at home.

f) I can't .... walking home in the rain! It's horrible!

g) I .... playing with my friends when I was little.

h) Gina .... to climb in through the window, but it was locked.

Unit 40 Verbs followed by prepositions

Explanations

Verbs followed
by prepositions

When you learn a new verb, it is advisable to check in a dictionary, so that you
know which preposition follows it. Some verbs are followed by different
prepositions, with and without change of meaning.

About

dream	*I dreamt about Harry last night.*
know	*Do you know a lot about economics?*
talk	*What are you talking about?*

At

laugh	*Don't laugh at me.*
look	*Look at that beautiful cherry tree!*

For

apologize	*I must apologize for being late.*
apply	*Jill has applied for a new job.*
ask	*Why don't we ask for the bill?*
look	*I'm looking for the bus station.*
pay	*Sheila paid for my ticket.*
wait	*I'll wait for you outside.*

In

believe	*Do you believe in ghosts?*
succeed	*Helen succeeded in collecting £35 for charity.*

Of

accuse	*Albert was accused of spying.*
remind	*This city reminds me of Buenos Aires.*
taste	*Does your coffee taste of soap?*

On

depend	*I might come. It depends on the weather.*
rely	*You can rely on Ann to work hard.*

To

belong	*Does this belong to you?*
explain	*Could you explain something to me please?*
lend	*Brian lent his car to me for the weekend.*

We can also say: Brian *lent me* his car.

listen	*You're not listening to me!*
talk	*Ellen was talking to her mother on the phone.*

be + adjective followed by a preposition

Note that most adjectives listed here have different meanings when used with other prepositions. It is advisable to check in a dictionary.

About   *angry, *annoyed, excited, happy, *pleased, right, sorry, upset*
       *Helen is **excited about** winning the prize.*
       *I'm **sorry about** your difficulties. Can I help?*

Adjectives marked * are followed by other prepositions when they refer to people. See *For, With* below.

At   *bad, good*
      *Dora is really **good at** maths.*

For   *famous, late, ready, sorry*
      *Our city is **famous for** its beautiful buildings.*
      *I was **sorry for** George when he came last in the race.*

From   *different*
      *This room is **different from** the other one.*

In   *interested*
      *Are you **interested in** computers?*

Of   *afraid, fond, frightened, full, jealous, tired*
      *My sleeping bag was **full of** ants!*

On   *keen*
      *I'm not very **keen on** fried food.*

To   *kind, married, used*
      *Ellen is **married to** Jack.*

With   *angry, annoyed, bored, pleased*
      *I'm really **angry with** you.*

Practice

1
Put **one** suitable word in each space.

a) Fiona is very different ...*from*....... her sister.

b) This house reminds me .... the house I grew up in.

c) Please try and listen .... my instructions.

d) My home town is famous .... its peaches.

e) Excuse me, but does this umbrella belong .... you?

f) What exactly was George talking .... ?

g) I think we should ask .... some information.

h) Kate is very keen .... growing her own vegetables.

i) I feel sorry .... Sam because he hasn't got any friends.

j) When I speak Italian, all the others in the class laugh .... me.

2

Rewrite each sentence so that it has a similar meaning and contains the word given.

a) Dick found his work boring.

bored

...*Dick was bored with his work*...

b) This town is a bit like Glasgow.

reminds

....

c) Paula has a good knowledge of biology.

knows

....

d) I'm trying to find the art gallery.

looking

....

e) I like cream cakes.

fond

....

f) Sue is Adrian's wife.

to

....

g) Dina always treats animals kindly.

kind

....

h) Ugh! This cake has a rubbery taste!

rubber

....

i) You make Lisa feel jealous!

is

....

j) Our new house makes me feel excited!

about

....

3

Complete the second sentence so that it has a similar meaning to the first sentence.

a) Do you find archaeology interesting?

Are you ...*interested in archaeology*.................... ?

b) You have made me angry.

I am ....

c) I'd like my lunch now.

I'm .... for lunch.

d) Geography is Richard's best subject.

Richard is very ....

e) The bad news made me feel upset.

I felt ....

f) My dog was in my dreams last night!

I dreamt ....

g) Sue is a reliable person.

You can ....

h) Jack borrowed my bike for the weekend.

I lent my ....

i) The dark makes me afraid.

I'm afraid ....

j) There were lots of people in the square.

The square was ....

4

Put **one** suitable word in each space.

a) We asked our teacher to ...*explain*... a difficult problem ..*to*.......... us.

b) The comic told a silly joke, but nobody .... it.

c) The ring I found .... an old lady who had lost it in the street.

d) We may come to your party, but it .... our finding a babysitter.

e) When Joe flew to Australia, his aunt .... his ticket.

f) Harry .... to his neighbours .... his bad behaviour.

g) You really .... my brother. You are very alike!

h) Tony .... passing his driving test at the first attempt.

i) See you in a minute! I'll .... you outside the cinema.

j) They spoke so quickly, that I didn't know what they were ....

....

5

Complete each part sentence a) to h) with one of the endings 1) to 8).

a) Ellen is not really interested ..*4*.

b) The hotel was different .....

c) Little Suzie was jealous .....

d) I was really annoyed .....

e) Paul is very keen .....

f) Jane is really good .....

g) At home, I'm used .....

h) I don't think I'm ready .....

1) at making new friends.

2) about losing my new calculator.

3) for another big meal.

4) in learning how to ski.

5) of her new sister at first.

6) to going to bed early.

7) from what we expected.

8) on collecting old bottles.

Unit 41 Pronouns

Explanations

Impersonal *one*

- In formal writing and in formal speech, *one* is used as an impersonal subject. In this context it means 'people in general'.
  One takes the train to the airport from the Central Station.

- There is a possessive form *one's*.
  One's luggage is carried in a special compartment.

- If *one* is used as a subject, all later references also use *one*.
  *One takes the train to the airport from the Central Station and **one can reserve one's seat** in advance.*

- In everyday speech it is common to use *you*, or to avoid using a personal subject, especially by using the passive.
  You take the train to the airport from the Central Station.
  Seats can be reserved in advance.

- For some speakers the use of *one* seems over-formal.

- If you use *one*, you must continue to use it. Do not mix *one* and *you*.

someone, somebody, something

- *Someone* and *somebody* describe an unknown person. *Someone* and *anyone* (see below) follow the same rules as *some* and *any*.
  *There's **someone/somebody** at the door.*
  Something describes an unknown thing.
  ***Something** is worrying me.*

- We use *someone, somebody, something* in questions about a definite idea.
  *Is **someone** coming to collect you?*
  *Can I ask you **something**?*

- Note that we refer to *someone* using *they/them*.
  ***Someone** phoned, and I told **them** you were out.*

everyone, everybody, everything

- *Everyone* and *everybody* describe a group of people. A singular verb is used.
  ***Everybody likes** Sue.*

- *Every one* has a different meaning. It is an emphatic way of saying *each single one*.
  *There were ten chocolates in the box and you have eaten **every one**!*
  Pronunciation: both words have equal stress.

● *Everything* describes all of a group of things.
   Everything *in the room was red.*
   Everything is used as a general subject instead of *all*.
   Everything *has gone wrong.*
   Pronunciation: the stress is normally on the first syllable.

anyone,
anybody,
anything

● *Anyone* and *anybody* describe unknown people. A singular verb is used. They are used in questions and with *not …* in negatives.
   Does anyone *know the answer?*
   There **isn't anybody** *at home.*

● *Anything* is used in a similar way about things. A singular verb is used.
   Is there anything *I can do to help?*

● See *someone* etc., on page 170, for the use of *someone* etc. in questions.

no one, nobody,
nothing

● *No one* and *nobody* describe people with a negative meaning. They are used with a positive singular verb.
   No one knows *the answer.*
   Nobody is *at home.*

● *Nothing* describes things in the same way.
   There **is nothing** *to eat.*

● Double negatives are not used. We cannot say: *No one doesn't know.*

Reflexives:
myself etc.

● Some verbs describe actions which refer to the same person who performs the action. In this case we use a reflexive pronoun.
   I have cut **myself.**   *He cut* **himself.**
   Did **you** *cut* **yourself**?   *We enjoyed* **ourselves.**
   She *introduced* **herself.**   *Have* **you** *hurt* **yourselves**?
   It's destroying **itself.**   **They** *introduced* **themselves.**

● Verbs often used in this way:
   cut, enjoy, hurt, introduce, kill
   At the end of the play, Cleopatra **kills herself.**
   Note that verbs may be reflexive in your language, but not reflexive in English.

● *Myself* etc. are also used for emphasis.
   Harry cooked all the food **himself.**
   This means that no one helped him.

Practice

1
Choose the correct word underlined in each sentence.

a) There isn't ~~anyone~~/no one in the garden.

b) Excuse me, could you move? I can't see anything/something.

c) There is anything/nothing to drink.

d) There's anyone/someone to see you outside.

e) You can do anything/something you want.

f) Anyone/Someone stole the money, but we don't know who.

g) I don't know anything/nothing about it.

h) No one/Someone would tell me the answer, so I guessed.

2
Complete the second sentence so that it has a similar meaning to the first sentence.

a) There was nothing I could do.
I couldn't ...*do anything*................................. .

b) I know Mary better than anyone.
No one ....

c) No one was on time yesterday.
Everyone ....

d) I haven't got any work.
I've got .... to do.

e) There's something I'd like to ask you.
May I .... ?

f) We are all milk drinkers here!
Everybody .... milk.

g) When I phoned, there was no reply.
No one ....

h) Are we going to be driven there?
Is .... ?

3
Rewrite each sentence so that it includes a suitable form of one of the verbs from the list, and a reflexive pronoun.

| ask behave blame cut dress |
| enjoy express hurt introduce talk |

a) Have a good holiday, both of you! And ...*enjoy*......... ..*yourselves*..

b) We leave little Jimmy's clothes beside his bed, and he ....

c) I keep .... why I didn't speak to him, but I just don't know.

d) Our teacher told us to stop shouting and to ....

e) When I fell off the horse, I didn't ....

f) Paula knows a lot of French, but can't .... easily.

g) Let me .... I'm Susan Perry.

h) The accident wasn't your fault. Don't ....

i) When I .... to .... , other people stare at me!

j) While Tom was picking up the broken glass, he ....

4

Rewrite each sentence so that it has a similar meaning and contains the word given.

a) The box isn't empty.
   something
   ...*There is something in the box.*...

b) All the people were dancing.
   everyone
   ....

c) I feel annoyed.
   something
   ....

d) We haven't got any food.
   nothing
   ....

e) The office is empty.
   no one
   ....

f) Helen is very popular.
   everybody
   ....

5

Put **one** suitable word in each space.

a) That's an easy question! ...*Everybody*..... knows the answer!
b) Is .... the matter? Can I help you?
c) .... is wrong with the car, and it won't start.
d) There's .... to see you. Shall I ask them to wait?
e) They introduced .... as Helen and Ann.
f) .... never really knows what will happen, does one?
g) .... I've done so far today has gone wrong!
h) .... you could say would make me change my mind, I'm afraid.

6

Underline the errors in these sentences. Rewrite each sentence.

a) Someone spoke to me, but I can't remember <u>its</u> name.
   ...*Someone spoke to me, but I can't remember their name.*...............................

b) All in the garden has been growing a lot lately.
   ....

c) Carol didn't do nothing yesterday.
   ....

d) There isn't no one waiting for you.
   ....

e) Peter and Kate enjoyed themselfs at the party.
   ....

f) One fills in an application form, and then you wait for an answer.
   ....

Unit 42 Possession

Explanations

Possessive apostrophe

- When a thing or things belong to a person, a possessive apostrophe *'s* is normally added to the thing or person.
    *This is **Jim's scarf.***   *Those are **Helen's gloves.***
    *Where is **the director's office**?*

- When a thing or things belong to a plural noun ending in *s*, the apostrophe only is added.
    *Those are the **students' coats.***

- A possessive apostrophe is sometimes used when a thing is part of another thing.
    *What is the **book's title**?*
    *What is this **plant's name**?*

- Note that names of shops and other services are often made by using the name of the shopkeeper or the business, with a possessive apostrophe.
    *George bought this melon in the **greengrocer's** / in **Smith's**.*
    *I went to the **doctor's** and the **dentist's** on the same day.*

- Note the common mistake of putting an apostrophe before the *s*-plural of plural words. We do not write: **Apple's sold here.*

- Note that an apostrophe is also used in a contraction, to show that letters are missing.
    ***It's** a lovely day.*   *It's = It is*   ***It's** got a battery.*   *It's = It has*

of and compound words

- *Of* is normally used to show that a thing or things belong to another thing.
    *The end **of the street.***
    *The last twenty pages **of the book.***

- Compound words are formed from two or more words. Compound words are often used when a thing is part of another thing, or used for a certain purpose.
    *I saw the shirt in a **shop window**.*
    *I bought some new **football boots**.*

- Compound words are very common in technical descriptions.
    *Loosen the **corner brackets** first.*

- Sometimes a hyphen is used to join the words. Check in a dictionary to see when a hyphen is used.
    *I bought a chocolate **ice-cream**.*

Possessive adjectives	● Possessive adjectives are used before nouns. *my your her its his our their*
	● We do not use an article with a possessive adjective. *Peter is **my** cousin. He doesn't live in **our** town.*
	● Possessive adjectives can be strengthened with *own*. *Paul cooks all **his own** meals.* *This isn't **my own** bike. I've borrowed it from a friend.*
Possessive pronouns	● Possessive pronouns are used instead of a possessive adjective and noun. They stand on their own, and are not used with another noun. *This is **my bike**.* (possessive adjective + noun) *This bike is **mine**.* (possessive pronoun) *mine yours hers his ours theirs* *Whose keys are these? Are they **yours** or **mine**?* ***Yours** are on the table. **These** are mine.* Note that there is not an apostrophe in possessive pronouns ending in *s*.
Double possessive	There are two common types. Both are normally used to describe the relationships between people. Possessive apostrophe and *of* *Jo is a friend **of my brother's**.* *Of* and possessive pronoun *I met a cousin **of mine** at the party.* It is possible to use *of* and possessive pronoun to describe things owned by people. *Do you like this new hat **of mine**?*

Practice

1
Choose the correct word or phrase underlined in each sentence.

a) Jane met a friend of her/hers in the street.

b) Helen does all herself/her own decorating.

c) Are these scissors your/yours?

d) The desk next to the window is my/mine.

e) Paul and Alice introduced me to a neighbour of their/theirs.

f) Excuse me, is this your/yours seat?

g) David asks if you have seen that old coat of his/him.

h) Peter has borrowed my/mine bike.

i) We haven't brought our/ours books with us.

j) The dog is black and white, and its/it's ears are very long.

2

Put an apostrophe where necessary.

a) Tell Susan its Marys turn, not hers.

...*Tell Susan it's Mary's turn, not hers.*.............................

b) Alices younger brothers called Bill.

....

c) Tims sandwiches were tastier than ours.

....

d) The films beginning is good but its ending is weak.

....

e) Are these keys yours or hers?

....

f) Kate fills in the patients record cards at the doctors.

....

g) When its raining, everybodys raincoats get wet.

....

h) The managers assistant reads all the customers letters.

....

i) Your sisters dog runs faster than ours.

....

j) Ones our teachers car and the others a visitors.

....

3

Make **two** compound words from the words listed.

a) football cheese boot sandwich ...*football boot*......... ...*cheese sandwich*...

b) window pocket coat shop ....

c) gate garden lamp bicycle ....

d) department cottage store country ....

e) engine singer rock fire ....

f) post sharpener office pencil ....

g) ground report school football ....

h) assistant shop station railway ....

i) mixer money food pocket ....

j) market street failure power ....

4

Complete the second sentence so that it has a similar meaning to the first sentence.

a) Naomi is a friend of my sister's.

Naomi is my ...*sister's friend*...................... .

b) These shoes belong to Sam.

These are ....

c) I met one of my friends outside the school.

I met a .... outside the school.

d) This is my favourite programme on television.

.... programme.

e) What are your teachers called?

What .... names?

f) Have you got a thing for opening tins?

.... opener?

g) Those bikes belong to our neighbours.

Those .... bikes.

h) I put my books on the table in the kitchen.

.... table.

i) Do you like my new umbrella?

Do you like this .... ?

j) This calculator doesn't belong to me.

.... calculator.

5

Underline the errors in these sentences. Rewrite each sentence.

a) There are two bus-<u>stop's</u> near my house.

...*There are two bus-stops near my house.*...............................

b) Our cat sleep's all day in it's bed.

....

c) Have you met the sister of Jane?

....

d) Creature's like these live at the sea's bottom.

....

e) This book is the mine.

....

f) I noticed these shoe's in a window's shop.

....

g) Everybodys drawing's were better than our's.

....

h) Are these your's or mine glove's?

....

i) The house stand's on it's own at the street's end.

....

j) Those are two friends' of my fathers.

....

Unit 43 Text organizers

Explanations

This unit includes words and phrases used to organize speaking and writing.

and, both, too, as well, also

- *And* is used to join words, phrases or clauses.
  *Helen put on her coat **and** picked up the suitcase.*

- To emphasize two actions or descriptions, *both ... and* is used.
  *Helen picked up **both** her suitcase **and** her umbrella.*

- *Too, as well* and *also* are used to describe two actions at the same time.
  *Helen picked up her suitcase **and** her umbrella **too**.*
  *Helen picked up her suitcase **and** her umbrella **as well**.*

- *As well* is also used with *as*.
  *Helen picked up her suitcase **as well as** her umbrella.*

- Note the position of *also*.
  *Helen picked up **both** her suitcase **and also** her umbrella.*

even

- When something is thought to be surprising, *even* is used to emphasize an action, or a thing. We do not use *and* to do this.
  *Sam studies very hard. He **even** gets up at 5.30 to study!*

- *Even* is also used to emphasize comparative adjectives.
  *This question is **even harder than** the last one.*

either, or

- *Either ... or* is used to describe a choice or an alternative.
  *We can **either** go to the cinema, **or** stay at home.*
  Or is not used at the beginning of sentences in writing. It is used in speech to complete someone else's sentence.
  'We could go to the cinema I suppose ...' *'... **or** we could stay at home and watch a video.'*

First (of all), secondly, etc., finally

When we list points in writing and formal speech, we often show that we are making a new point, so that our point of view is easier to understand.
  *Television has changed our lives in several ways. **First of all**, it has ...*
  ***Secondly**, more people ... **Finally**, it has changed the way that ...*

As well as this, besides this

These are used in writing and formal speech to show that we are adding a point.
  Television has changed our lives in several ways. First of all, it has ...
  Secondly, more people ...
  ***As well as this/Besides this**, more people ...*

In my view, *personally*	These are used in formal speech and writing to introduce our own ideas.
	Some people believe that television has killed the art of conversation. **In my view/Personally**, *I think it gives people something to talk about.*

In conclusion	This is used in formal speech and writing to introduce our final point.
	In conclusion, *we can say that television has both good and bad features.*

except	*Except* describes something not included. *For* is sometimes used with it.
	We have painted all the house, **except (for)** *the front door.*
	They gave presents to everyone **except** *me.*

for example, *such as*	● *For example* is used either before or after the examples.
	Diet varies from place to place. **For example**, *in hot countries, people tend to eat more fruit.*
	In hot countries, **for example**, *people tend to eat more fruit.*
	● *Such as* follows a general idea and gives examples.
	In hot countries, **such as** *Greece, people tend to eat more fruit.*
	● *Such as* cannot be used at the beginning of a sentence.

in fact, actually	*In fact* is used when we give more detail, or contradict what has been said.
	Dave has several dogs. **In fact**, *he's got twelve.* (more detail)
	I thought Gina was a doctor but, **in fact**, *she's a vet.* (contradiction)
	I thought Gina was a doctor but, **actually**, *she's a vet.* (contradiction)

instead (of)	● This is used to describe a change.
	Instead of *cooking I ordered a take-away meal.*
	Jill came to the party **instead of** *her sister.*
	● At the end of a sentence, *instead* is used without *of*.
	I didn't cook. I ordered a take-away meal **instead**.

Time words with other meanings	The meaning of a word depends on its use. Many common words have other uses. The following tend to be used more in writing.
	since meaning *as* I couldn't swim, **since** I had a cold.
	yet meaning *although* No one replied to my knock, **yet** all the lights were on.
	while meaning *although* The first two buses were full, **while** the next was completely empty.

Practice

1

Choose the correct word or phrase underlined in each sentence.

a) Mrs Davis taught us except for/(instead of) Mr Taylor.

b) We can either/or wait here, or phone for a taxi.

c) Helen plays the guitar and also/too writes songs.

d) There is a very cold winter in countries for example/such as Finland.

e) Everyone in the team played badly also/except Sam.

f) All the shops were closed, since/yet it was a public holiday.

g) Jack studies and/both geography and history.

h) The Peakworth tent is strong and waterproof, since/yet light to carry.

i) Jane felt wet and miserable both/too.

j) The shelf was so high that and/even our teacher couldn't reach it.

2

Rewrite each sentence so that it has a similar meaning and contains the word given.

a) Paula visited both the castle and the museum.

too

...Paula visited the castle and the museum, too...

b) Jack was the only person who came late.

except

....

c) Although I said it was raining, it isn't!

fact

....

d) Helen hurt her leg, so she couldn't play.

since

....

e) My opinion is that smoking is bad for you.

view

....

f) I ate the chocolate cake and the lemon pie.

as well as

....

g) Jim played in goal, in his brother's place.

instead

....

h) Finally, I'd like to thank the head teacher, Ann Coles.

in

....

i) Though I have written twice, I have not received a reply.
   yet
   ....

j) We can wait for the bus or take a taxi.
   either
   ....

3
Decide which
answer, a), b), c)
or d), best fits the
space.

Nowadays there are many good reasons for using bicycles (1) ..c.. cars to travel
in city centres. (2) ..... , bicycles are (3) ..... silent and clean, (4) ..... are easy to
park. (5) ..... , using a bicycle (6) ..... keeps people fit. However, city centres must
(7) ..... have cycle lanes (8) ..... be free of private cars completely. Some large
cities, (9) ..... Amsterdam in the Netherlands, are already organized in this way.
(10) ..... , a combination of the use of bicycles with very cheap or free public
transport solves the problem of traffic jams and makes the city centre a more
pleasant place.

1) a) but   b) except for   c) instead of   d) such as
2) a) as well   b) first of all   c) in fact   d) personally
3) a) both   b) and   c) too   d) as well
4) a) also   b) for example they   c) except   d) and as well as this
5) a) and   b) yet   c) while   d) secondly
6) a) and   b) both   c) also   d) too
7) a) in conclusion   b) either   c) besides this   d) both
8) a) such as   b) yet   c) also   d) or
9) a) such as   b) as well   c) in my view   d) while
10) a) personally   b) finally   c) for example   d) actually

4
Complete each
sentence with a
word or phrase
from the list. Use
each word or
phrase once only.

actually	as well as this	both	either
except	instead	personally	such as

a) Everyone ...*except*........... Julia remembered to bring their dictionaries.

b) We've repaired the roof, and .... we've repainted the whole house.

c) .... I don't think that there are aliens or flying saucers.

d) I managed to lose .... my passport and my wallet.

e) I was going to go to the cinema, but I went to the theatre ....

f) People think that Tim is shy, but .... he is very talkative.

g) Some illnesses, ... the common cold, do not have a cure.

h) We're going to .... go camping, or stay with some friends.

5

Complete the spaces a) to j) using 1) to 10).

(a) ..5.. I'd like to thank everyone who has helped with the school play. (b) .....
the actors, and the stage hands, have worked very hard, and everyone who made
the costumes worked hard (c) ..... . I would (d) ..... like to thank all those who
have sold tickets. This year we had an (e) ..... larger audience than last year, and
(f) ..... Tuesday evening, every single seat was sold. This year the play ran for a
week (g) ..... for two days. We did not have a lot of time for rehearsals, and
(h) ..... the play was a great success. (i) ..... , I feel that we should congratulate all
the actors for their wonderful performance. (j) ..... , I'd like to give Judy Walker,
the director, this present from everyone at the school.

1) even
2) yet
3) as well
4) except for
5) first of all
6) in conclusion
7) also
8) personally
9) both
10) instead of

Unit 44 Capital letters and punctuation

Explanations

Capital letters

- Capital (or upper-case) letters are used:

  to begin a sentence   *This is a beautiful place.*
  for names of people   *Jim, Helen*
  for addressing people   *Mrs Jones, Uncle Peter, Mum*
  for personal pronoun *I*   *I saw Ellen last night.*
  for titles of books etc.   *'Three Men and a Baby' is a funny film.*
  for names of places   *France, Hungary*
  for calendar information   *Wednesday, March, New Year's Day*

- Note that words like *and*, *a/the* and prepositions do not have capitals, unless they are at the beginning of the title.

  'In the Heat of the Night' is a good film.

- Some words can be written with capitals, or in lower-case. These are:

  names of the seasons   *in Spring, in spring*
  decades   *the Fifties, the fifties*
  jobs   *Sanderson was a good president.*   (used generally)
       Paul met President Brunswick.   (named jobs)
  compass points   *I live in the north of Scotland.*
       Sally works in the Far East.

Punctuation

- Full stop (.)
  At the end of a sentence.
  After each letter which stands for a word in an abbreviation.

  e.g.   *etc.*

  Full stops are often left out after the abbreviations *Mr* and *Mrs*

- Comma (,)
  A comma represents a pause. It is used in lists.

  I bought some bananas, some oranges and some potatoes.

  If the last two items of the list are long we use a comma.

  All day we cleaned the floors, washed the walls, and tidied the house.

  Openings
  Some words or phrases at the opening of a sentence are followed by commas.

  First of all, this can be dangerous.

Parentheses
These are phrases put between the subject and the verb.
> *Ann, on the other hand, did not agree.*

Non-defining clauses – see Unit 23.
> *Tony, who is usually late, turned up at 10.30.*

Commas are not used after reporting verbs in reported speech.
> *Jim said he would be late.*

Compare direct speech, where a comma is needed:
> *Jim said, 'I'll be late.'*

Commas separate clauses and phrases, and cannot be used to join sentences.
> *Two men were walking down the street. They were carrying a box.*
> *Two men carrying a box were walking down the street.*
> **Two men were walking down the street, they were carrying a box.*

The last sentence is not acceptable in formal writing.

- Semi-colon (;)
  We can join two sentences, with related meaning, using a semi-colon.
  > *Road users annoy pedestrians; pedestrians annoy road users.*

  A semi-colon is also used to separate long items in a list.
  > *Students are asked not to leave bicycles by the entrance; not to leave bags*
  > *in the sitting room; and not to leave coats in the dining room.*

- Colon (:)
  A colon introduces items in a list, or an explanation of the previous part of
  the sentence.
  > *There are two rules: One, don't do it; two, don't get caught.*
  > *Finally, we had to stop: we were tired and it was dark.*

- Quotation marks (" ") (' ')
  Quotation marks (or speech marks) are used with direct speech.
  Punctuation goes inside the marks. Quotation marks can be double or
  single.
  > *"Why are we leaving so early?" Helen asked.*
  > *'It might rain later,' I explained.*

  Titles of books, films, plays etc. are usually put inside single quotation marks
  when using handwriting. Punctuation is put outside in this case.
  > *We went to a performance of Ibsen's 'Ghosts'.*

  In printed text, the titles of books, films, plays etc. are usually put in italics.

- Question mark (?) and Exclamation mark (!)
  Question marks only occur after the question.
  > *What's the time?*

  Exclamation marks are used in informal writing, but are not considered
  appropriate in formal writing.
  > *You'll never guess what! I've just got engaged!*

Practice

1

Tick (✓) the sentence which is punctuated correctly.

a) 1) 'Would you mind telling me where we are?' Tina asked. ✓
   2) 'Would you mind telling me, where we are Tina asked?'
   3) 'Would you mind telling me, where we are,' Tina asked?

b) 1) I agreed, that a cottage in the mountains, would be better.
   2) I agreed that a cottage in the mountains would be better.
   3) I agreed that a cottage, in the mountains would be better.

c) 1) Helen who arrived after I did, asked me when the play finished?
   2) Helen, who arrived after I did, asked me when the play finished.
   3) Helen, who arrived after I did asked me, when the play finished.

d) 1) Peter told me, not to wait and said 'I'll see you later.'
   2) Peter told me not to wait and said, 'I'll see you later.'
   3) Peter told me not to wait and said I'll see you later.

e) 1) In the end I went home, I was wet and hungry, and felt ill.
   2) In the end I went home; I was wet and hungry; and felt ill.
   3) In the end I went home: I was wet and hungry and felt ill.

f) 1) I bought some flour, some eggs, two lemons and some sugar.
   2) I bought some: flour, some: eggs, two: lemons and some sugar.
   3) I bought some flour some eggs two lemons, and some sugar.

g) 1) Ann told us that nobody had asked her for her passport.
   2) Ann told us that, nobody had asked her, for her passport.
   3) Ann told us that nobody had asked her, for her passport.

2

Rewrite each group of words so that it contains the punctuation listed.

a) First of all who is going to carry the suitcase asked Sue
   (one full stop, one comma, one question mark, speech marks)
   ....*'First of all, who is going to carry the suitcase?' asked Sue.*...........................

b) Kate said she would be on time but I didn't believe her
   (one full stop, one comma)
   ....
   ....

c) Jack said that he had missed the train got lost and been arrested
   (one full stop, two commas)
   ....
   ....

d) When the bell rang our teacher stood up and said Stop writing please
   (one full stop, three commas, speech marks)
   ....
   ....

e) On the other hand we could go to the cinema couldn't we said David
(one full stop, two commas, one question mark, speech marks)

....

....

f) Hello Alan said Tina how do you feel today
(one full stop, one comma, one question mark, speech marks, one capital letter)

....

....

g) If I were you I'd ask for some help or perhaps start again
(one full stop, two commas)

....

....

h) The old stadium was eventually demolished very few people went there and it was becoming dangerous
(one full stop, one comma, one colon)

....

....

3
Rewrite each sentence putting in any necessary capital letters.

a) we're meeting uncle david on tuesday evening at eight.
...We're meeting Uncle David on Tuesday evening at eight..............

b) last february i met mrs wilkinson for the first time.

....

c) tim lives in the south of france near cannes.

....

d) we saw a great film at the abc called 'the remains of the day'.

....

e) carol works as the manager of a tourist agency.

....

f) we went to a party at mrs harrisons' house on new year's eve.

....

g) julia's reading 'a portrait of a lady' by henry james.

....

h) when jean met the prime minister she asked some difficult questions.

....

....

Unit 45 Spelling and pronunciation 1

Explanations

Adding *-ing* to verbs

- One- syllable words which end in one vowel and one consonant double the last consonant.
  *swim/**swimming***   *put/**putting***
  Compare these words which do not double the consonant:
  shoot/shooting   *lift/lifting*

- Two-syllable words which end in one vowel and one consonant double the last consonant when the stress is on the second syllable.
  *begin/**beginning***   *control/**controlling***
  Compare these words with the stress on the first syllable.
  *wonder/**wondering***   *threaten/**threatening***
  One exception to this rule in GB English is *travel/travelling*.
  Words which end in one vowel, one consonant and *-e* drop the final *-e*.
  *write/**writing***   *leave/**leaving***

Words ending in *-ful*

The suffix *-ful* has only one *l*.
  beautiful   *successful*
When *-ly* is added for adverbs, a double *l* is formed.
  beautifully   *successfully*

-ie or *-ei*?

There is a useful rule: *i* before *e* except after *c*, when the sound is /iː/.
  field   *niece*   but   ***receive***

Silent letters

- Many words contain letters which do not obviously form the sound. These are sometimes referred to as 'silent letters'. The silent letters are underlined.
  bt/mb   *doubt   plumber   thumb*
  kn   *knee   knife   know*
  ps   *psychology   psychiatrist*
  sc   *descend   ascend*
- *q* and *u*
  The letter *q* is always followed by *u*.
  question squid acquire

Practice (Words commonly spelled wrongly are also included here.)

1

Correct the spelling where necessary.

a) decideing ...*deciding*.........   g) thier   ....
b) swiming   ....   h) beatiful ....
c) foto   ....   i) reciept   ....
d) qestion   ....   j) begining   ....
e) whistle   ....   k) phychiatrist ....
f) knowen   ....   l) sucesfull   ....

2

Use the letters to make a word which fits the space.

a) Sue said she'd ..*phone*.... (nehop) me but I haven't ...*received*.... (iredvece) a call.

b) When the referee blew the .... (stewlih) the players left the .... (edlif).

c) Ellen .... (feclyslusucs) completed the course in nuclear .... (shipscy)

d) I didn't .... (wonk) how to cut the string without a .... (inkef).

e) The police arrested the .... (itfeh) as he was .... (negvial) the bank.

f) Jim asked a .... (siqontue), but his teacher wasn't .... (nilsigent).

g) At the .... (nigengibn) of the film, I had a poor .... (wive) of the screen.

h) These ancient .... (mulcosn) are .... (yitbuelfual) made.

3

Write each verb with an -*ing* ending.

a) control ...*controlling*...   e) fly   ....   i) write   ....
b) thicken ....   f) make   ....   j) improve ....
c) grip   ....   g) upset   ....   k) swim   ....
d) choose ....   h) hook   ....   l) ride   ....

4

Correct the spelling in this letter.

Dear Tina,

I am sory that I have not writen to you for so long. I'm afriad I've been very bussy at shool, and I haven't had much time for writeing leters. Last week I finised my examenations, so now I'm geting redy to go on holyday.

I was wundering wether you wood like to come to stay for a fiew days? You cann meat my freinds, and we coud all go swimeing. The wheather is realy good now hear in Italy, and I'm shure you will engoy yourself.

best wishes,

Maria

5

Correct these words commonly spelled wrongly.

a) tommorow ...*tomorrow*.......   g) neccessarry ....
b) Wensday ....   h) dissappointed ....
c) advertisment ....   i) wheather   ....
d) neihbour ....   j) rember   ....
e) thrugh   ....   k) libary   ....
f) greatfull ....   l) anser   ....

Unit 46 Spelling and pronunciation 2

Explanations

Same sound, different spelling

Both vowel and consonant sounds in English have several ways of spelling the same sound. In each group, the sound underlined is the same.

Vowels

c*o*mpany br*o*ther l*o*ve tr*ou*ble r*u*bbish bl*oo*d

r*oa*d m*o*st h*o*me th*ough* l*ow*

*ea*rth f*u*rther w*o*rd h*u*rt

w*ai*t gr*ea*t l*a*te w*eigh*t

n*ow* sh*ou*t dr*ow*n pl*ough*

Consonants

rela*ti*on *sh*ock *s*ure con*sci*ous deli*ci*ous

*ch*urch furni*tu*re wat*ch*

lei*s*ure mea*s*ure confu*si*on

Same pronunciation, different spelling and meaning

Common examples are:

court/caught	stair/stare	sore/saw	allowed/aloud
lesson/lessen	find/fined	waste/waist	fare/fair
warn/worn	wait/weight	no/know	two/too

Words which look similar

Some words are similar to other words, but have a different meaning.

later/latter	quiet/quite
recent/resent	accept/except
through/thorough	formerly/formally
insure/ensure	lose/loose

Words with a syllable which is not pronounced

Some words appear to have more syllables than they actually have when pronounced. Examples which are often spelled wrongly:

temperature	library	Wednesday
vegetable	people	interesting

Nouns and verbs with *c* and *s*

Noun	advice	practice
Verb	advise	practise

How to improve spelling

Use a dictionary to check the pronunciation of new words, and relate their spelling to words you know. Make lists of the words you usually spell wrongly. Reading widely will give you experience of the way words are spelled.

Practice (Words commonly spelled wrongly are also included here.)

1
Find pairs of words with the same sound underlined.

a) (dirt)   g) c<u>o</u>mpany   m) p<u>a</u>rk

b) pl<u>u</u>m   h) d<u>ou</u>bt   n) r<u>u</u>le

c) h<u>ea</u>rt   i) mea<u>s</u>ure   o) br<u>o</u>wn

d) ca<u>tch</u>   j) furni<u>t</u>ure   p) cau<u>t</u>ion

e) ph<u>o</u>ne   k) t<u>oa</u>st   q) (w<u>or</u>d)

f) <u>s</u>ure   l) f<u>oo</u>d   r) confu<u>s</u>ion

2
Choose the correct word in each sentence.

a) Please stop looking at me like that! It's very rude to <u>stair/stare</u>.

b) I think you should <u>practice/practise</u> diving every day.

c) The doctor gave Martin a <u>through/thorough</u> examination.

d) Could you give me some <u>advice/advise</u> about language courses?

e) We wanted to go by train, but we couldn't afford the <u>fair/fare</u>.

f) Could you wait a moment? I'm not <u>quiet/quite</u> ready.

g) Reading <u>allowed/aloud</u> is hard unless you have time to check first.

h) Sorry I didn't come to your party, but I just felt <u>two/too</u> tired.

3
Tick (✓) if a pair of words rhymes.

a) sweet/eat   ✓   f) thought/short .....   k) abroad/afford .....

b) worse/horse .....   g) later/latter .....   l) quite/diet .....

c) worn/torn .....   h) word/heard .....   m) friend/leaned .....

d) lose/loose .....   i) chose/bruise .....   n) blood/food .....

e) tea/bee .....   j) low/go .....   o) weight/height .....

4
Correct the spelling in this letter.

Dear Maria,

Thanks for your leter and your invittation to Italy! I have never traveled abraod before, and I am realy looking forwerd to staying with you and your familly. I have spokken to my parrents and they have aggreed. They say they are going to phone soon to discus the arangements.

I've dicided to have some Italian lessons so that I can practice when I come to Italy. I'd like you to write some simple sentences for me. Please note my new adress. We moved last weak and now I've got a much biger bedroom.

best wishes,   Tina

5
Correct these words commonly spelled wrongly.

a) vegtable   *...vegetable...........*   g) intresting   ....

b) langage   ....   h) biscit   ....

c) qeueu   ....   i) cieling   ....

d) recieve   ....   j) difrent   ....

e) peple   ....   k) knowlige   ....

f) beatiful   ....   l) indipendant   ....

Problems, Errors, Consolidation 5

Used w
L. Friend KN. "/5/??

1

Choose the correct words underlined in each sentence.

a) Paula keeps talking about that new bike of (hers)/her/her's.

b) I asked my teacher for help, but she refused to help/helping me.

c) David isn't interested at/for/in collecting stamps.

d) Sue couldn't swim although/as she had a bad cold.

e) It's really dark. I can't see anything/something/nothing.

f) I really enjoy to spend/spending time with you!

g) Ann is not very good at/by/for French.

h) Helen hasn't told me anything/nothing about the trip.

2

Decide which answer, a), b), c) or d), best fits the space.

An unfortunate misunderstanding

Last year we (1) ..h.. to have an expensive holiday, so we (2) ..... to visit some friends, Brian and Ann, who (3) ..... to live by the sea. They (4) ..... to put us up for two weeks, and as we always (5) ..... seeing them, it (6) ..... to be a good idea. They asked us if we (7) ..... sleeping on the sofa, and said that they would (8) ..... to make us comfortable. We (9) ..... to get there by bus, and when we arrived we could (10) ..... Brian and Ann sitting in the garden. They (11) ..... to be glad to see us, but it was obvious that they hadn't (12) ..... to see us. They said that we had (13) ..... to tell them when we were arriving, and they (14) ..... asking us how long we were going to stay. We (15) ..... feeling embarrassed, so the next day we went home.

1) a) continued   b) couldn't afford   c) liked   d) promised
2) a) fancied   b) tried   c) wished   d) decided
3) a) meant   b) kept   c) hoped   d) happened
4) a) offered   b) admitted   c) enjoyed   d) intended
5) a) denied   b) imagined   c) enjoyed   d) preferred
6) a) began   b) seemed   c) imagined   d) expected
7) a) minded   b) suggested   c) wanted   d) remembered
8) a) practise   b) mean   c) learn   d) try
9) a) suggested   b) tried   c) managed   d) started
10) a) watch   b) see   c) keep   d) wait
11) a) intended   b) pretended   c) expected   d) suggested
12) a) preferred   b) forgotten   c) promised   d) expected
13) a) forgotten   b) denied   c) seemed   d) chosen
14) a) loved   b) wanted   c) kept   d) couldn't stand
15) a) imagined   b) minded   c) couldn't help   d) seemed

191

3
Complete the second sentence so that it has a similar meaning to the first sentence.

a) Tim was the only student who forgot the test.
   Everyone remembered the test ...*except Tim*.. .

b) Helen knows this town better than anyone.
   No one ....

c) These two pairs of gloves belong to the twins.
   These are ....

d) Sam wouldn't carry my bag.
   Sam refused ....

e) Peter is reliable.
   You can ....

f) Mary is one of my brother's friends.
   Mary is a ....

g) The snow began yesterday evening.
   It ....

h) The classroom is empty.
   There's ....

i) Do you think you could close the window?
   Would you mind .... ?

j) Bill borrowed Sue's calculator.
   Sue lent her ....

4
Look carefully at each line. Some lines are correct but some have a word which should not be there. Tick each correct line. If a line has a word which should not be there, write the word in the space.

Winning a million

Life changed completely for Carol Miles when she won	1) .....✓.......
£1,000,000 in the lottery. 'I decided that to buy a ticket	2) ...*that*....
while I was waiting for take the bus. I didn't get excited	3) ....
about it, because I didn't expect me to win. In fact, I	4) ....
completely forgot it to check my numbers, until a	5) ....
friend reminded for me to do it. You can imagine how	6) ....
surprised I was!' Carol had often been dreamt about	7) ....
being rich, but she has got discovered that having lots	8) ....
of money doesn't always mean being happy. 'I can't	9) ....
enjoy for anything now. When I go out with my friends,	10) ....
for example, they either expect me to pay or the bills,	11) ....
or they are angry with me when I offer to pay it. Some	12) ....
people they are jealous of my good luck, I think, and	13) ....
accuse me of thinking only about money. Nobody seems	14) ....
to have understand. I thought I would enjoy myself, but	15) ....
everyone has started to treat me with differently, except for	16) ....
one friend of mine who has asked me to lend it him £10,000!'	17) ....

5

Put **one** suitable word in each space.

An afternoon at the bus station

Kate had been waiting (a) ...*for*....... a colleague of (b) .... father's to collect her from the bus station for more than an hour, and she was tired (c) .... waiting. There was (d) .... else there, and it had (e) .... raining. A friend of (f) .... had lent her an umbrella to take on her trip, but she (g) .... to be getting wet. Perhaps her father was angry (h) .... her, she thought, or had simply (i) .... to collect her. There wasn't (j) .... a phone-box in the bus station. Why did (k) .... always go wrong when she travelled by bus? (l) .... the bus was crowded and she felt very uncomfortable, or it (m) .... stopping and the journey lasted for hours. Suddenly she (n) .... a car stopping outside. (o) .... was waving at her. It was her father!

6

Rewrite this letter, correcting the spelling and adding any necessary capital letters and punctuation.

17 Harford Street,
Bilsworth,
BK3 4JG
Tel: 08143 6783

dear david

it was grate too here from you after so long i enjoied hearing all youre knews i didn't reallize that you had spent a year abbroad you must have had a realy good time in greece ive dicided to go their next sumer praps we coud go twogether

ive had a fantastick year at colidge the work is harder than the work we did at scool but its more intresting im studing bussiness administration and computer sience at the momment ive also maid lots of new freinds

im thinkeing of comming to bristol for a few days to vissit my sister woud you like to meat you coud show me the sites and we coud talk abowt our old scooldays

why dont you give me a ring and we coud discus it it woud be wunderfull to see you agane
best wishes
ellen wilson

7

Put **one** suitable word in each space.

a) ...*Instead*. ...*of*......... going out to lunch, we stayed at home.
b) There were a dozen oranges in the bowl but you've eaten .... one.
c) I thought it was Wednesday today, but .... it's Tuesday!
d) .... , I would like to thank everyone who has given help.
e) Ted is a friend .... brother's, but isn't a friend of ....

f) Joe bought two shirts and a jacket ....

g) I really like this new coat of .... Where did you buy it?

h) Kate fell over and cut .... on a piece of broken glass.

i) I suppose it depends .... whether you believe .... UFOs.

j) The test was so hard that .... our teacher didn't know the answers.

Problem check

1   What is the difference between these pairs of sentences?
   a I tried to take an aspirin.
          I tried taking an aspirin.
   b I remember to do my homework.
          I remember doing my homework.
   c The boys stopped having a rest.
          The boys stopped to have a rest.

2   Many verbs or adjectives can be followed by different prepositions. Check these meanings in a dictionary:
   a You remind me of my brother.
          Can you remind me about the test?
   b We're pleased with him.
          We're pleased for him.
          We're pleased by him.

3   Only use *one* in formal speech and writing. Don't mix *one* and *you*.

4   Remember that using an apostrophe can mean that a letter is missing (*it's = it is*) or it can show possession (*Ann's hat*).

5   The best way to improve your punctuation and spelling is through wide reading. Make lists of words you often spell wrongly.

Vocabulary
1 Dealing with vocabulary

When you find a new word

If you are reading, and you come across a word you do not know, you may not need to look it up immediately. Ask yourself:

Do I need to know the exact meaning?
Do I think it's a useful word?

There are a number of actions you might take. This will probably depend on whether you are reading for pleasure or for information, whether you have time and whether you can get any help.

Leave it and come back later if it seems important.
Guess it from the context if possible.
Compare it with words you know that look similar, then guess.
Ask someone.
Use a dictionary.

Making sense of words

It is hard to remember words in isolation, and you need useful information about the word. Sometimes a word is really several words e.g. a multi-word or phrasal verb. Which information in this list do you find most useful?

Grammatical class (e.g. noun)
Pronunciation
Translation
Collocation (words which this word is often found with)
An example of how the word is used
Frequency (how common it is)
Usefulness
Formal or informal

Making the most of your dictionary

Choose a dictionary which has all the information you need. To use a dictionary effectively you need to know:

- how to find words in alphabetical order
- what the abbreviations in each entry mean

- how to look for words if you don't find them at first (e.g. look for other words in the family or the collocation)
- when to carry it with you
- when to use it and when not to use it (you might get bored if you use it too much)

Keeping a written record

If you organize the words you come across into a written record, then you are more likely to remember them. If your record is organized so that you make sense of the new words, this will help your memory. Here are some ways of recording words. What are the advantages and disadvantages of each one?

- Choosing words because they:
  are the most useful
  interest you
  cause you problems

- Recording them in alphabetical order

- Large topic areas

- Idioms and expressions

- Word field   (This is a group based on a closely related topic.)

  Garden
  lawn   hedge   shed   flowerbed

- Word family   (This is a group based on word formation.)

  beauty   noun
  beautiful   adjective
  beautify   verb

Word fields and families can be written as diagrams.

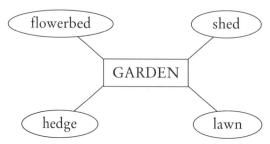

2 Word formation

Words can be formed by adding a prefix to the beginning or a suffix to the end. There are many prefixes and suffixes included in this unit, and Unit 3. Use a dictionary to find words formed with prefixes and suffixes.

Examples of prefixes: *un-, dis-, im-, mis-*

> *un- + certain* **uncertain**   *dis- + appear* **disappear**
> *im- + possible* **impossible**   *mis + understand* **misunderstand**

Examples of suffixes: *-ness, -ful, -less, ship*

> *happy + -ness* **happiness**   *care + -ful* **careful**
> *end+ -less* **endless**   *friend + -ship* **friendship**

Words of two or more syllables ending in -*y* change -*y* to -*i*. See Unit 45.

1

In each sentence, add a word from the list to the prefix to make a negative word.

advantage agree appear appointed correct employed fortunately interesting patient understanding

a) I didn't read all of the book because I found it un*interesting*.

b) Cycling to school has one dis.................... . It makes you feel hot and sweaty.

c) Paula had a ticket for the theatre, but un.................... she fell ill that night.

d) Terry can't stand waiting in queues, because she is very im.................... .

e) My brothers always dis.................... when it's time to do the washing-up.

f) My teacher underlined the word in red because it was in.................... .

g) After Jack lost his job, he was un.................... for three months.

h) I'm sorry, but I completely dis.................... with you. I think it was a great film.

i) Because of a mis.................... , half the class went to the wrong classroom.

j) Ann felt really dis.................... when she didn't get the job.

2

Add a prefix from the list to the word in each sentence.

out- over- under- inter- re-

a) My alarm clock didn't go off, and so I ...*over*.slept this morning.

b) Peter packed some shirts and socks, some ....wear, and his jeans.

c) You have to go to the ....national airport to catch a plane to the USA.

d) It's very cold this morning, so wear your ....coat.

e) Helen decided to ....line all the important words in her French book.

f) Our team was completely ....played by the team from Wales.

g) I've decided to ....write my letter, because I made too many mistakes.

h) Bill ....cooked the meat, and it was burnt in places.

i) I have to go to the library today and ....new my ticket.

j) The staff went on strike because they were ....paid and overworked.

197

3

Complete the word in each sentence with a suffix from the list. Make any other necessary changes to the word.

-er -let -ess -hood -ship -ful -ery

a) After two years of friend*ship...* , Kate got to know David really well.

b) If you don't speak the language you feel more like a foreign......... .

c) Sarah spent a very happy child......... on a small island.

d) I asked a steward......... what time the plane arrived, but she didn't know.

e) Every teenage......... knows that parents worry a lot.

f) Don't forget to add a spoon......... of sugar, and some milk.

g) We live in a beautiful neighbour......... on the outskirts of the city.

h) Tina picked up a hand......... of snow, and threw it in my face.

i) Under the floor there was a rumbling sound of machine......... .

j) The college sent Sue a small book......... describing its courses.

4

Complete each sentence with a noun made from the verb given.

a) There are over one million ...*inhabitants*.... in this city.
inhabit

b) Greg often suffers from .... in the school holidays.
bore

c) This is the tallest .... in the whole of the country.
build

d) Some students can't find suitable ....
accommodate

e) I was upset by Carol's .... to help me.
refuse

f) It took Tim years to become a successful ....
act

g) Every .... in this company has received a pay rise.
employ

h) You need a lot of .... to write a good story.
imagine

i) Don't forget to turn off the .... before you leave.
cook

j) I read an interesting .... in the local paper.
advertise

5

Complete each sentence with a noun ending in *-ness* made from a word in the list. Make any necessary changes.

| dark | friendly | happy | lonely | short |
| sick | silly | thin | tired | thorough |

a) The ...*shortness*.. of the journey surprised me, as I thought it would be longer.

b) Sue was impressed by the .... of everyone in her new school.

c) We knew it was going to rain because of the .... of the sky.

d) Old Mrs Holt's .... was cured when she was given a pet cat.

e) The doctor told Peter that his .... was a result of overwork.

f) Wendy's teacher was impressed by the .... of her work.

g) We wished the bride and groom .... in their new life together.

h) Joe's teachers began to grow tired of his .... in class.

i) I felt rather cold when I arrived because of the .... of my clothes.

j) Jean took a travel .... pill, and then she felt much better.

6

Complete the word in each sentence with one of the suffixes in the list.

| -ful | -less | -ly | -like | -y | -ish | -ic | -al | -ous |

a) On rain*y*... days, we spend a lot of time indoors watching television.

b) The mystery creature has a long snake..... body, and six legs.

c) Paul received most of his music..... education from his mother.

d) The government is going to provide more houses for home..... people.

e) Mary's mother..... qualities made her a favourite with the children.

f) This road is extremely danger..... when the weather is bad.

g) We didn't have any difficult..... in finding your house.

h) It was very fool..... of you to leave all the doors and windows open.

i) Everyone thanked the fire-fighters for their hero..... efforts.

j) Lisa's party was the most success..... she had ever had.

3 Word formation

1

Choose the correct word underlined in each sentence.

a) By 11.00 I felt so (tired)/tiring that I went to bed.

b) I heard the film was good, but it was very disappointed/disappointing.

c) Being alone in an old house at night can be frightened/frightening.

d) Julie was so embarrassed/embarrassing that her whole face turned red.

e) Jim gets bored/boring if he has to study too much.

f) It's very confused/confusing to be taught in so many classrooms.

g) Andy said that the twenty-mile walk was <u>exhausted/exhausting</u>.

h) Are you <u>interested/interesting</u> in going to the beach tomorrow?

i) I was really <u>surprised/surprising</u> when my boss gave me the day off.

j) Why don't you go away and stop being so <u>annoyed/annoying</u>!

2

Complete the word underlined in each sentence with a prefix or suffix from the list. Make any other necessary changes to the word.

| -age   dis-   -ful   im-   un-   -y   -ness |

a) I suppose Paul might help us, but it seems <u>likely</u>.   *...unlikely.......*

b) Fred can't fill his pool because there's a water <u>short</u>.   ....

c) I found most of the maths questions completely <u>possible</u>.   ....

d) Jan has taken up <u>photograph</u> as a hobby.   ....

e) Thanks for those notes. They were really <u>use</u>.   ....

f) I <u>like</u> winter sports so I never go skiing.   ....

g) When it's time for bed I start feeling <u>sleep</u>.   ....

h) This is a really <u>usual</u> stamp. I've not seen one like it before.   ....

i) I really like Dan. He's always so happy and <u>cheer</u>.   ....

j) I'm writing to thank you for the <u>kind</u> you showed me.   ....

3

Complete each sentence with a word made from the word given.

a) It's ...*unusually*...... cold today, considering it's still summer.
   usual

b) Actually I found Tony's book was .... interesting.
   surprise

c) ...., my father used to go to school with your father.
   interest

d) The police managed .... to find the missing children.
   success

e) Jean's compositions are always .... written.
   beautiful

f) I am .... ashamed of your behaviour!
   thorough

g) This question is .... difficult, isn't it!
   awful

h) Mike tried .... to phone Cathy several times.
   success

i) These instructions seem .... complicated.
   necessary

j) Someone had .... left the front door open.
   obvious

4
Complete each word using the word given.

a) I can't sit on this chair. It's really un*comfortable*.... .
   comfort

b) Ann has left home and is in..................... of her parents.
   depend

c) These old envelopes are re..................... so we can save money.
   use

d) Not being chosen for the team was a great dis..................... .
   appoint

e) Maria and Louis have a really good ....ship.
   relate

f) Being un..................... means that you share with others.
   self

g) Not taking exercise is rather un..................... .
   health

h) David has a really un..................... temper, and gets angry easily.
   control

i) These trousers won't get smaller. They're un..................... .
   shrink

j) They didn't give Gary the job as he was in..................... .
   experience

5
Complete each sentence with a word made from the word given.

a) Harry asked for a ...*receipt*...... and the cashier gave him one.
   receive

b) Nina wants to be a .... and join the government.
   politics

c) No one knows the exact .... of the water here.
   deep

d) You have to have a lot of .... to go fishing.
   patient

e) .... is a serious matter, and you have to think about it.
   marry

f) Tom sent in his .... for the job the next day.
   apply

g) Helen's mind is filled with all kinds of unusual ....
   know

h) There was no .... for the crash of the airliner.
   explain

6
Complete each sentence with a word made from the word given.

a) The ...*theft*......... of the diamonds baffled the police.
thief

b) Most people have no real .... in ghosts.
believe

c) Tina had no .... that anything was wrong.
suspect

d) We measured the .... of the room with a ruler.
long

e) Our teacher was really .... when she found out.
anger

f) George won a medal for ....
brave

g) Looking in the mirror too much is an example of ....
vain

h) Do you think you have the .... to pass the test?
able

i) Eddie put the .... food in the freezer.
freeze

j) Sheila has got the right .... for the job.
qualify

4 Expressions

1
Complete the expression based on the word *time* in each sentence, using a word from the list.

being	high	in	lose	matter
on	pass	spare	tell	time

a) Come on John! It's ...*high*........ time you started doing some work!

b) What do you most enjoy doing in your .... time?

c) I don't go sailing often, but I enjoy doing it from time to ....

d) When I have to wait at the airport, I do a crossword to .... the time.

e) When Carol was given her first watch, she learned to .... the time.

f) We have decided to stay with friends for the time ....

g) Sally is never late. She is always .... time for her lessons.

h) It's only a .... of time before someone finds out the truth!

i) Thank goodness the doctor hurried. She saved Jim's life just .... time.

j) Hurry up. We've no time to .... The train leaves in five minutes!

2

Complete the sentences with the most suitable verb from the list.

burst	caught	got	had	lost
made	paid	spent	told	took

a) Peter's father ...*made*..... lots of money by selling old cars.

b) Sue .... a party last week and most of her friends came.

c) I .... some very good photos of our dog with my new camera.

d) David .... a lot of money on rebuilding his motorbike.

e) The ending of the film was so sad that many people .... into tears.

f) According to the story, George Washington always .... the truth.

g) Kate .... into trouble at school for playing a joke on her teacher.

h) You didn't understand because you .... no attention to the instructions.

i) I .... a cold last week so I couldn't play in the football match.

j) We .... our way completely and had to ask for directions.

3

Complete each sentence with a word from the list.

alone	breath	difference	discussion	facts
leaf	mad	mess	secret	temper

a) It's hard to believe the news, but we have to face the ...*facts*......... .

b) I made a complete .... of one exam, and had to take it again.

c) When I swim underwater I can hold my .... for two minutes.

d) Peter told the boy to leave his little brother ....

e) Can you tell the .... between butter and margarine?

f) The loud music from the house next door drove Mary ....

g) When I stepped on Helen's foot, she tried not to lose her ....

h) I'll tell you, but only because I know that you can keep a ....

i) Bob wanted to change his ways and turn over a new ....

j) We had a very interesting .... about the problems of pollution.

4

The words underlined are in the wrong sentences. Find the correct sentence for each one.

a) Now that my summer holidays have begun I feel as free as <u>pie</u>.   ...*a bird*......

b) Without my glasses I am as blind as <u>a pig</u>.   ....

c) After our search, suddenly David turned up as large as <u>rain</u>!   ....

d) As cool as <u>a bat</u>, the robber asked for all the money in the bank!   ....

e) I didn't have any problems with the test. It was as easy as <u>houses</u>.   ....

f) Our dog eats too much, and is getting as fat as <u>a picture</u>.   ....

g) My boss has no feelings at all! He's as hard as <u>life</u>.   ....

h) Little Sarah looked as pretty as <u>a cucumber</u> in her new dress.   ....

i) Take this medicine, and in a few days you'll be as right as <u>nails</u>.   ....

j) Don't be frightened of being on this plane. It's as safe as <u>a bird</u>.   ....

5

Replace each phrase underlined with one of the expressions in the list.

| feel dog tired   get ready   have an early night   have fun |
| have nothing to do   sleep like a log   take a day off   take it easy |

a) I'm really tired. I'm going to <u>go to bed before it gets late</u>.
   ...*have an early night*...............

b) I've been working very hard, so I'm going to <u>relax and have some rest</u>.
   ....

c) I felt ill last Tuesday, so I decided to <u>stay at home and not go to work</u>.
   ....

d) Let's go out tonight and <u>enjoy ourselves</u>.
   ....

e) I <u>don't have any work</u> this evening, so we can go to the cinema.
   ....

f) Last night I managed to <u>have a good sleep, and didn't wake up at all</u>.
   ....

g) That was a long day. <u>I'm completely exhausted</u>.
   ....

h) I think we should <u>prepare ourselves</u> for the trip as early as we can.
   ....

6

Complete the expressions underlined in each sentence, with a word from the list.

| day   down   life   round   seek |
| soul   sound   then   time   wide |

a) It's extremely important. In fact, it's <u>a matter of ...*life*.... and death</u>.

b) Ann is great fun, and is always <u>the life and .... of the party</u>.

c) The police have been searching <u>far and ....</u> for the stolen jewels.

d) We were completely lost, and drove <u>round and ....</u> for hours.

e) I've told you <u>........... and again</u> not to write tests in pencil!

f) The two missing explorers have been found <u>safe and ....</u> .

g) That man has been walking <u>up and ....</u> outside the house all day.

h) The children decided to <u>play hide and ....</u> in the garden.

i) I don't see Paul very often, but I visit him <u>now and ....</u> .

j) Sheila worked <u>night and ....</u> to finish her book on time.

5 Compound words

1

Complete each compound word with a word from the list.

| ache | clip | cut | glasses |
| lace | path | post | table |

a) Make sure you walk on the foot*.path.*.... , because the road is dangerous.

b) I need to fix these two sheets together. Have you got a paper .... ?

c) As I was doing up my shoe, the shoe............ in one of them broke.

d) On our first day at school, we copied down our time............ .

e) Tom had a hair............ yesterday and his friends made fun of him.

f) It's really sunny today, and I've forgotten my sun............ .

g) Could I have a couple of aspirins? I've got a terrible head............ .

h) The bus swerved to avoid a dog and hit a lamp-............ .

2

Complete each sentence with a compound word made from two words from the list.

| air   alarm   birthday   central   clock |
| conditioning   fiction   heating   machine |
| party   report   school   science   stick |
| walking   washing |

a) I love ...*science*... ..*fiction*.... films with robots in them.

b) Old Mr Low has a bad leg and always leans on his ....

c) David's teachers wrote lots of good things in his ....

d) As soon as the .... rings, I jump out of bed.

e) When it's hot, I turn on the ....-................ and it cools the room.

f) Julia invited all her friends from school to her ....

g) This house has .... and there is a radiator in every room.

h) If you have any dirty clothes, just put them in the ....

3

The compound words underlined are in the wrong sentences. Find the correct sentence for each one.

a) I couldn't unscrew the <u>shed door</u>, so I couldn't drink my cola.
   ...*bottle top*...........................

b) On my way to school, I saw a fantastic bike in a <u>bathroom mirror</u>.
   ....

c) My bike had a flat tyre, and I didn't have my <u>television screen</u> with me.
   ....

d) As the girls were leaving, they saw their teacher at the <u>pocket money</u>.
   ....

e) As she was eating the chocolate bar, Ann threw the <u>bottle top</u> away.
   ....

f) When I saw my face in the <u>school entrance</u>, I knew I really was ill.

....

g) During my favourite serial, a newsflash appeared on the <u>door handle</u>.

....

h) The <u>sweet wrapper</u> was locked, so I couldn't use the lawn mower.

....

i) Paul's parents gave him a small amount of <u>bicycle pump</u> every week.

....

j) Susie was too small to reach the <u>shop window</u>, so she knocked.

....

4

Match each situation with an object from the list.

> bottle opener   coffee maker   dishwasher   fire extinguisher
> food mixer   hairdrier   lawn mower   pencil sharpener
> stain remover   water heater

a) Comb it first and then use this.   ...*hairdrier*...............

b) Just put all the dirty plates in here.   ....

c) I've dropped ink all over my white trousers.   ....

d) Use this in an emergency.   ....

e) I've just broken mine, and I can't write.   ....

f) I'm really thirsty but I can't open this lemonade. ....

g) That grass really needs cutting.   ....

h) It's much quicker preparing a cake with this.   ....

i) If you need a bath, I'll turn it on.   ....

j) If you'd like a cup, I've just put it on.   ....

5

Make a compound word which describes the person in each sentence, using one of the words underlined, and a word from the list.

> bather   dreamer   fighter   keeper
> lifter   maker   manager   sitter

a) Someone who spends all <u>day</u> lost in pleasant thoughts.   ...*day-dreamer*.........

b) Someone who owns or runs a <u>shop</u>.   ....

c) Someone who is lying in the <u>sun</u> to get a tan.   ....

d) Someone who looks after a <u>baby</u> while you are out.   ....

e) Someone who exercises with objects of great <u>weight</u>.   ....

f) Someone who is a member of the <u>fire</u>-brigade.   ....

g) Someone who is in charge of the branch of a <u>bank</u>.   ....

h) Someone who is away from home on <u>holiday</u>.   ....

6
Complete each compound word by adding a word from the list.

> about bringing coat come doors
> ground pour set skirts stairs

a) Jane has a high in.*come*......., but she works very hard to earn it.

b) I'm sorry I said that. I hope you're not up............... .

c) You have to turn left at the next round............... .

d) Kevin fell down............... and hurt his ankle.

e) It's cold today, so you'd better wear your over............... .

f) On our way home we got soaked in a terrific down............... .

g) It's a lovely day. Why don't we have lunch out............... ?

h) They live in a small house on the out............... of the town.

i) It's easy to travel in London if you use the Under............... .

j) That child is so polite. She obviously had a good up............... .

6 Money and shopping

1
Replace the words underlined with one of the phrases from the list.

> in a sale pay you back save up in debt
> second-hand be well-off annual income can't afford it

a) Kate's car was <u>owned by someone else before her</u>.
   ...*second-hand*......................

b) We're not going on holiday this year, because we <u>are short of money</u>.
   ....

c) Don't worry, next week I'll <u>give you the money you lent me</u>.
   ....

d) We decided to <u>put money aside</u> so we could buy a small boat.
   ....

e) I don't want to end up <u>owing a lot of money</u> to the bank.
   ....

f) What exactly is the amount of your <u>earnings every year</u>?
   ....

g) I bought my CD-player <u>when the prices were reduced</u>.
   ....

h) Mary used to <u>have a lot of money</u>, but she wasted most of it.
   ....

2

Choose the correct word or phrase underlined in each sentence.

a) Dora (earns)/gains/wins more money in her job than I do.

b) The factory workers asked for a rise in their <u>income/reward/wages</u>.

c) Paul <u>borrowed/lent/loaned</u> some money from me but didn't pay it back.

d) I'm sorry, but we don't accept credit cards, only <u>cash/coins/money</u>.

e) Is it all right if I pay <u>with cheque/by cheque/from cheque</u>?

f) We don't exchange goods unless you still have the <u>bill/cheque/receipt</u>.

g) I'm afraid I've only got a £50 note. Do you have <u>change/money/rest</u>?

h) I still <u>debt/owe/own</u> the bank more than £5000.

3

Complete the shopping situations a) to h) with a remark from 1) to 8)

a) I can't decide whether to buy it or not, so I think ..6..

b) Have you got a pair like this in red? .....

c) Can I pay by credit-card? .....

d) Can I help you? No thanks, ...

e) That's £49.99, please. .....

f) Thanks very much for your help. .....

g) There isn't a price label on this shirt. .....

h) This computer looks difficult to use. .....

1) Not at all, madam. It's a pleasure.
2) I'm just looking.
3) Could you explain how it works?
4) How would you like to pay?
5) We're out of stock at the moment. Sorry.
6) I'll leave it.
7) Sorry, we only accept cash or cheques.
8) How much is it?

4

Complete each phrase with a suitable word from the list.

| loaf   box   carton   packet   bunch   tube   bar   tin |

a) a ..*packet*.. of biscuits

b) a .... of toothpaste

c) a .... of tomatoes

d) a .... of milk

e) a large .... of tissues

f) a .... of chocolate

g) a .... of bananas

h) a .... of bread

5

Choose the most suitable word for each space.

Shopping in the street

When I (1) ..c.. shopping, I enjoy visiting street (2) ..... and looking for (3) ..... . I wander around looking at each (4) ..... , and asking about (5) ..... . Many (6) ..... on sale are less (7) ..... than those in high-street shops, though the (8) ..... is not always as good. It also depends on how much you want to (9) ..... . Clothes are often (10) ..... , but it is difficult to (11) ..... them on. It's always (12) ..... looking at second-hand books, because you can (13) ..... a lot of money in this way. Fresh fruit and vegetables are usually good (14) ..... , and there is always an excellent selection. The main problem is whether you can carry home lots of (15) ..... bags!

1) a) like   b) make   c) go   d) do
2) a) markets   b) trades   c) shops   d) sales
3) a) values   b) cheaper   c) special   d) bargains
4) a) counter   b) table   c) stall   d) department
5) a) costs   b) prices   c) values   d) figures
6) a) produces   b) shopkeepers   c) offers   d) goods
7) a) expensive   b) cost   c) priced   d) cheaper
8) a) expense   b) package   c) kind   d) quality
9) a) spend   b) use   c) make   d) cash
10) a) fashion   b) cheaper   c) worn   d) logical
11) a) purchase   b) carry   c) try   d) wrap
12) a) worth   b) more   c) been   d) time
13) a) borrow   b) spend   c) save   d) count
14) a) health   b) value   c) time   d) taste
15) a) hand   b) papers   c) more   d) heavy

6

Complete the sentence with a compound word made from two words in the list. A word may be used more than once. Some compounds are written as one word.

account   assistant   bag   bank   book   carrier
cash   cheques   cut   department   desk   money
pocket   price   shop   store   traveller's   window

a) Most teenagers are given some ...*pocket money*....... to spend by their parents.
b) Pat saw the suit in the .... and decided to buy it.
c) Perhaps you left your wallet at the .... when you paid.
d) Jane buys all her CDs cheap in a/an .... store.
e) I bought the new novel by Richard Francis in my local ....
f) You can buy nearly anything in a big ....
g) You can't write cheques unless you have a/an .... !
h) The .... who served me helped me buy what I was looking for.
i) When I go abroad I always take .... with me.
j) I brought my shopping home in a strong ....

7 Living space

1
Complete each sentence with a word from the list.

| carpet | curtains | cushion | drawer |
| pillow | radiator | settee | socket |

a) Is that chair comfortable, or would you like to use a ...*cushion*.... ?

b) Peter couldn't use his computer as there wasn't a .... in the room.

c) This house has central heating, and there's a .... in every room.

d) I was so tired that I fell asleep as soon as my head touched the ....

e) Could you draw the .... ? Someone is staring through the window.

f) My bedroom has a fitted .... which covers the whole floor.

g) The knives and forks are in the second .... on the left.

h) Come over here and sit next to me on the ....

2
Complete each part sentence a) to h) with one of the endings 1) to 8).

a) Please sit down and make yourself ..*4*..

b) Many of our language students share .....

c) I like Do-It-Yourself, but I've decided to have .....

d) Alan seems to have so many clothes that he can never find .....

e) If you can't find the house you can always ask for .....

f) Susan lives on the tenth floor of .....

g) If you are short of money you can buy .....

h) As we live in a semi-detached house, we hear .....

1) room for all of them in the wardrobe.
2) a block of flats on the south side of the city.
3) directions at the bus-station.
4) at home, while I make some tea.
5) accommodation in the villages nearby.
6) the decorating done by a local firm.
7) a lot of noise through the wall from the family next door.
8) furniture from the street market near the cathedral.

3
Each sentence contains an inappropriate word or phrase. Underline this word, and then replace it with a word or phrase from the list.

| bookcase | chimney | fence | floor |
| gate | pane of glass | step | towel |

a) Unfortunately the ball hit the window and broke a <u>glass</u>.
   ..*pane of glass*......................

b) I washed my hands in the bathroom and dried them with a cloth.
   ....

c) There was a small wooden door leading into the garden.
   ....

d) As I sat down at the kitchen table, I knocked my cup onto the ground.

....

e) In the corner of Joe's room was a small library for his books.

....

f) All round the garden there was a high wooden wall.

....

g) On the roof-tops Tina could see a tall fireplace pouring out smoke.

....

h) The floor of the kitchen is a bit lower, so mind the stair.

....

4

Choose the correct word underlined in each sentence.

a) Will you be at home/at house later this evening?
b) Paul's room is at the top of the stairs/steps opposite the bathroom.
c) Can you remember to clean the wash-basin/sink in the bathroom?
d) The rooms downstairs are so low I can touch the roof/ceiling.
e) Tony is a keen cooker/cook and always uses an electric cooker/cook.
f) You'll find plates in the cupboard/wardrobe next to the fridge.
g) Ann was sitting at/to her desk, but Chris was sitting in/on an armchair.
h) I won't be long. I'm just going upstairs for a bath/a bathe.
i) Lisa didn't like doing homework/housework, so she paid a cleaner.
j) Under the house there's a cave/cellar where we keep our old things.

5

Use **two** words from the list to make a word and use the new word to complete the sentence. One word is used twice.

dust   room   book   down   flower   stairs
wash   ash   basin   chair   bin   key   arm
bed   case   dish   hole   tray   washer

a) It's very cold in my ...*bedroom*........ , and I find it hard to sleep.
b) Sarah spent all afternoon sitting in a large .... in front of the TV.
c) I left my socks soaking in the .... in the bathroom.
d) Do you think you could put all your rubbish outside in the .... ?
e) There is a beautiful .... full of roses right outside my window.
f) Don't worry about the washing-up. We'll put everything in the

....

g) I can't open the front door. Something is stuck in the ....
h) If you really insist on smoking, please use this ....
i) Can you come .... ? There's someone at the door for you.
j) In this .... are the dictionaries and an encyclopedia.

6

Complete each sentence with a verb from the list in a suitable form. You can use a verb more than once.

drop	finish	get	look	move	put	take	turn

a) I've got nowhere to stay tonight. Can you ...*put*.... me up?

b) We've bought a new house but we can't .... in until next month.

c) Adrian doesn't .... on with his neighbours, because they are so noisy.

d) Jan likes cooking, but she says it .... up a lot of her time.

e) Don't forget to .... off the television before you go to bed.

f) Helen has done most of the decorating and plans to .... it off tomorrow.

g) I have a large room, and it .... out onto a beautiful garden.

h) Karen and Mike live next door and they often .... in for a chat.

8 Personal matters

1

Choose the correct word underlined in each sentence.

a) When her bicycle was stolen, Jill became extremely (angry)/nervous.

b) Peter felt ashamed/embarrassed when he had to make a speech.

c) I always write thank-you letters, just to be gentle/polite.

d) You never do anything to help me! You're so lazy/tired.

e) Sue never does anything silly. She's very sensible/sensitive.

f) The children had to stay in the house all day and felt bored/tired.

g) Tina doesn't worry about anything and is always cheerful/sympathetic.

h) Mr Jackson is very annoyed/bad-tempered and often shouts at people.

i) When he heard about the accident, Alan was very damaged/upset.

j) I've got an important exam tomorrow and I'm a bit jealous/nervous.

2

Complete each sentence with one of the verbs from the list. Use each verb once only.

cheer   complain   nod   cry
shake his head   shout   smile   whistle

a) Please look at the camera and ...*smile*......... . Say 'cheese'!

b) If you agree with what I say, just ....

c) The food in the restaurant was terrible so we decided to ....

d) I had to .... Ann's name three times before she heard me.

e) The little boy fell over and then started to ....

f) At the end of the President's speech, the crowd began to ....

g) Paul hardly ever says 'no'. He tends to .... instead.

h) When I try to .... I put my lips together but I can't do it!

3

Complete each sentence with a word formed from the word underlined.

a) You can't <u>rely</u> on Joe. He is very ...*unreliable*... .

b) Carla has very little <u>patience</u>. She is very ....

c) Jack shows no <u>interest</u> in this subject. He is ....

d) Pat is lacking in <u>honesty</u>. She is ....

e) Bill doesn't act like a <u>friend</u>. He is ....

f) Lisa doesn't have much <u>experience</u> of this work. She is ....

g) Peter never acts <u>politely</u>. He is ....

h) The official did not <u>help</u> us very much. She was ....

i) Graham doesn't <u>consider</u> other people. He is ....

j) Ann refused to <u>co-operate</u> with the police. She was ....

4

Complete each sentence with an adjective from the list. Use each once only.

| ashamed annoyed disappointed excited exhausted |
| fascinating glad jealous selfish terrified |

a) When her team lost the cup final, Sue felt very ..*disappointed*. .

b) I was .... when Jack accepted my invitation to dinner but didn't come.

c) Mark was .... when he saw smoke coming from the plane's engine.

d) Thanks for your letter. I'm .... to hear that you are feeling better.

e) David was .... to tell his parents that he had been sent to prison.

f) After running for fifteen kilometres, Christine felt completely ....

g) Helen felt .... when she saw her boyfriend talking to another girl.

h) I felt really .... while I was waiting to meet the star of the film.

i) Mrs Hobson told us about her life. She is a .... person.

j) Tom doesn't think about others, and is rather ....

5

Replace the words underlined in each sentence with **one** of the phrases from the list.

| are fond of   fancy   fed up with   get on my nerves |
| give up   let me down   longing for   put me off |

a) I'm really <u>looking forward to</u> a few weeks' holiday!
...*longing for*.........................

b) Sarah has decided to <u>do without</u> eating chocolate.
....

c) I wanted to study biology, but my teacher <u>discouraged me</u>.
....

d) Sports programmes on television really <u>annoy me</u>.
....

e) Do you <u>feel like</u> going to the cinema this evening?
....

f) Why can't you tell the truth? I'm <u>tired of</u> your excuses!

....

g) Terry and I <u>like</u> going for walks in the country.

....

h) George agreed to help me, but then <u>disappointed me</u>.

....

6
Complete each sentence with a word from the list.

conscience	death	hand	heart	mood
tears	temper	thanks	trouble	voice

a) The children were happy because their teacher was in a good ...*mood*...... .

b) .... to Mr Dawson, our car was repaired in time for our holiday.

c) Ruth was helpful, and went to a lot of .... to make us comfortable.

d) Harry was leaning out of the window and shouting at the top of his ....

e) When Alice heard the bad news, she burst into ....

f) Neil is a very kind person. His .... is in the right place.

g) If you do something bad, it will be on your .... for a long time.

h) I was really angry, and lost my .... , and shouted at people.

i) We need some help. Could you give us a .... ?

j) The first time I saw a horror film, I was scared to ....

9 Family and friends

1
Complete each sentence with one of the words from the list.

alike	children	couple	elder	engaged
friendship	housewife	husband	single	twin

a) Jane got married to her ...*husband*... , Bob, four years ago.

b) Jane's friends think that she and Bob are the perfect ....

c) They haven't got any .... yet, but they want a large family.

d) Jane's .... sister, Mary, was born half an hour before she was.

e) Jane and Mary look .... but are not exactly the same.

f) Mary isn't married. She says she prefers to be ....

g) She says she believes in .... , but doesn't believe in marriage.

h) Diana is Jane and Mary's .... sister. She calls them her 'little sisters'.

i) Diana has been .... for three years, but hasn't got married yet.

j) She has a career and doesn't like the idea of being a ....

2

Complete each sentence with a noun formed from a verb in the list.

> acquaint bear behave celebrate die
> engage greet marry relate resemble

a) All Sue's friends and ...*relations/relatives*... came to her party.

b) I occasionally meet Terry, but he is more a/an .... than a friend.

c) Mary received many cards congratulating her on the .... of her baby.

d) When Paul arrived, he received a warm and friendly ....

e) Six months after their .... , Michael and Lisa got married.

f) There was a great .... in the village when their team won the cup.

g) In an ideal .... , husband and wife share each other's problems.

h) Dina and her mother look alike. There is a strong .... between them.

i) There was no trouble, and the .... of the football fans was excellent.

j) Tim cried when he heard about the .... of his old dog.

3

Choose the correct word underlined in each sentence.

a) Children are not allowed to see this film. It's for (adults)/old only.

b) By the time the vet arrived, the injured cat was already dead/died.

c) Unfortunately it rained on Nick and Helen's wedding/marriage day.

d) David and Diana have two sons and one daughter/girl.

e) I think we should try to understand the problems of aged/old people.

f) There should be more facilities for youth/young people in this town.

g) Julie is very popular and has a wide company/circle of friends.

h) More than fifty relatives/parents were invited to Jack's party.

i) Old Mrs Turner now lives in an old people's home/house.

j) It's my anniversary/birthday today. I'm eighteen years old.

4

Complete each part sentence a) to j) with an ending from 1) to 10).

a) I have started going

b) When little Tina is grown

c) I wonder if you could put

d) Carol doesn't really get

e) Everyone says that Tom

f) Let's have some friends

g) Do you think you could look

h) Why don't we all get

i) Ellen and Laura were brought

j) If I have time I'll drop

1) takes after his father.

2) together again next Friday evening?

3) up by an aunt after their parents died.

4) in on Steve for a chat.

5) after my dog while I'm away?

6) out with George's younger sister.

7) round and play charades on Friday.

8) on well with her mother-in-law.

9) up she wants to be an astronaut.

10) us up for a few days next week?

5
Match each
sentence a) to h)
with a sentence
from 1) to 8)
which helps to
explain the
meaning of the
word underlined.

a) We've got a new <u>neighbour</u> called Helen Willis. ..5..

b) This is Sue. She's a <u>colleague</u> of mine. .....

c) Andrew is going to be our <u>best man</u>. .....

d) At the end of the evening I thanked our <u>host</u>. .....

e) I'm sure that Mary will be a wonderful <u>bride</u>. .....

f) Next week I'm going to stay with my <u>grandparents</u>. .....

g) I've always got on well with my <u>sister-in-law</u>. .....

h) Georgina is the ideal <u>guest</u>. .....

1) I was happy that he had invited me to his party.

2) Even before she married my brother we had become good friends.

3) She always offers to help in the house when she stays with us.

4) We both work in the same department at the bank.

5) She moved into the house next door yesterday.

6) They are both in their seventies, but they live a very full life.

7) When John and I get married, he'll stand next to John.

8) She's a dressmaker, and has designed her own wedding dress.

6
Complete each
sentence with a
word or phrase
from the list. Use
each word or
phrase once only.

| after against away in |
| on on and off out over |

a) It would be nice to meet again. I'll get ...*in*......... touch with you next week.

b) I'm afraid Karen isn't here. She went .... for the weekend.

c) I keep leaving and coming back. I've lived here .... for several years.

d) George brought up the children .... his own after his wife died.

e) The baby was called Mary, ... its grandmother.

f) After their final quarrel, Carrie told Luke their relationship was ....

g) Ann decided to get married .... the wishes of her parents.

h) Peter is .... at the moment but he'll be back in half an hour.

10 The body and clothes

1
Choose the
correct word
underlined in
each sentence.

a) The trousers are the right length, but the <u>stomach/waist</u> is too small.

b) I like this watch, but the strap is too small for my <u>palm/wrist</u>.

c) The hand has four fingers and a <u>thumb/toe</u>.

d) When Jim is nervous he tends to bite his <u>nails/joints</u>.

e) This bag has a strap and I can carry it on my <u>neck/shoulder</u>.

f) Gina twisted her <u>ankle/elbow</u> and she can't walk very easily.

g) Paul dropped the stone on his foot and broke two <u>toes/fingers</u>.

h) When you are worried lines appear on your <u>eyebrows/forehead</u>.

2
Choose the most suitable word for each space.

Clothes

Choosing clothes can be difficult. Some people want to be (1) ..*c*.. , but they don't want to look exactly (2) ..... everybody else. Not all clothes are (3) ..... for work or school, perhaps because they are not (4) ..... enough, or simply not (5) ..... . It is easy to buy the (6) ..... size, and find that your trousers are too (7) ..... , especially if you are a little bit (8) ..... . Very (9) ..... clothes make you feel (10) ..... , but when they have (11) ..... in the washing machine, then you have the same problem! If you buy light (12) ..... clothes, then they might not be (13) ..... enough for winter. If your shoes are not (14) ..... , and if you are not (15) ..... for the cold, you might look good, but feel terrible!

1) a) of fashion   b) fashioned   c) fashionable   d) fashion
2) a) alike   b) like   c) similar   d) same
3) a) fitted   b) suitable   c) comfort   d) equal
4) a) formal   b) strict   c) uniform   d) suited
5) a) comforting   b) comfort   c) comforted   d) comfortable
6) a) false   b) mistake   c) wrong   d) error
7) a) straight   b) close   c) stiff   d) tight
8) a) slim   b) overweight   c) thin   d) enormous
9) a) loose   b) lose   c) loosened   d) lost
10) a) thin   b) slim   c) narrow   d) spare
11) a) lessened   b) reduced   c) decreased   d) shrunk
12) a) of cotton   b) in cotton   c) cotton   d) cottoned
13) a) warm   b) cold   c) hot   d) cool
14) a) tight   b) enclosed   c) firm   d) waterproof
15) a) worn   b) clothed   c) dressed   d) fitted

3
Complete each sentence with a verb from the list. Use each verb once only.

disguise   dress up   fit   go with
look   put on   suit   wear

a) This dress doesn't ...*fit*......... me. It's far too big.

b) The children decided to .... as astronauts for the party.

c) Sue always seems to .... trousers. She says they are more comfortable.

d) I like your new haircut. It makes you .... younger.

e) It's a nice pullover, but the colour doesn't .... you.

f) The escaped prisoner managed to .... himself as a policeman.

g) I got up late and had only a few minutes to .... my clothes.

h) I don't think that yellow socks .... a black suit.

4
Match the words
with the
definitions.

| blouse   cap   dress   shorts   skirt   sleeve   sock   suit |

a) part of an item of clothing for covering the arm
...*sleeve*........

b) woman's or girl's clothing that covers the body from shoulders to knee or
below

....

c) jacket together with trousers or skirt made from the same material

....

d) a soft covering for the head worn by soldiers, and in some sports

....

e) trousers that end above or at the knee

....

f) item of clothing for women or girls that hangs from the waist and covers all
or part of the legs

....

g) loose item of clothing for women or girls covering the upper half of the body

....

h) soft item of clothing that covers the lower leg and foot inside the shoe

....

5
Complete each
expression
underlined with
one of the parts
of the body from
the list.

| arms   eye   face   foot   hair |
| hand   head   heart   leg   tongue |

a) The word is on the <u>tip of my ...*tongue*...</u> , but I just can't remember it.

b) Crossing the mountains on my own was a ....-raising adventure.

c) I know this is hard to believe, but you must <u>............... the truth</u>.

d) It is now over thirty years since man first <u>set .... on</u> the moon.

e) After his long trip Tom's parents <u>welcomed him with open</u> ....

f) Peter knows the songs <u>by</u> .... and doesn't need to look at a book.

g) Try to stay calm, and don't <u>lose your</u> .... , and everything will be fine.

h) Have I really won the prize, or are you only <u>pulling my</u> .... ?

i) Lisa needs some help with her suitcase. Could you <u>give her a</u> .... ?

j) I waved at Ann, hoping <u>to catch her</u> .... , but she didn't see me.

11 Everyday problems

1
Complete each sentence with a verb from the list.

> blocked   collapsed   collided   crashed   exploded
> flooded   had   injured   sank   trapped

a) Sam ...*had*........ an accident while he was driving home from college.

b) Yesterday a lorry .... into a bus at the traffic lights.

c) The falling roof tiles .... several passers-by, though not seriously.

d) The old wooden building .... in a high wind.

e) A terrorist bomb .... at the railway station last week.

f) The river burst its banks and .... the town during the night.

g) Rocks and mud from the mountain .... the main road yesterday.

h) A train .... with a car on a crossing just outside the town.

i) The storm at sea .... several small fishing boats.

j) The rising water .... two families in their homes for six hours.

2
Choose the correct word or phrase underlined in each sentence.

a) The doctor gave Sue a prescription/recipe for some medicine.

b) Tim's mother used a thermometer to take his fever/temperature.

c) It took Julia a long time to get over/get off her illness.

d) The cut on Karen's leg took a long time to cure/heal.

e) I couldn't run because I had a hurt/pain in my leg.

f) I bought these sea-sickness pills from the chemist's/physician's.

g) David was ill with a flu/flu for two weeks.

h) Dick couldn't speak because he had a throat ache/sore throat.

3
Complete each sentence with a compound word made out of two words from the list.

> air   bus   car   city   centre
> failure   hour   jam   park   parking
> pollution   power   rush   shortage   stop
> strike   ticket   traffic   train   water

a) The roads were crowded and I was stuck in a ...*traffic*.... ...*jam*.......for hours.

b) The .... is bad in this city. It's getting hard to breathe!

c) All the lights went out because there was a ....

d) I left my car in the wrong place and the police gave me a ....

e) I couldn't use the railway yesterday because there was a ....

f) I had to pay a fortune to leave my car in a multi-storey ....

g) I waited at the .... for hours but all the buses were full.

h) There is always a lot of traffic during the ....

i) It doesn't rain a lot here, and at the moment there is a ....

j) The Government has decided to ban all cars from the ....

4

Match the sentences which have a similar meaning.

a) They arrived too late to see her. ..*k*.

b) They didn't think it was safe. .....

c) They asked her to come next week instead. .....

d) They argued with her. .....

e) They were injured. .....

f) They didn't know where they were going. .....

g) They asked someone to tell them the way. .....

h) They've cancelled their party. .....

i) They asked for directions. .....

j) They had a row with her. .....

k) They missed her. .....

l) They were hurt. .....

m) They put her off for a week. .....

n) They felt it was dangerous. .....

o) Their party is off. .....

p) They'd lost their way. .....

5

Choose the best ending 1) to 10) for each sentence a) to j).

a) Fire-fighters managed to put ..*6*.

b) After a few minutes a fire .....

c) It was believed that someone set .....

d) Luckily Paul carried a fire .....

e) The fire was started by a .....

f) Metal melted from the intense .....

g) I could hardly breathe because of the .....

h) The old theatre caught .....

i) The wooden hut was burnt to .....

j) In seconds the building burst ....

1) fire accidentally.

2) a heap of ashes.

3) thick cloud of smoke.

4) into flames.

5) heat inside the burning car.

6) out the fire after two hours.

7) spark from a passing train.

8) -extinguisher in his car.

9) fire to the house deliberately.

10) engine arrived at the blaze.

6

Complete each sentence with a word from the list.

ambulance bandage blood hospital operation patient surgeon ward

a) A long white ...*bandage*... was wound around my arm.

b) This .... was built only two years ago, but is already too small.

c) The .... in the bed next to mine was a man with a broken leg.

d) The doctor told Jim that he would have to have a/an ....

e) David's bed is in a small .... with two others.

f) Paula was operated on by the best .... in the city.

g) Some people feel faint when they see ....

h) Helen was hurt in an accident and a passer-by called a/an ....

12 Travel and holidays

1
Choose the most suitable word for each space.

Holidays

Most people enjoy going (1) ..c.. for their holidays, and having the opportunity to (2) ..... in an interesting city or a seaside (3) ..... . If you speak (4) ..... languages, you can make new friends, and (5) ..... home some interesting (6) ..... as presents. But before you can do that, you have to (7) ..... your destination, and that is often a problem! If you fly, then you may find that your flight has been (8) ..... . (9) ..... by train can also be difficult, since trains are often (10) ..... in the summer, and you might have to reserve a (11) ..... in advance. Whichever way you (12) ..... , you can have problems with your (13) ..... , and it is often difficult to find good (14) ..... . Apart from this, you might not be able to afford the (15) ..... !

1) a) out   b) forward   c) abroad   d) foreign
2) a) remain   b) pass   c) spend   d) stay
3) a) resort   b) post   c) too   d) one
4) a) strange   b) stranger   c) foreigner   d) foreign
5) a) fetch   b) take   c) go   d) get
6) a) memories   b) souvenirs   c) memoirs   d) recollections
7) a) reach   b) arrive   c) go   d) travel
8) a) waited   b) reversed   c) delayed   d) booked
9) a) Journeys   b) Travels   c) Voyages   d) Passes
10) a) filling   b) occupied   c) overdone   d) crowded
11) a) post   b) chair   c) seat   d) position
12) a) voyage   b) travel   c) trip   d) tour
13) a) baggages   b) luggage   c) goods   d) sacks
14) a) staying   b) homes   c) lodges   d) accommodation
15) a) fare   b) fair   c) far   d) fur

2
Complete each sentence with a word formed from the word given.

a) They told me to ask at the ...*information*.... desk.
   inform
b) The plane gathered speed as it roared along the ....
   run
c) The .... of our plane has been delayed.
   depart
d) The plane made a bumpy .... and I felt ill.
   land
e) The clerk asked me if I had made a ....
   reserve
f) I got a seat because of another passenger's ....
   cancel

g) We arrived late at the .... , and missed the plane.
   air

h) We fastened our seatbelts and prepared for ....
   take

3

Complete each sentence with **one** of the words from the list. Use each word once only.

after back down for off in on out up with

a) The car broke ..*down*.. in the mountains, and we couldn't find a garage.

b) Harry had to set .... at dawn to catch the early train.

c) Sue's bike passed me, and I had to ride fast to catch .... with her.

d) I arrived at the airport, checked .... , and then had some coffee.

e) All the people in the queue were pushing, trying to get .... the bus.

f) We were making .... Paris, but we were not in a hurry to get there.

g) Paul enjoyed camping, but couldn't put up .... the insects!

h) When we realized we had forgotten our passports, we turned ....

i) Jill ran .... of money after a week, and had to go home.

j) Our next-door neighbours looked .... our dog while we were away.

4

Complete each part sentence a) to j) with one of the endings 1) to 10) and make a compound word.

a) I sent my friend a post
b) I fastened my seat
c) We stayed on a small camp
d) I always forget my guide
e) Don't forget to take your swim
f) If you lose your pass
g) We stayed in a quiet guest
h) The train time
i) I used to like going to the sea
j) Nowadays I'm afraid that hitch

1) suit with you to the beach.
2) table turned out to be wrong.
3) belt, and waited for takeoff.
4) port , you must tell the police.
5) hiking can be dangerous.
6) side when I was little.
7) card of the town where I stayed.
8) book when I visit old cities.
9) house down by the river.
10) site just outside the town.

5

Choose the correct word underlined in each sentence.

a) In Greece we visited several (ancient)/antique temples.

b) Whenever Helen travels by boat she feels seasick/dizzy.

c) Brighton is a popular/touristic seaside town.

d) Holidays in the mountains are always more relaxed/relaxing.

e) We always eat the local/topical food when we are abroad.

f) On my summer holidays I like getting suntanned/sunburnt.

g) It may not be easy to find accommodation at reasonable/logical prices.

h) After cycling all day, Bill was completely exhausted/tired.

i) The owner of the hotel gave us a hospitable/warm welcome.

j) Jack likes spending most of his holiday in the open/plain air.

6

The words underlined are in the wrong sentences. Find the right sentence for each one.

a) We spent two weeks in a lovely seaside <u>station</u>.
...*resort*...............

b) Jim stayed the night in a small bed and <u>hostel</u>.
....

c) Karen was exhausted after her fifteen-mile <u>holiday</u>.
....

d) Martin and Carol had a great time on their camping <u>cheques</u>.
....

e) As it was cheaper, I bought a return <u>stop</u>.
....

f) We managed to find some petrol at a remote filling <u>village</u>.
....

g) The bus made an overnight <u>breakfast</u> in a town near the border.
....

h) The family rented a cottage in a country <u>walk</u> for the summer.
....

i) If you are a student, you can save money by staying in a youth <u>ticket</u>.
....

j) David never carried cash on holiday. He always takes traveller's <u>resort</u>.
....

13 Interests and free time

1

Choose the most suitable word underlined in each sentence.

a) United managed to <u>beat</u>/win City in the last minute of the match.
b) At the end of the play, everyone in the theatre <u>applauded/exploded</u>.
c) If you want to <u>enter for/sign on</u> the competition, you'll need a form.
d) The cycling club is <u>doing/holding</u> a meeting next Thursday.
e) The youth orchestra has <u>acted/performed</u> all over Europe.
f) I'm <u>doing/going</u> fishing next week. Do you want to come?
g) The final score was 2–2, so Rovers <u>drew/equalled</u> the game.
h) David <u>spends/passes</u> an hour every day playing computer games.
i) Did you <u>enjoy/please</u> yourself at the folk festival?
j) We were late and so we <u>lost/missed</u> the beginning of the film.

2

Match each word in the list with **one** of the explanations.

| athletes audience cast competitors fans |
| group members spectators team viewers |

a) People who watch a sporting performance.
...*spectators*...........................

b) People who exercise and take part in games of speed and strength.
....

c) People who support a sport, or a famous person.
....

d) People who together take part in a sport.
....

e) People who all belong to the same club.
....

f) People who play rock music together.
....

g) People who listen to or watch a play or performance.
....

h) People who watch television.
....

i) People who act together in a play.
....

j) People who are all trying to win the same prize.
....

3

Complete each sentence with a word from the list.

| exhibition line medal prize queue |
| rod screen ticket tyre whistle |

a) Helen won first ...*prize*........... in the competition.
b) When Jim won the race, he was given a gold ....
c) We had to wait in a .... before we could get into the cinema.
d) Mary had to push her bike after she got a flat ....
e) There was so much shouting that no one heard the referee's ....
f) I've got a spare .... for tomorrow's concert. Do you want to come?
g) Have you seen the new .... of paintings at the National Gallery?
h) I'm going fishing tomorrow. I've just bought a new ....
i) Kate was the first runner to cross the finishing ....
j) We didn't enjoy the film because we were very close to the ....

4

Complete each sentence with a word from the list.

> drop fall go join knock
> live make put stand turn

a) Lenny 'The Fist' Smith, the boxer, said he would ...*knock*.... out his opponent.

b) Carol won the match because the other player failed to .... up.

c) The singer asked the audience to .... in and all sing together.

d) It was a reasonable film, but didn't really .... up to my expectations.

e) The first performance of the play was .... off because an actor was ill.

f) Tom and Sue used to .... out together.

g) From my seat, I couldn't .... out what was happening on the stage.

h) The referee made it clear that he would not .... for bad behaviour.

i) Peter had to .... out of the race after his car broke down.

j) Ann started off in the lead, but started to .... behind and finished last.

5

Choose the most suitable word for each space.

Music

What kind of music do you (1) ..*b*. ? Some people like going to (2) ..... concerts, and listening to (3) .... The (4) ..... wear very formal clothes, and the (5) ..... is silent until the end of the (6) ..... . Perhaps you are a rock music (7) .... . Rock concerts are often held at football (8) ..... or in parks. (9) ...... of the audience dance to the music, or sing the songs. (10) ..... music is (11) ..... at weddings and parties in many countries, and some people (12) ..... their own music at home. Nowadays we (13) ..... music in shops and lifts, and many people (14) ..... their own music with them, or even (15) ..... to music when they study. Music is everywhere!

1) a) listen   b) enjoy   c) have   d) preferring
2) a) classic   b) classics   c) classical   d) classified
3) a) a group   b) an orchestra   c) a band   d) a record
4) a) musicians   b) actors   c) musicals   d) instruments
5) a) spectators   b) people   c) guests   d) audience
6) a) happening   b) action   c) music   d) performance
7) a) fan   b) enthusiasm   c) reader   d) friend
8) a) matches   b) grounds   c) pitches   d) pools
9) a) Members   b) Selections   c) Persons   d) Those
10) a) Historical   b) Nation   c) Traditional   d) Ancient
11) a) acted   b) formed   c) done   d) played
12) a) do   b) get   c) make   d) take
13) a) listen   b) hear   c) perform   d) understand
14) a) carry   b) wear   c) lift   d) play
15) a) hear   b) have   c) follow   d) listen

6

Match each activity a) to h) with a place 1) to 8).

a) Sunbathing and wearing swimming costumes.
b) Watching elephants dancing.
c) Doing keep fit exercises.
d) Crossing the finishing line.
e) Taking a dog for a walk.
f) Celebrating someone's birthday.
g) Riding a ghost train or a big wheel.
h) Speaking clearly so the audience can hear.

1) a park
2) a party
3) a running track
4) a stage
5) a funfair
6) a circus
7) a beach
8) a gym

14 Places

1

Choose the most suitable word for each space.

A house in the country

The house is situated among beautiful (1) ..h. , two miles from the nearest village, surrounded by (2) ..... . On a (3) ..... a short distance from the house is a (4) ..... , and a small (5) ..... flows past the end of the garden, which also contains a small (6) ..... . The name of the house, Rose Cottage, is on the garden (7) ..... , from which a (8) ..... leads to the (9) ..... door. On the (10) ..... floor there is a large (11) ..... room, a dining room, a kitchen, and (12) ..... and toilet . (13) ..... there are three bedrooms. There is also a garage next to the house. The village has a post (14) ..... , pub and supermarket, and there is a railway (15) ..... three miles away.

1) a) view   b) scenery   c) sights   d) looks
2) a) grass   b) flats   c) earth   d) fields
3) a) mountain   b) peak   c) hill   d) summit
4) a) wood   b) greenery   c) jungle   d) forest
5) a) river   b) channel   c) stream   d) canal
6) a) lake   b) bath   c) water   d) pond
7) a) gate   b) door   c) opening   d) entrance
8) a) road   b) path   c) way   d) pavement
9) a) forward   b) front   c) first   d) further
10) a) bottom   b) back   c) ground   d) earth
11) a) lounge   b) seating   c) saloon   d) living
12) a) bathroom   b) bath   c) basin   d) washing
13) a) Over   b) Up   c) Upstairs   d) Higher
14) a) shop   b) centre   c) place   d) office
15) a) station   b) stop   c) post   d) base

2

Complete each sentence with **one** word from the list.

> block   centre   crossing   hall   junction
> part   place   station   traffic   zone

a) The police officer asked me to come with him to the police ...*station*.... .

b) When you reach the road .... turn right.

c) The mayor's office is in the town ....

d) Margaret lives on the top floor of a .... of flats.

e) Cars have to stop for you if you use a pedestrian ....

f) Which .... of town do you live in?

g) You can buy fresh fish in the market .... every Friday.

h) Take the first turning on the left after the next set of .... lights.

i) The centre of town is now a traffic-free .... and cars are banned.

j) A new shopping .... has been opened on the edge of the town.

3

Replace the words underlined by **one** of the words from the list.

> capital   crowded   international   isolated
> local   neighbouring   rural   urban

a) It's much healthier to live in a <u>country</u> area, far away from the city.
...*rural*...............

b) Sue has just moved to a <u>nearby</u> town.
....

c) We lived in the middle of nowhere in an <u>out of the way</u> cottage.
....

d) Paris is the <u>most important</u> city of France.
....

e) There is not a lot of <u>world</u> news in this newspaper.
....

f) I do my shopping at the <u>neighbourhood</u> shops, not in the town centre.
....

g) At weekends the town centre is always <u>full of people</u>.
....

h) There is far too much pollution nowadays in <u>city</u> areas.
....

4

Choose the most suitable word underlined in each sentence.

a) We arranged to meet in the centre of town in the main <u>place</u>/(<u>square</u>).

b) Their cottage is in the heart of some beautiful <u>country/countryside</u>.

c) The children spent all day playing on the sandy <u>beach/seaside</u>.

d) I dropped my ice-cream on the <u>earth/ground</u>, so I couldn't eat it.

e) This <u>footpath/pavement</u> leads across the fields to the village.

f) There was a wonderful <u>scenery/view</u> from my hotel room.

g) You can't stop here. <u>Car-park/Parking</u> is not allowed in this street.

h) Helen decided to leave the <u>country/land</u> and work abroad.

i) Buses pass the bus <u>station/stop</u> outside my house every ten minutes.

j) Jan's house was at the end of a narrow country <u>lane/street</u>.

5

Fill each space with a word from the list and make a compound word.

> about   bridge   ground   path
> park   roads   side   skirts

a) Our children spend a lot of time having fun at the local play*ground* .

b) When you reach the cross.............. , take the road to Linton.

c) You have to turn left when you reach the next round.............. .

d) We can't leave the car here. We'll have to look for a car.............. .

e) Follow this foot.............. until you reach the main road.

f) There was an old woman selling fruit at the road.............. .

g) Paula lives on the out.............. of the town, where the countryside begins.

h) You can cross the railway line by walking over a foot.............. .

6

Match the words from the list with the explanations.

> bridge   bungalow   caravan   castle   cottage
> semi-detached house   terraced house   tower

a) A strong building made in the past to defend people against enemies.
...*castle*..........................

b) A small house on wheels which is pulled by a car.
....

c) A house which is one of a pair of houses joined together.
....

d) A small house with only one floor.
....

e) This carries a road or railway over a river.
....

f) A house which is part of a row of houses all joined together.
....

g) A small house in the country.
....

h) A tall building standing alone, or as part of a castle or church.
....

15 Food and drink

1
Choose the correct word underlined in each sentence.

a) Would you like a bread/roll with your soup?

b) The first course/plate consisted of cold fish and salad.

c) The kettle/teapot is boiling. Do you want to make some tea?

d) That was a really lovely food/meal. Please let me pay for you.

e) I felt so thirsty that I drank two cans/tins of Corky Cola.

f) Nowadays many people buy frozen/iced food instead of fresh food.

g) Could you give me the receipt/recipe for this cake? It's delicious!

h) This pie is fantastic! It's really tasteful/tasty.

i) Helen is a really good cook/cooker.

j) Can I have a fork/spoon so I can stir my coffee?

2
Complete each sentence with a suitable verb from the list.

| add bake boil chop fry |
| grate mix peel roast squeeze |

a) John decided to ...*roast*...... the beef in the oven for two hours.

b) Put all the ingredients in a bowl and .... them together well.

c) First .... the onions into small pieces.

d) I wanted to .... some cakes this morning, but I didn't have time.

e) Taste the soup, and .... salt and pepper if necessary.

f) .... the potatoes, and then cut them into large pieces.

g) These vegetables taste great if you .... them for a minute in hot oil.

h) .... some cheese, and sprinkle it over the spaghetti.

i) .... a lemon and sprinkle the juice over the salad.

j) .... the rice in salted water for ten minutes.

3
Complete each phrase with a suitable word from the list.

| bacon biscuits butter chips |
| fork salt saucer vinegar |

a) pepper and ..*salt*.......

b) knife and ....

c) egg and ....

d) bread and ....

e) fish and ....

f) oil and ....

g) cup and ....

h) tea and ....

4

Complete each phrase with a suitable word from the list.

> bar   carton   cup   glass
> jar   loaf   pinch   slice

a) a ..*slice*........ of bread or cake
b) a .... of chocolate
c) a .... of jam
d) a .... of tea

e) a .... of bread
f) a .... of water
g) a .... of salt
h) a .... of milk

5

Match each description with the name of a kind of food from the list.

> cheese   chop   grape   lamb
> lettuce   onion   pie   plum

a) Green or purple fruit which grows in bunches.
    ...*grape*..............

b) Small vegetable with a strong smell and taste.
    ....

c) Plant with large green leaves used in salads.
    ....

d) Meat from a young sheep.
    ....

e) Meat, vegetables or fruit baked in pastry.
    ....

f) Small sweet fruit with red or yellow skin, and a stone in the centre.
    ....

g) Solid food made from milk.
    ....

h) Piece of pork or lamb with a bone, cut from the ribs of the animal.
    ....

6

Complete each sentence with a word from the list.

> bill   book   dessert   dish
> menu   takeaway   tip   waiter

a) We weren't sure what to have, so we asked for the ..*menu*........ .
b) Tony finished his meal, paid the ...., and left the restaurant.
c) After two courses we felt full, so we didn't have any ....
d) We had a very tasty Indian .... for the main course.
e) Mary tried to call the ...., but couldn't attract his attention.
f) We got a .... from the Chinese restaurant and ate at home.
g) This is a popular restaurant and you have to .... a table.
h) The service was excellent so we left a large .... on the table.

7

Complete each sentence with *a* or *some*, or leave the space blank.

a) I'd like ...*a*.... chicken please, a large one for roasting.

b) Could I have .... bread please?

c) Do we have time for .... snack before our bus leaves?

d) Would you like to come to .... lunch with me on Thursday?

e) There's .... milk jug in the cupboard near the fridge.

f) George has decided to go on .... diet, starting next week.

g) I'm going to have .... cheese and tomato sandwich.

h) For breakfast I eat .... toast and marmalade, and drink a glass of milk.

i) Do you like .... yoghurt? Personally, I can't stand it!

j) Tim managed to eat .... chicken, but felt too ill to eat anything else.

16 Work and study

1

Choose the correct word underlined in each sentence.

a) Penny took three exams and managed to (pass)/succeed them all.

b) Most people would prefer a job/work which was near home.

c) Tim had to learn/teach fifty children how to swim.

d) I can't come to the cinema tonight. I'm reading/studying for a test.

e) Rita did very well, and was given maximum grades/marks.

f) Every Friday, the building workers are given their salary/wages.

g) It's hard reading aloud/loudly when you don't understand the words.

h) The manager told David to make an application/invitation for the job.

i) Ann works in advertising and earns/wins a very high salary.

j) Would you like to come into my bureau/office? We can talk there.

2

Complete each sentence with one of the words from the list.

business	date	heart	phone
practice	rules	time	work

a) Before her history exam, Laura learnt a list of dates by ..*heart*...... .

b) The manager will be with you in a moment. He is on the ....

c) I haven't spoken Spanish for ages and I'm a bit out of ....

d) Ever since Tim lost his job he has been out of ....

e) Bringing your mobile phone to the class is against the .... !

f) This factory is not very modern. Most of the machines are out of ....

g) Our maths teacher is always late. He's never on ....

h) Mrs Smith isn't here at the moment. She's away on ....

3
Complete each
sentence with a
word formed
from the word
given.

a) Nowadays it is very important to get a good ...*education*.... .
   educate

b) Our company helps .... people to find new jobs.
   employ

c) Paul has good ideas, but writes very ....
   care

d) Helen has become a .... businesswoman.
   succeed

e) I hope to leave school with some useful ....
   qualify

f) Mr Dale was my .... for ten years, and paid me well.
   employ

g) According to the .... , the French lesson starts at ten.
   time

h) Cathy has three jobs, so she has a high ....
   come

i) John's .... of history is amazing for a boy of his age.
   know

j) All the .... in this company are given free meals.
   employ

4
Complete each
sentence with
one of the words
from the list.

| fill get hand keep look make |
| pick stand take write |

a) If you don't know the answer, ...*look*... it up in the back of the book.

b) If you speak so fast I can't .... down what you are saying.

c) Stop talking, and .... on with your work!

d) George finds it hard to .... up with the rest of the maths class.

e) I can see the blackboard, but I can't .... out what the words say.

f) Carol had a holiday in France and managed to .... up the language.

g) Could you .... in this form please, with your personal details.

h) My boss wouldn't let me .... time off to go to a football match.

i) Don't forget to check over your work before you .... it in.

j) Mrs Wood is going to .... in for your teacher while he is away.

5

Choose the most suitable word for each space.

The wrong age for school!

Are the years you (1) ..*d*. at school the best years of your life? Personally, I found most (2) ..... rather uninteresting. We had to sit at our (3) ..... in silence and (4) ...... attention. The teachers used to (5) ..... on the blackboard and (6) ..... us difficult questions. We also had to (7) ..... lots of homework, and (8) ..... it in on time. We had to wear a school (9) ..... , and we had to obey lots of (10) .... I (11) ..... school as soon as I could and started (12) .... I read books at the public (13) ..... , and later I decided to (14) ..... college. I really enjoyed studying because I was older and knew that I wanted some (15) ..... . When I was at school, I was just the wrong age!

1) a) go   b) have   c) pass   d) spend
2) a) lectures   b) lessons   c) them   d) class
3) a) chairs   b) desks   c) posts   d) parts
4) a) pay   b) make   c) have   d) follow
5) a) read   b) sit   c) write   d) talk
6) a) make   b) do   c) get   d) ask
7) a) answer   b) do   c) take   d) finish
8) a) write   b) hand   c) pass   d) complete
9) a) uniform   b) robe   c) dress   d) cloth
10) a) ways   b) rules   c) laws   d) time
11) a) passed   b) qualified   c) examined   d) left
12) a) job   b) labour   c) employee   d) work
13) a) bookshop   b) shelves   c) library   d) university
14) a) go   b) attend   c) study   d) follow
15) a) qualifications   b) examinations   c) papers   d) grades

6

Match each sentence a) to j) with a sentence 1) to 10) with a similar meaning.

a) She was given the sack.
b) She got a rise.
c) She got a promotion.
d) She retired.
e) She applied for the job.
f) She resigned.
g) She was unemployed.
h) She did it for a living.
i) She was ambitious.
j) She was conscientious.

1) She was given a better job.
2) She answered an advertisement.
3) She decided to leave.
4) She did the job carefully.
5) She didn't have a job.
6) She earned her money that way.
7) She was dismissed.
8) She wanted a better job.
9) She was old and stopped work.
10) She was given more money.

233

17 The natural environment

1

Choose the correct word underlined in each sentence.

a) Before we set off, we listened to the climate/(weather) forecast.
b) Paula saw a flash of lightning/thunder and then heard a deep boom.
c) The traffic had to slow down because of the thick fog/vapour.
d) There won't be much rain. It's only a short shower/stream.
e) Spring is my favourite season/term of the year.
f) Last summer was very hot, and there was a real heatwave/temperature.
g) Look at those clouds! There's going to be a blast/storm.
h) On a hot day in summer, I look forward to the chilly/cool evening.
i) We were caught in the rain and damp/soaked to the skin.
j) In the morning there was half a metre of ice/snow blocking the road.

2

Choose the word which best matches the description.

a) Large white water bird with a long neck.   duck/(swan)
b) Four legged animal with horns, good at climbing.   goat/sheep
c) Sea animal with a shell and five pairs of legs.   crab/frog
d) Insect with large beautifully coloured wings.   butterfly/bee
e) Small reptile with four legs and a long tail.   lizard/snake
f) Small flying insect which drinks blood from the skin.   fly/mosquito
g) Small long-eared animal that lives in a hole.   mouse/rabbit
h) Animal with long legs and neck and orangey skin.   camel/giraffe
i) Eight-legged creature which catches insects.   bat/spider
j) Young animal which barks, often a pet.   kitten/puppy

3

Complete each sentence with a word from the list.

| bark berry blossom branch bud |
| leaf root stem thorn trunk |

a) Sue managed to reach the ...*branch*.... of a tree and climb up to the window.
b) I felt ill after I ate a red .... from a bush in the woods.
c) The wall was cracked by the .... of a tree growing underneath it.
d) On the end of each .... there are two or three yellow flowers.
e) In the autumn, every .... on the tree turns yellow and then falls off.
f) Liz hurt herself on a .... while she was picking some roses.
g) The .... of this tree can be removed and used as a kind of paper.
h) In spring all the apple trees are covered in white ....
i) Before the flower opened it was a large green ....
j) An oak tree has a very broad .... , sometimes two metres thick.

4

Choose the best ending from 1) to 10) for each sentence a) to j).

a) In cities the air is hard to breathe because of car
b) The earth's climate is changing because of
c) Not having enough of something is called a
d) Air, sea and land can suffer from
e) Throwing things away unnecessarily is called
f) A mixture of smoke and fog is called
g) Things which we throw away are called
h) To avoid wasting things we can use
i) The paper people drop in the street is called
j) Areas with low rainfall often suffer from

1) waste
2) pollution
3) recycling
4) global warming
5) rubbish
6) litter
7) drought
8) exhaust fumes
9) shortage
10) smog

5

Choose the most suitable word for each space.

The threat to the Environment

Nowadays people are more aware that wildlife all over the world is in (1) ..a.. . Many (2) ..... of animals are threatened, and could easily become (3) ..... if we do not make an effort to (4) ..... them. There are many reasons for this. In some cases, animals are (5) ..... for their fur or for other valuable parts of their bodies. Some birds, (6) ..... as parrots, are caught (7) ..... , and sold as pets. For many animals and birds, the problem is that their habitat – the (8) ..... where they live – is (9) ..... . More (10) ..... is used for farms, for houses or industry, and there are fewer open (11) ..... than there once were. Farmers use powerful chemicals to help them grow better (12) ..... , but these chemicals pollute the environment and (13) ..... wildlife. The most successful animals on earth – human beings – will soon be the only ones (14) ..... , unless we can (15) ..... this problem.

1) a) danger   b) threat   c) problem   d) vanishing
2) a) marks   b) more   c) species   d) forms
3) a) disappeared   b) vanished   c) empty   d) extinct
4) a) harm   b) safe   c) protect   d) serve
5) a) hunted   b) chased   c) game   d) extinct
6) a) like   b) such   c) or   d) where
7) a) lively   b) alive   c) for life   d) for living
8) a) spot   b) point   c) place   d) site
9) a) exhausting   b) departing   c) escaping   d) disappearing
10) a) earth   b) land   c) soil   d) area
11) a) spaces   b) air   c) up   d) parts
12) a) products   b) fields   c) herbs   d) crops
13) a) spoil   b) harm   c) wound   d) wrong
14) a) survived   b) over   c) missing   d) left
15) a) answer   b) calculate   c) solve   d) explain

6

Complete each
sentence with a
pair of verbs
from the list with
opposite
meanings.

> clean up   cut down   destroy   let   plant
> pollute   prevent   protect   recycle   waste

a) People should be encouraged to ...*protect*.... the environment, rather than
   ...*destroy*.... it.
b) We should try to .... disasters happening, not just .... them
   happen.
c) Everyone should try to .... beaches, and not .... them.
d) It would be a good idea to .... more trees, not to .... trees.
e) We can use things again if we .... rather than .... them.

18 Tools and technology

1

Choose the
correct word
underlined in
each sentence.

a) I am bad at maths, so I always carry a pocket (calculator)/computer.
b) The bed was too big to fit into the lorry/van with the doors closed.
c) In Britain most private cars run on gas/petrol or diesel.
d) Ann's friends bought her an electric/electrical mixer for her birthday.
e) When I turned on the light, the bulb/lamp broke.
f) Peter had to push his bike when he got a flat tyre/wheel.
g) This car has got a really powerful engine/machine.
h) When the machine is on, a little red light/torch comes on.
i) The noise of the workmen banging in nails/screws was disturbing.
j) The radiators will have to be fitted by a heater/plumber.

2

Match the words
from the list with
the explanations.

> answer machine   camera   cash dispenser   dishwasher
> photocopier   mobile phone   sewing machine   vacuum cleaner

a) Use this if you can't stay in to take your calls.   ...*answer machine*..
b) Use this to keep in touch when you're out and about.   ....
c) Use this to do your own dressmaking.   ....
d) Use this to get rid of dust and dirt.   ....
e) Use this when you need some money after the banks
   are closed.   ....
f) Use this to take a snapshot for your album.   ....
g) Use this to deal with dirty cutlery and crockery.   ....
h) Use this if you need several pages all the same.   ....

3

Complete each phrase underlined with a verb from the list.

| blow | break | cut | go | ring |
| plug | run | turn | warm | wear |

a) I'm sorry I can't talk now, but I'll ..*ring*.. back in half an hour.

b) The police think that a car bomb was used to .... up the building.

c) These tyres are strong, and won't .... out for ages.

d) Jane's old car used to .... down all the time.

e) You can .... in the computer to the socket by the window.

f) If you don't pay the electricity bill they will .... you off.

g) I think it's time to .... off the television and go to bed.

h) Whenever there is a thunder storm, all the lights .... out.

i) It's not necessary to .... up the engine first, although it's so cold.

j) If you leave the radio on all night the battery will .... out.

4

Replace the group word in each sentence with an example word from the list.

| car | cello | electric toothbrush | oven |
| frying pan | gun | ladder | saw |

a) The police discovered the <u>vehicle</u> more than twenty miles away.

...*car*....................................

b) My sister bought me this <u>gadget</u> as a present.

....

c) The builders left their <u>equipment</u> outside the house.

....

d) The cost of the kitchen includes an <u>electrical appliance</u>.

....

e) This <u>kitchen utensil</u> is lightweight and non-stick.

....

f) I had to use a <u>tool</u> to cut the floorboards in half.

....

g) One of the robbers was carrying a <u>weapon</u>.

....

h) This <u>instrument</u> is rather heavy to carry.

....

5

Complete each sentence with a word from the list.

| battery | button | dial | handle | key |
| lock | plug | socket | switch | wire |

a) Lisa turned the door ...*handle*... , opened the door and entered the room.

b) My watch stopped working because the .... had run out.

c) The television won't work in this room, as there isn't an electric ....

d) Bill pressed the light .... , but none of the lights was working.

e) To wind up this old clock you need a special kind of ....

f) Mary put the key in the .... , but it wouldn't turn.

g) I've bought an electric kettle, but the lead hasn't got a .... on it.

h) Choose the programme on the washing machine by turning the ....

i) Don't press this red .... unless there is an emergency.

j) The electric bell didn't work because the .... had been cut.

6

Match each sentence with the necessary object from the list.

| binoculars | compass | hairdrier | iron | lawnmower |
| pump | razor | scissors | thermometer | tin-opener |

a) There is no air in either of these tyres.   ...*pump*..............

b) Do you fancy some tinned beans for lunch?   ....

c) The grass in the back garden is awfully long.   ....

d) Sam has been letting his beard grow but now he's going to shave.   ....

e) When it's long like this you need more than a towel.   ....

f) I've got to cut the ends off the legs of my new jeans.   ....

g) Do you think I've got a temperature?   ....

h) It's difficult to see wild animals when they are so far away.   ....

i) Jean was completely lost, and needed to know where north was.   ....

j) You can't go out with all those creases in your shirt.   ....

19 Everyday objects

1

Choose the correct word underlined in each sentence.

a) I have to do some sewing. Do you have a pin/needle?

b) You need special glue/sticker when you make model aeroplanes.

c) I always carry a carving knife/penknife in my pocket.

d) Paul keeps his papers together with a rubber band/rubber ring.

e) Sheets of paper can be fastened together with a paper clip/zipper.

f) I wrapped up the parcel using brown paper and rope/string.

g) Helen took the cutters/scissors and started trimming Mary's hair.

h) Oh bother! One of my shirt bottoms/buttons has fallen off.

i) As David was tying his shoelace/shoestring, it broke.

j) Little Susie usually ties up her hair with a red ribbon/strip.

2

Match each sentence with the necessary object from the list.

diary   dictionary   envelope   eraser   file
notepad   notice   ruler   sharpener   stamp

a) It's important to let everyone know what time the meeting starts.

...*notice*...............................

b) Hang on a minute, I'll just write down those details.

....

c) Oh dear, I've written my name in the wrong place.

....

d) Write down the date of the next match so you don't forget.

....

e) I've written my letter but I've got nothing to put it in.

....

f) I keep losing the sheets I wrote my homework on.

....

g) How long is this piece of paper exactly?

....

h) What a nuisance! My pencil has broken.

....

i) My letter's ready for the post. How much will it cost?

....

j) I'm not really sure what this word means.

....

3
The words underlined are in the wrong sentences. Find the best sentence for each word.

a) You can hang your coat on the <u>fireplace</u> behind the door.
..*hook*.............................

b) It's time for lunch. Can you put the <u>doormat</u> on the table?
....

c) I've bought a beautiful <u>hook</u> with long leaves for your room.
....

d) Don't forget to put all the rubbish from the kitchen into the <u>broom</u>.
....

e) Cathy pulled back the <u>plant</u> and peeped out at the street.
....

f) You can sweep the floor with the <u>curtain</u> in that cupboard.
....

g) My mother insists that we all wipe our feet on the <u>tablecloth</u>.
....

h) Some logs were blazing and crackling in the <u>dustbin</u>.
....

4
Match the words from the list with the explanations.

| street sign   hedge   kerb   lamp-post   pavement |
| pedestrian crossing   post-box   gate   subway   verge |

a) This is a safe place to go from one side of the street to the other.
..*pedestrian crossing*............

b) This has a light at the top in the street.
....

c) This is where people walk in the street.
....

d) This is a kind of wall made of a living plant.
....

e) This closes the opening in an outside wall.
....

f) This is a line of stones between the footpath and the road.
....

g) This helps you know where you want to go.
....

h) This is where you put your letters in the street.
....

i) This is a way of crossing under the road.
....

j) This is a strip of grass at the side of the road.
....

5

Complete each sentence with a word from the list.

alarm comb gown hanger mirror pillow slippers table toothpaste towel

a) My hair is in an awful mess. Have you got a ...*comb*......... ?

b) When I get up I put on my dressing .... and go downstairs.

c) It's sometimes a shock to see your own face in the ....

d) Helen always sits at her dressing .... and brushes her hair.

e) When I'm in the house I take off my shoes and put on ....

f) I want to clean my teeth but I can't find any ....

g) Every morning at 6.30 the .... clock goes off and I wake up.

h) You can wash your hands here, and there's a .... behind the door.

i) I can't get to sleep unless I have a really comfortable ....

j) You can put your coat in the wardrobe on a coat ....

6

Complete the text with the words from the list.

bowl jug kettle mug saucer tap teapot teaspoon tray washing-up

Every morning Mrs Dawson comes downstairs into the kitchen. First she does the (a) ...*washing-up*... from the previous day. She turns on the cold (b) ...., and fills the (c) .... When the water boils, she makes tea in the (d) .... , and also makes some toast. She pours the tea into a (e) .... She doesn't use a cup and (f) .... She puts some breakfast cereal into a (g) .... , and takes a (h) .... of milk from the fridge. She puts some milk in her tea, and some on the cereal. She puts some sugar in her tea with a (i) .... and stirs it. Then she puts everything on a (j) .... and carries it upstairs. After breakfast in bed she goes back to sleep.

20 People

1
Choose the
correct word
underlined in
each sentence.

a) Mrs Grant is a good employee/(employer) and pays her staff well.

b) Excuse me, but are you the ower/owner of this bike?

c) Tom works in a local garage as a car engineer/mechanic.

d) I want to borrow some money, so I'm seeing the bank boss/manager.

e) Little Jimmy has got a new professor/teacher at his primary school.

f) Helen joined the army as an officer/official, and is now a captain.

g) The house really needed decorating so I called a painter/wallpaper.

h) Please ask the cash/cashier for a receipt.

i) Have you thought about getting a job as a typewriter/typist?

j) I waited for my letters, but the poster/postman was late as usual.

2
Match a person
from the list with
each problem.

> carpenter   dentist   electrician   gardener   guide
> hairdresser   optician   photographer   plumber   vet

a) The lawn is really long and there are weeds everywhere.
   ...*gardener*.........................

b) I want to visit as much of the old city as possible in an afternoon.
   ....

c) The taps don't work, and there is water all over the floor.
   ....

d) I want to have a special portrait made for my eighteenth birthday.
   ....

e) One of my fillings has come out, and I've got terrible toothache.
   ....

f) I want to use the wood from these shelves to make a bookcase.
   ....

g) When I turn on the television, all the lights go off.
   ....

h) I can't see to read very well and I think I need glasses.
   ....

i) Benny hurt one of his paws when I was taking him for a walk.
   ....

j) It's far too long at the back and too curly at the front.
   ....

3

Complete each sentence with a word from the list.

assistant   colleague   flatmate   employee   guest
host   member   partner   supporter   team-mate

a) Peter has just become a/an ...*member*... of the fishing club.

b) I started this business with my .... , Dora, about ten years ago.

c) There is a spare room, so I have decided to let it and get a/an ....

d) We provide every .... in the hotel with whatever he or she needs.

e) At the end of the party, Bill thanked his .... and then left.

f) Ann is a/an .... of mine. We work together at Dawson and Co.

g) Any .... who wishes to work at weekends should see the manager.

h) I've been a/an .... of Hull City FC for as long as I can remember.

i) Mary was my .... last year in the basketball tournament.

j) This job is a lot for one person, so we think you need a/an ....

4

Complete each sentence with a group word from the list.

audience   cast   crew   crowd   group
queue   society   staff   team   trio

a) The ...*crew*........ of the ship cheered as the new captain came on board.

b) Paula has just joined the dramatic .... at school.

c) The head teacher thanked the .... for working so hard.

d) There was a long .... of people waiting in the post office.

e) A huge .... had assembled outside the president's palace.

f) The members of the .... play the violin, the piano and the cello.

g) A small .... of us went on a trip to Rome last summer.

h) When the music stopped, the .... applauded for ten minutes.

i) Last year Helen was the captain of the basketball ....

j) When the play ended all the .... came on stage and took a bow.

5

Complete each sentence with a word formed from the word given.

a) This city has over half a million ...*inhabitants*... .
   inhabit

b) Margaret has decided to have a career as a ....
   politics

c) Every .... in this country has the right to vote.
   city

d) Eric studied hard to become a rock ....
   guitar

e) After the crash, Carla was the only ....
   survive

f)   David's mother is a famous ....
     science

g)   At nineteen, Tony became a professional ....
     crime

h)   I've always wanted to be a jazz ....
     music

i)   It will take Kate years to become a ....
     law

j)   Jack was my .... in the tennis match.
     oppose

6
Match each word
in the list with an
explanation.

> celebrity   coward   expert   favourite   fool
> genius   liar   miser   optimist   pessimist

a)   Someone who does not have any courage.
     ...*coward*..............................

b)   Someone who hates spending money and becomes rich by keeping it.
     ....

c)   Someone who says that a bottle is half full.
     ....

d)   Someone who is very well known in the media.
     ....

e)   Someone who is loved more than any other.
     ....

f)   Someone who has special knowledge or training.
     ....

g)   Someone who does something silly or mistaken.
     ....

h)   Someone who has very great ability or special talent.
     ....

i)   Someone who says that a bottle is half empty.
     ....

j)   Someone who does not tell the truth.
     ....

Formation rules

1
Tenses

Present simple

I/you/we/they like.   She/he/it likes.
Do you like?   Does she like?
You don't like.   He doesn't like.

Present continuous

I am going.   You/we/they are going.
She/he/it is going.
Are you going?   Am I going?
I am not going.   Is she going?
She isn't going.   You aren't going.

Present perfect

I/you/we/they have left.   She/he/it has left.
Have they left?   Has she left?
They haven't left.   He hasn't left.

Present perfect continuous

I/you/we/they have been waiting.   She/he/it has been waiting.
Have you been waiting?   Has she been waiting?
We haven't been waiting.   He hasn't been waiting.

Past simple

1 I/you/she/he/it/we/they started. (regular)
   Did you start?
   You didn't start.
2 I/you/she/he/it/we/they went. (irregular)
   Did you go?
   You didn't go.

Past continuous

I/he/she/it was going.   You/we/they were going.
Was he going?   Were you going?
She wasn't going.   You weren't going.

Past perfect

I/you/she/he/it/we/they had left.
Had he left?
They hadn't left.

Future perfect

I/you/she/he/it/we/they will have finished.
Will they have finished?
They won't have finished.

2
Reported Speech

'I always drink milk.'	He said (that) he always drank milk.
'I'm leaving.'	She said she was leaving.
'I'll be back soon.'	He said he would be back soon.
'I've forgotten it.'	She said she had forgotten it.
'I took it.'	He said he had taken it.
'I was reading.'	She said she had been reading.
'I had left by then.'	He said he had left by then.
'I must go.'	She said she had to go/must go.
'I can help.'	He said he could help.
'I would like to help.'	She said she would like to help.

3
Passive Tenses

Active	Passive
He helps.	He is helped.
He is helping.	He is being helped.
He has helped.	He has been helped.
He helped.	He was helped.
He was helping.	He was being helped.
He will help.	He will be helped.
He will have helped.	He will have been helped.

4
Infinitives

Present:	to like
Present passive:	to be liked
Past:	to have liked
Past passive:	to have been liked

5
Participles (-*ing* forms)

Present:	liking
Present passive:	being liked
Past:	having liked
Past passive:	having been liked

Irregular verbs

Infinitive	Past simple	Past participle
be	was/were	been
beat	beat	beaten
become	became	become
begin	began	begun
bend	bent	bent
bite	bit	bitten
blow	blew	blown
break	broke	broken
bring	brought	brought
build	built	built
burn	burnt/burned	burnt/burned

burst	burst	burst
buy	bought	bought
catch	caught	caught
choose	chose	chosen
come	came	come
cost	cost	cost
cut	cut	cut
deal	dealt	dealt
dig	dug	dug
do	did	done
draw	drew	drawn
dream	dreamt/dreamed	dreamt/dreamed
drink	drank	drunk
drive	drove	driven
eat	ate	eaten
fall	fell	fallen
feed	fed	fed
feel	felt	felt
fight	fought	fought
find	found	found
fly	flew	flown
forbid	forbade	forbidden
forgive	forgave	forgiven
freeze	froze	frozen
get	got	got
give	gave	given
go	went	gone
grow	grew	grown
hang	hung	hung
have	had	had
hear	heard	heard
hide	hid	hidden
hit	hit	hit
hold	held	held
hurt	hurt	hurt
keep	kept	kept
know	knew	known
lay	laid	laid
lead	led	led
learn	learnt/learned	learnt/learned
leave	left	left
lend	lent	lent
let	let	let
lie	lay	lain

light	lit	lit
lose	lost	lost
make	made	made
mean	meant	meant
meet	met	met
pay	paid	paid
put	put	put
read	read	read
ride	rode	ridden
ring	rang	rung
rise	rose	risen
run	ran	run
say	said	said
see	saw	seen
sell	sold	sold
send	sent	sent
set	set	set
shake	shook	shaken
shine	shone	shone
shoot	shot	shot
show	showed	shown
shut	shut	shut
sing	sang	sung
sink	sank	sunk
sit	sat	sat
sleep	slept	slept
speak	spoke	spoken
spell	spelled/spelt	spelled/spelt
spend	spent	spent
stand	stood	stood
steal	stole	stolen
stick	stuck	stuck
swim	swam	swum
take	took	taken
teach	taught	taught
tear	tore	torn
tell	told	told
think	thought	thought
throw	threw	thrown
understand	understood	understood
wake	woke	woken
wear	wore	worn
win	won	won
write	wrote	written

Grammar index

Grammar answers

In some cases more than one answer is acceptable.

Unit 1

1. a) *Present perfect continuous/ progressive. Continuing time up until the present.*
   b) Present continuous with future reference. A fixed arrangement in the future.
   c) Past simple used here as an unreal or imaginary tense in a conditional sentence. There is no reference to past time.
   d) Present simple. A habitual action.
   e) Past perfect. The earlier of two past events.

2. a) *2*
   b) All are possible. 2 is least polite, 1 polite, 3 possibly over-polite!
   c) 2 is most appropriate. 3 is over-formal and more appropriate in formal writing.
   d) 3

3. a) *1 is correct. 2 is not possible as this kind of state verb is not usually used in a continuous form i.e. own is already a continuous activity.*
   b) Both are correct. *By car* describes a general means of transport. When an owner is named, *in* is used.
   c) Both are correct. 2 is an indirect question and so the *where* question is not inverted as a normal question is.
   d) 1 is correct. 2 is not possible as this kind of state verb is not used in a continuous form i.e. *like* is already a continuous activity.

Unit 2

1. a) *do you go*   f) is happening
   b) are you waiting   g) do you know
   c) doesn't know   h) I'm having
   d) I'm having   i) doesn't work
   e) do you leave   j) are you doing

2. a) *does Sue live*
   b) you know Jim
   c) are you doing at the moment
   d) you sitting here
   e) we change trains here
   f) are you wearing two pullovers
   g) David staying with Tom
   h) does Kate come home

3. a) *Naomi and Bill aren't watching television.*
   b) Peter doesn't like chocolate cake.
   c) Carol doesn't drive a little red sports car.
   d) I'm not using this pencil at the moment.
   e) The children aren't having lunch in the kitchen.
   f) The sun doesn't set in the east.
   g) I don't get up early on Saturday.
   h) Kate isn't writing a novel.
   i) Sue doesn't live in London.
   j) We aren't waiting for you.

4. a) *Do you like*   f) It's snowing
   b) does the sun rise   g) are you talking
   c) are you reading   h) goes
   d) I'm having   i) Do you wear
   e) don't watch videos j) She is building

5. a) *writing*   i) using
   b) digging   j) waiting
   c) taking   k) washing
   d) deciding   l) riding
   e) swimming   m) flying
   f) having   n) studying
   g) lying   o) going
   h) reading

Unit 3

1. a) 2 b) 1 c) 1 d) 2 e) 1 f) 2
   g) 2 h) 1

2. a) *I don't believe*   f) I'm driving
   b) has   g) are we eating
   c) I'm leaving   h) tastes
   d) are you doing   i) are you going
   e) You are being   j) I don't understand

3. a) *hate*
   b) are you going with
   c) do you wear
   d) think
   e) doesn't usually sit
   f) are you looking at
   g) does this bus stop
   h) am not taking/is giving

4. 1) *a* 2) g 3) b 4) e 5) f 6) h
   7) d 8) c

5. a) *do you usually do*
   b) only eats
   c) Do you know
   d) are you staring
   e) do you speak
   f) is staying
   g) You are putting
   h) Are they speaking

Unit 4

1. a) *was washing/rang*
   b) did you feel
   c) reached/received
   d) went swimming
   e) bit/screamed
   f) sang/ate
   g) fell/happened
   h) was washing-up/broke
   i) didn't see/missed
   j) were you doing/phoned

2. a) *I didn't enjoy the concert.*
   b) Did Sue like the party?
   c) Did you eat all the bread?
   d) Tom spent a lot.
   e) I didn't feel well yesterday.
   f) Ann bought a car.
   g) Did they win the prize?
   h) Paul speaks Polish.
   i) I didn't pay all the bills.
   j) Did Ruth make a mistake?

3. a) *while*   e) While   h) in
   b) Last week   f) ago   i) When
   c) when   g) when   j) ago
   d) at

4. 1) *c* 2) a 3) f 4) e 5) b 6) g
   7) h 8) d

5. a) *woke up/told*
   b) did you leave/went
   c) was waiting/arrived
   d) finished/took
   e) wanted/chose
   f) was studying/phoned
   g) found/was looking for
   h) was watching/arrived
   i) went out/was lying
   j) went/did you eat

6. a) *sitting*   i) shopping
   b) felt   j) heard
   c) tried   k) hiding
   d) crying   l) waited
   e) wasn't   m) played
   f) enjoyed   n) went
   g) thought   o) fitted
   h) living

Unit 5

1. a) *When we had eaten lunch, we sat in the garden.*
   b) While I was looking for my keys, I remembered I had left them at home.
   c) Anna used to play badminton when she was at school.
   d) When I got into bed, I fell asleep immediately.
   e) When I finally found the house, I knocked at the door.
   f) After Jill gave/had given Nick his books, she went home.
   g) Maria used to live in Sweden when she was a child.

h) I used to get up early when I went sailing.
i) The Vikings sailed to North America a thousand years ago.
j) Sue was sure she had seen the tall man before.

2 a) *was waiting/noticed/had not been*
  b) went/found/had stolen
  c) met/knew/had met
  d) got off/was walking/realized/had left

3 a) *had broken*   f) needed
  b) wanted   g) did not know
  c) had stolen   h) had flown
  d) thought   i) had been
  e) had done   j) took place

4 a) *used to have*
  b) would/used to read
  c) would/used to meet
  d) didn't use to like
  e) used to write
  f) used to live
  g) used to be
  h) would/used to cheer

5 a) *Michael had taken*
  b) didn't use
  c) sure he had not forgotten
  d) used to get up
  e) I had seen/read
  f) used to play tennis
  g) took a taxi because we had missed
  h) would spend

Unit 6

1 a) *Have you cut*
  b) hasn't sunk
  c) Have your sisters written
  d) have had
  e) has never seen
  f) has stolen
  g) have not slept
  h) have just broken
  i) hasn't won
  j) Have you ever eaten

2 a) *have been married*
  b) have been
  c) have written
  d) have never eaten
  e) have loved
  f) have broken

3 a) since   e) yet   h) So far
  b) always   f) for   i) often
  c) ever   g) never   j) already
  d) just

4 a) *have worked here for* (Note: present perfect continuous is also possible, *have been working here for.* See Unit 7.)
  b) haven't been on a plane
  c) My pen has
  d) have left
  e) have just seen
  f) haven't finished (writing)

g) you been to South America
h) have left
i) have not spoken
j) Anna/she woken

Unit 7

1 a) *I have lived here*
  b) has just stolen
  c) left
  d) I lost
  e) I've decided
  f) It's started
  g) have visited
  h) I've been standing
  i) has been
  j) went

2 a) *lost/have just lost*
  b) work/have decided
  c) have been/have come
  d) Have you seen/left
  e) had/caught
  f) have never eaten/ate
  g) hope/have cooked
  h) have taken up
  i) reached/weren't
  j) has had/has gone

3 1) *Have you seen/am looking forward*
  2) have been studying/have not finished
  3) have been phoning/has gone
  4) Have you heard/has robbed
  5) have broken/has written

4 a) *so*   f) teaching
  b) since   g) yet
  c) been   h) has
  d) met   i) practising
  e) recently   j) taught

5 a) *have been living here*
  b) has gone
  c) have been learning
  d) haven't finished
  e) just left
  f) have written/have finished
  g) haven't been
  h) haven't eaten
  i) forgotten
  j) has changed

6 a) *My penfriend has been writing to me for years but has never sent me a photo.*
  b) We started this course three weeks ago.
  c) 'What have you been doing all day?' 'I've been writing letters.'
  d) When did you arrive in this city?
  e) Have you ever been to India?
  f) Paula has been staying in a hotel by the sea.
  g) I've been feeling ill for three weeks.
  h) I have lived in this city since I was born.
  i) I have been waiting here a long time. Where have you been?
  j) Tony has left his books on the bus.

Unit 8

1 a) 2 b) 2 c) 1 d) 1 e) 1 f) 1

2 a) *is joining/is going to join*
  b) won't be
  c) will snow/it's going to snow
  d) am going out
  e) are going to knock
  f) will probably ride
  g) is going to give/is giving
  h) am going
  i) are going to hit
  j) will probably win

3 a) *am having a party*
  b) going to rain
  c) our team will
  d) won't be
  e) is going to finish
  f) will meet you
  g) are we having/are we meeting
  h) of tourists will come to
  i) am not going to sell
  j) you doing

4 a) *I am going swimming next Saturday. Would you like to come?*
  b) ✔
  c) The boat is turning over! I think it's going to sink!
  d) ✔
  e) I've read the weather forecast, and it's definitely going to be sunny tomorrow.
  f) ✔
  g) ✔
  h) Sorry I won't see you tomorrow. I have to go to London.
  i) ✔
  j) Bye for now. I'll see you later this evening.

5 a) *I'm going to study engineering in France.*
  b) I'm going to have a party next Friday.
  c) The score will be 3–0.
  d) We're going to the doctor's, so we can't come.
  e) Paula will probably get the job.
  f) Martin's wife is going to have another baby.
  g) Sarah isn't going to get married yet.
  h) It will possibly snow tomorrow.

Unit 9

1 a) *will be lying*
  b) rings
  c) will be moving
  d) does your train leave
  e) leave
  f) will you be working
  g) I'll be
  h) won't stop
  i) it'll bite

2 a) 6 b) 2/4 c) 1 d) 8 e) 3
  f) 5 g) 2/4 h) 7

3
a) *Shall we play tennis?*
b) I'm going to study Arabic in Cairo.
c) I'll be home by midnight.
d) I'll meet you later.
e) Will you go to the shops for me?
f) We won't make too much noise.
g) Shall I help you with those bags?
h) We'll come back later if you like.
i) I'll have a lemonade.
j) Will you take the dog for a walk?

4
a) ✓
b) When you grow older, you'll change your mind about this.
c) ✓
d) I won't leave until you give me the money.
e) As soon as the taxi arrives, I'll let you know.
f) Will you be using the video next lesson?
g) By the time we get to Helen's house, she'll have left.
h) 'Do you want me to carry this?' 'No that's all right, I'll do it.'
i) ✓
j) By the time we arrive, the play will have started.

5
a) *will have finished*
b) meet next/again, I'll phone
c) I check the spelling
d) let me share her
e) we have
f) leave/go until I
g) the lesson has finished
h) you be doing

Problems, Errors, Consolidation 1

1
a) *I used to ride*
b) Shall I
c) Have you seen her
d) have you been working
e) I haven't finished
f) I was washing
g) are you staring
h) I'm having
i) stops
j) did you last go

2
a) *do you do*
b) ran
c) was sitting
d) don't understand
e) realized
f) am studying
g) was reading
h) know
i) am staying
j) did you do

3
a) *before*
b) since
c) all week
d) yet
e) As soon as
f) never
g) lately
h) at
i) for
j) By the time

4
1) *c* 2) a 3) d 4) d 5) b 6) a
7) c 8) c 9) d 10) b 11) b
12) d 13) a 14) c 15) a

5
a) *arrived, Steve had*
b) I help
c) do you usually
d) has been playing tennis for
e) I'll
f) was eating/having my meal
g) gone
h) is staying
i) haven't seen David
j) you doing

6
1) *been* 7) ✓ 13) ✓
2) ✓ 8) are 14) been
3) ✓ 9) been 15) ✓
4) have 10) will 16) have
5) had 11) shall 17) be
6) ✓ 12) have

7
a) *it had stopped*
b) I haven't played it before.
c) When did Peter write to you last?
d) Do you ever go to the cinema?
e) I went to the beach every day.
f) She is playing basketball.
g) I've been waiting here for ages!
h) How long have you lived in this flat?

8
a) *Have you finished yet?*
b) I'll see you tomorrow!
c) Did you have a nice time?
d) Do you know what I mean?
e) Are you coming out for a drink later?
f) Have you been waiting long?
g) Are you enjoying yourself?
h) Have you heard the latest?

Unit 10

1
a) *Sally said that she had lost her keys.*
b) Chris said that he must leave early.
c) Maria and Tony said they would see us tomorrow.
d) Tom said, 'I'm coming to your party.'
e) Sue said that she had written a letter to Lisa.
f) Steve told us/said that he was arriving at 8.00.
g) 'I have bought a new bike,' Pam told us.
h) 'What's the matter?' Ellen said/asked.
i) Jim says that he needs some help.
j) Joe said that he didn't feel well yesterday.

2
a) *I've finished*
b) I'll be back at 6.00.
c) I'm going to go shopping
d) I want to make a phone call
e) I've forgotten my homework
f) I have to be back by 3.30
g) I'll let you know
h) I'm going to be late

3
a) *3* b) 5 c) 2 d) 1 e) 4

4
a) *told*
b) spoke/said
c) said/told
d) told/saying
e) told/tell
f) told/spoke
g) say/told
h) told/said

5
a) *wouldn't be there because she was having a party*
b) had lost the map and (he) didn't know the way
c) she had finished the book she was going to watch television
d) was doing some homework but he wouldn't be long
e) liked swimming but (she) didn't go very often
f) had got up late and (had) missed the bus
g) was going to visit friends in Fiji but (she) wasn't sure when
h) wanted to buy it but (he) hadn't brought any money

Unit 11

1
a) *whether/was*
b) when/would
c) if,whether/had
d) if,whether/took
e) where
f) if,whether/had

2
a) *Are you having lunch or going out*
b) What did you do yesterday
c) Do you often go sailing
d) How many German books have you read
e) Are you going to change schools
f) Who do you sit next to in class
g) Will you be here tomorrow
h) Where do you live

3
a) *if/whether I was staying there all summer*
b) what 'procrastinate' meant
c) if/whether I had done my homework
d) when her birthday was
e) if/whether I had remembered to lock the door
f) why I had turned off the television
g) if/whether I spoke Italian
h) how much he had paid for his bike

4
a) *what the time is*
b) what this means
c) how much this costs
d) what time the museum opens
e) if/whether I am in the right seat
f) where Asham Street is
g) if/whether this is Trafalgar Square
h) when this bus leaves

5
a) *Mike promised Sue that he would definitely be at her house before 8.00.*
b) Chris invited Jean to the cinema.
c) Patsy advised Dave not to eat too much.
d) George suggested going for a walk.
e) Carol apologized for breaking the window.
f) Bill offered to do the washing-up.
g) Tina's mother congratulated her on passing her driving test.
h) Pat refused to go to the dentist's.

Unit 12

1. a) *we're/will be*
   b) lived/we'd see
   c) take/we'll arrive
   d) don't hurry/we'll be
   e) were/would be able to
   f) don't wear/you'll feel
   g) studied/would get
   h) had/I'd ride
   i) lend/I'll let
   j) had/I'd give

2. a) *fall in/will get*
   b) were/would go
   c) knew/would tell
   d) run/will catch
   e) rains/will go
   f) had/would join
   g) lived/would eat
   h) study/will pass

3. a) *would*   f) Would
   b) unless   g) would
   c) would   h) If
   d) Unless   i) would
   e) Would   j) unless

4. a) *8* e) 1 h) 2 b) 6 f) 3 i) 5
   c) 9 g) 4 j) 7 d) 10

5. a) *had/would be able*
   b) take/will feel
   c) ate/would live
   d) became/would buy
   e) leave/will give
   f) follow/will come
   g) used/wouldn't be
   h) touch/won't bite
   i) leave/will give
   j) owned/would not visit

Unit 13

1. a) *What would you do if you had wings?*
   b) If I were you, I'd leave now.
   c) How would you feel if you lived on Mars?
   d) If I were you, I'd buy a bike.
   e) What would you do if you were rich?
   f) What would you say if Jim came with us?
   g) If I were you, I'd take the bus.
   h) What would you do if you owned a robot?

2. a) *had phoned/would have given*
   b) took/might feel
   c) had driven/wouldn't have crashed
   d) had come/would have enjoyed
   e) I'd known/would have sent
   f) helped/might be
   g) had scored/could have won
   h) wore/wouldn't get

3. a) *had left early/wouldn't have missed*
   b) had bought more milk/would have had
   c) had taken a map/wouldn't have got lost

   d) had gone to bed/would have woken up
   e) had made a shopping list/ wouldn't have forgotten to buy
   f) had realized you were tired/I wouldn't have asked you to go
   g) had sailed across the Atlantic/ would have reached
   h) had turned left at the station/ wouldn't have lost

Unit 14

1. a) *hadn't sunbathed*   e) could see
   b) could stay   f) didn't sit
   c) could swim   g) had
   d) I had   h) enjoy

2. a) *2* d) 2 g) 2 b) 2 e) 1 h) 1
   c) 1 f) 2

3. a) *had brought*   e) had taken
   b) had bought   f) hadn't bought
   c) went   g) had finished
   d) knew   h) spoke/could speak

4. (Suggested answers)
   a) *I had a sandwich*
   b) you have a good
   c) had been here/had come here/had visited it
   d) lived
   e) danced/could dance

Unit 15

1. a) *by someone*   e) –
   b) –   f) by the postman
   c) by a doctor   g) by the police
   d) –   h) by someone

2. a) *was questioned*
   b) is watched
   c) will be finished
   d) has been elected
   e) is being rebuilt
   f) has been closed
   g) is written
   h) was stolen
   i) will be met
   j) was won

3. a) *Many pet dogs are lost every year.*
   b) The ill man was taken to hospital.
   c) A new bridge is being built across the river.
   d) All the food at the party was eaten.
   e) Nothing will be decided before next Saturday.
   f) The match is being played on Friday evening.
   g) The robber unlocked the door with a false key.
   h) This book was written by Sam's father.

4. a) *has been discovered by archaeologists in the Valley of the Kings*
   b) will be opened by the President on Saturday
   c) was painted by one of the most famous painters in the world
   d) of the competition will be announced tomorrow
   e) is being redecorated during the summer holidays
   f) have been arrested (by the police) in New York
   g) are sold by our company every week
   h) is being built in the city centre
   i) was discovered by Alexander Fleming in 1928
   j) is used by two million people every day

5. a) *The casino has been closed.*
   b) The flat was broken into last week.
   c) English is spoken all over the world.
   d) The new swimming-pool has been opened.
   e) This purse was left in the classroom yesterday.
   f) Traffic has been banned from the city centre.
   g) A new government has been elected.
   h) The match has been postponed.

Unit 16

1. a) *cut*   e) broken
   b) taken   f) offered
   c) sent   g) were you born
   d) serviced   h) repaired

2. a) *had his*
   b) was lent to me by
   c) had one of my teeth taken
   d) was born
   e) sold a rock concert ticket
   f) his house broken into
   g) were you
   h) was given this ring by my

3. a) *I am having my car serviced tomorrow.*
   b) I had my bike stolen yesterday.
   c) We had our house painted last year.
   d) I am having my tooth taken out tomorrow!
   e) I have just had my hair cut.
   f) We are having our new carpet fitted tomorrow.
   g) Ann has just had her portrait painted.

Unit 17

1. a) *might*   f) may not
   b) can't be   g) can't be
   c) must be   h) must be
   d) could be   i) could be
   e) might   j) can't come

2 a) *can swim really*
b) might
c) can't be
d) must work
e) can't come
f) might see you tomorrow
g) your teacher can't come
h) must be very hot
i) can I open
j) must be

3 a) *same*   f) different
b) different   g) same
c) same   h) same
d) different   i) different
e) same   j) different

4 a) *You ought to see a dentist.*
b) We don't have to go to school tomorrow.
c) That can't be John, because he's in Paris.
d) Ann could/might/may be at home.
e) You had better wear a warm coat today.
f) I may be late.
g) I don't think that you should go/ought to go skiing.
h) You can't leave your bike here.
i) I might see you on Thursday evening.
j) You have to write this test in pencil.

5 a) *have*   f) had
b) should   g) can't
c) must   h) have
d) may/might i) able
e) must   j) ought

6 a) *I think you'd better/you should take more exercise.*
b) The plane should land soon.
c) You can't use a dictionary.
d) That can't be Sue. She's abroad.
e) I may/might come to your party.
f) You mustn't drop litter in the street.
g) You don't have to wait.
h) I think you should stay/If I were you I'd stay in bed today.

Unit 18

1 a) *You must have dropped your wallet at the bus-stop.*
b) Joanna might have missed the last bus.
c) Peter was able to skate when he was twelve.
d) Emma should have told you the answer.
e) We didn't have to pay to get in.
f) I didn't need to buy any food yesterday.
g) Diana can't have taken your books.
h) David might not have noticed you.
i) Terry needn't have arrived early.
j) We shouldn't have been rude to the policeman!

2 a) *have studied so late*
b) you able to stop him
c) have to work hard
d) have lost his way
e) have hurt yourself
f) have told me
g) have enjoyed it
h) have helped her
i) not to have left
j) have done it

3 a) *should have taken an umbrella*
b) must have left it on the bus
c) couldn't get through
d) should have bought her a present
e) can't stand orange
f) might have forgotten the address
g) ought to have studied harder
h) could have had a good time

Problems, Errors, Consolidation 2

1 a) *asked*
b) had
c) had
d) said she didn't want me to
e) can't have stolen
f) had
g) you'd better
h) would be
i) have been
j) we'd remembered

2 1) ✓   2) *if*   3) they   4) to   5) paint
6) to   7) ✓   8) must   9) have
10) if   11) can   12) have   13) ✓
14) was   15) if   16) been   17) us
18) ✓

3 1) *c*   6) d   11) d   2) a   7) b   12) a
3) b   8) c   13) c   4) a   9) a   14) b
5) d   10) c   15) d

4 a) *knew the answer, I would help you*
b) you run fast, you'll feel tired
c) was arrested by an off-duty policewoman
d) had left early, we wouldn't have missed the train
e) I hadn't eaten all the ice-cream
f) tell me where the bus station is
g) is being built by the local council
h) were you, I'd go to the doctor's
i) was broken with a hammer
j) Sue to buy some milk

5 a) *I didn't have to go to work yesterday.*
b) I wish I were rich!
c) I'm having my hair cut tomorrow.
d) David might have missed the bus.
e) Radio was invented by Marconi.
f) You shouldn't have forgotten the keys!
g) We'd better take an umbrella.
h) Maria must have worked very hard.

i) Richard was given a camera by Helen.
j) We needn't have bought so much food.

6 a) *don't have to*
b) mustn't
c) might have
d) have to
e) must
f) could
g) had to
h) must have
i) should
j) didn't have to

7 a) *We are having our house*
b) Peter had his car
c) George told Kate that he had
d) I wouldn't take the job if I
e) Could you tell me when the play
f) Let's go for a picnic unless
g) If I had felt tired I wouldn't have
h) can't have met
i) Mary asked Ann if she had to leave
j) I asked Peter

8 a) *'War and Peace' was written by Leo Tolstoy.*
b) That can't be David! He's on holiday in Bermuda.
c) David asked a passer-by where the railway station was.
d) If I had lived in Ancient Greece, I might have been a slave!
e) In the army, you have to wear a uniform.
f) Kate told me that she had to/must finish her homework.
g) I think someone must have opened your bag. That's the only explanation.
h) I wish I were taller!
i) I have my car repaired by a qualified mechanic.
j) If I saw a snake, I'd scream and run away!

Unit 19

1 a) *so that*
b) to
c) in order to
d) dressed/could
e) for
f) couldn't/wouldn't
g) can
h) could
i) wouldn't
j) to

2 a) *I went to the shops for some eggs.*
b) Ann came here to meet the director.
c) We went on holiday for a rest.
d) Peter plays chess to relax.
e) I opened the window for some air.
f) Helen went shopping for some new clothes.

g) I went to a private school to learn English.
h) Sam went to a specialist for treatment.

3 a) *left work early/he could go*
b) was rebuilt/make it
c) gave Jack her phone number/he could call
d) put on some suntan oil/I don't/won't get
e) hid the presents/nobody would/could see
f) had the party in a large hall/people would
g) arrived early/he could/would get
h) changed seats in the cinema/I could see
i) wore a funny hat/his friends noticed/would notice
j) some sandwiches/wouldn't feel hungry

Unit 20

1 a) *such*   f) so much
b) so many   g) in the end
c) too   h) so much
d) so few   i) tall enough
e) so   j) so little

2 a) *too*   f) so few
b) as/because/since   g) enough
c) so much   h) so
d) so many   i) so little
e) so   j) As/Since/ Because

3 a) *I stayed at home and had a rest because I felt really tired.*
b) I didn't use that piece of string, because it wasn't long enough.
c) It was such a difficult question that I had to ask for help.
d) There were too few seats for all the guests.
e) There were too many guests and not enough seats.
f) I couldn't take any more clothes as there was too little space in my suitcase.
g) The play was so good that the audience cheered.
h) I've got so much work that I can't go out.
i) She had so many children that she didn't know what to do.
j) I have too little time to do all my work.

4 a) *Sorry, but I haven't got enough time.*
b) Helen is not old enough to drive a car.
c) Paul has so many friends that he is always busy.
d) We had too little time to go sight-seeing.
e) It's so hot that I can't think!
f) There was so much snow that we couldn't travel.

g) It was such a long way that we decided to drive there.
h) As I had run a long way, I felt exhausted.

5 a) *slow to be in the running team*
b) to the house, because/as it's not very far
c) such a long film that we missed our last bus
d) unhappy that she cried
e) much money that they don't know what to do with it
f) old enough to get married
g) enough money to buy this bike
h) enough plates I'm afraid

Unit 21

1 a) *however*   e) but
b) Although   f) despite
c) Although   g) In spite of
d) On the other hand h) although

2 a) *Although*   f) although
b) but   g) Despite
c) However   h) spite
d) even   i) However
e) still   j) still

3 a) *the snow, we went out for a walk*
b) some experts think the world is growing warmer, others disagree
c) I don't enjoy rock music, I went to the concert anyway
d) losing at half-time, City won in the end
e) it was hot, Diana wore her winter clothes
f) but this year they have gone down
g) having a headache/his headache, Jim still read until late
h) but he still did well in the test

Unit 22

1 a) 4 b) 2 c) 7 d) 10 e) 6 f) 3
g) 9 h) 1 i) 5 j) 8

2 a) *Would you mind*
b) If I were you, I'd write
c) go
d) Could you
e) Would you like
f) I won't do it
g) Shall I help
h) Why don't you go
i) Could I borrow
j) should go

3 a) *I'll be back*
b) I'll have ice-cream
c) I think you should talk it over with your parents.
d) Shall I carry it?
e) How about going to the cinema?
f) Can I leave school early?
g) Can you tell me how much it costs?
h) Would you like some lemonade?

i) Could you open the window?
j) No, I won't.

4 a) *you mind taking a seat*
b) have fruit juice
c) you wait for me
d) I leave the room
e) you turn off the television
f) about going for a walk
g) won't talk to Richard again
h) I help you
i) you mind telling me when the plane arrives
j) were you, I'd see a doctor

5 a) *should*
b) Would/Could/Can
c) Would/Could/Can
d) Will
e) Let's
f) mind
g) rather
h) Would/Could/Can
i) Would
j) may/can

Unit 23

1 a) *who*   f) which
b) who   g) that
c) that   h) whose
d) whose   i) whose
e) who   j) which

2 a) *whom* f) whom
b) who   g) who
c) whom   h) who
d) who   i) whom
e) whom   j) who

3 a) *whose* f) whose
b) that   g) that
c) who   h) who
d) whose   i) who
e) who   j) that

4 a) D b) N c) N d) D e) N
f) N g) D h) N

5 a) *The book that John was reading was a bit frightening.*
b) The travel agency which sold me the ticket was near my office.
c) The name of the girl who lived next door was Ellen.
d) In the end, our holiday was the best that we had ever had.
e) The dentist who I go to isn't very expensive.
f) The film which we saw last week was much better than this one.
g) The people who were leaving couldn't find their coats.
h) The garden, which wasn't very large, was full of flowers.
i) The car which David bought was not in good condition.
j) The girl who I sit next to in class in my best friend.

6 a) *These are the boys I went on holiday with.*
b) This is the letter I have been waiting for.
c) That is the shop Sue bought her bike from.
d) That is the bed-and-breakfast I stayed at.
e) Tim is someone I hardly ever write to.
f) Do you know who this book was written by?
g) Ravenna was the most interesting town (that) we stayed in.
h) United were the best team (that) we played against.

7 a) *Friday was the last time that I saw Jim.*
b) The island that /which we visited was extremely beautiful.
c) The girl that/who I met was a friend of Harry's.
d) The meal that/which we ate was not very tasty.
e) Mary was the first person that I asked.
f) The book that/which I read didn't explain the problem.
g) The teacher that/who we usually have was away ill.
h) The friends that/who I met last night send you their love.
i) Unfortunately I've lost the pen that/which I always use.
j) The bus that/which I catch stops outside the university.

Unit 24

1 a) *which* f) that
b) What g) whose
c) who h) who
d) whose i) which
e) that j) who

2 a) ✓ b) his c) ✓ d) it e) she
f) it g) ✓ h) they

3 a) *The museum that we want to visit opens at 12.00.*
b) The boy whose bike was taken visited the police station.
c) The friend who met me at the airport carried my suitcase.
d) The meal that Tom cooked was delicious.
e) The friend who is staying with me comes from Paris.
f) The man whose wallet I found gave me a reward.
g) The shop in the centre that I go to is cheaper.
h) The girl whose party I went to phoned me.
i) I know someone who likes you.

4 a) ✓ b) what c) ✓ d) what
e) ✓ f) what/who g) ✓ h) What

Unit 25

1 a) *What time do you usually get up?*
b) What were you reading?
c) Why did you go there?
d) What have you done so far today?
e) What do I have to do now?
f) How did you feel yesterday?
g) What are you doing at the moment?
h) Why have the lights gone out?
i) Where did you leave your bike?
j) Who is coming to your party?

2 a) *Who lives next door?*
b) Who do you play with?
c) Who teaches you maths?/What does Mrs Dawson teach you?
d) What do you usually eat for lunch?
e) What frightens you?
f) Who do you talk to most?
g) Who do you sit next to in English?
h) What do you do every evening?
i) Who makes you laugh?
j) What helps you study?

3 a) *I haven't* e) I didn't
b) I am f) I can't
c) I did g) I do
d) I will h) he isn't

Unit 26

1 a) *I haven't* f) they can
b) I do g) I won't
c) I am h) she hasn't
d) she didn't i) it is
e) he has j) she didn't

2 a) *Have we* f) Is there
b) Don't you g) Has she
c) Did she h) Haven't you
d) Don't you i) Isn't there
e) Is he j) Did you

3 a) *aren't we* f) don't they
b) have you g) do you
c) aren't you h) don't you
d) will you i) hasn't he
e) isn't he j) should I

4 a) *Paul doesn't like football, does he?*
b) You've got a sister, haven't you?
c) You haven't done your homework, have you?
d) You didn't sit next to Ellen, did you?
e) The guests haven't arrived, have they?
f) Your name is John, isn't it?
g) Your name isn't John, is it?
h) I didn't leave my wallet on the desk, did I?
i) William hasn't got married, has he?
j) This book is by Martin Aimless, isn't it?

5 a) 2 b) 2 c) 2 d) 1 e) 2 f) 2
g) 1 h) 2

Unit 27

1 a) *there* e) there/there
b) It's f) It's
c) they're g) their
d) its h) its

2 a) *There/It* e) It
b) It/it f) There/it
c) It/there g) It/there/there
d) It h) there/It

3 a) *There is a small restaurant*
b) It is strange that you went
c) There is a big tree at the end of my
d) It seems that the plane had
e) It seems that Brian
f) It is really cold
g) It is a long way from here
h) There aren't any batteries in your
i) It appears that we are
j) It is strange that the police

Unit 28

1 a) *at* b) on c) to d) in e) below
f) in g) over h) on i) on j) in

2 a) ✓ b) in c) in d) at e) by
f) ✓ g) on h) ✓ i) in j) over

3 a) *in* b) on c) on d) in e) on
f) inside g) on h) out i) on j) at

4 a) *in* b) at c) in d) in e) on
f) to g) in h) over

5 a) *in* e) opposite
b) next to f) near
c) to g) on
d) inside h) on

6 a) *in* e) on/over
b) over f) on
c) near g) on
d) under h) at

Problems, Errors, Consolidation 3

1 a) *in order to* f) because
b) too g) Although
c) they're h) in
d) whose i) so
e) for j) In spite of

2 a) *but we decided to go for a walk*
b) John is someone I used to work
c) such a difficult exam that I couldn't finish it
d) the rain, we worked in the garden
e) about spending the afternoon at the beach
f) There are four large bedrooms
g) take some sandwiches/we don't/won't feel
h) It's strange that the cat hasn't come
i) enough money to go on holiday
j) you mind telling me where the National Muscum is

3 1) *b* 2) c 3) c 4) a 5) d 6) d
7) b 8) a 9) d 10) b 11) c
12) b 13) d 14) a 15) c

4 a) *on* b) beside c) to d) at
e) near f) on g) at h) opposite
i) inside j) at

5 1) ✓ 2) *who* 3) to 4) Then 5) so
6) who 7) she 8) them 9) much
10) you 11) ✓ 12) that 13) he
14) at 15) ✓ 16) it 17) so

6 a) *read a book which she really*
b) who visited me brought me a
c) that I stayed in was cheaper than
d) friend whose bike I borrowed
wanted it
e) to buy the vase that I saw in the
f) who sings in the group has got
g) I met a girl whose brother is in my
h) that we are taking leaves
i) who knocked at the door was selling
j) which I saw with Tom was

7 a) *You have got* f) can't you
b) won't they g) You weren't
c) Let's go h) do you
d) 're not leaving i) weren't they
e) haven't they j) didn't forget

Unit 29

1 a) *one day*
b) Nowadays
c) This morning
d) by
e) the day after tomorrow
f) During
g) afterwards
h) on

2 a) *we had/had had lunch, we went for a coffee*
b) on time for lessons
c) until 8.00
d) three months ago
e) at 12.00
f) first of January
g) day after tomorrow
h) for three

3 a) *on* b) ago c) later d) during
e) At f) nowadays g) in
h) afterwards i) for j) later

4 a) *I go to the seaside in summer.*
b) I'll see you later.
c) I've been at this school since 1997.
d) George had a bath and then washed his hair.
e) Diane was at my house until 10.00.
f) The train arrived on time.
g) I'll arrive by 2.00.
h) Paul tried hard but in the end he gave up.
i) I wasn't in time to say goodbye to Lisa.
j) I started learning English two years ago.

5 a) *last* b) During c) After d) for
e) one f) on g) afterwards h) at

Unit 30

1 a) *How much* b) are c) some
d) some e) much f) is
g) How many h) a i) some j) was

2 a) *an* b) a c) some d) –
e) many/– f) – g) a h) a
i) some j) any/many

3 a) *give you some advice*
b) any clean trousers
c) There isn't much
d) needs washing
e) Where are my
f) was not in the book
g) How much did
h) aren't any sandwiches left

4 a) *some wood*
b) There was
c) some advice
d) any
e) a chicken
f) was very useful
g) How many
h) It's green
i) they're on their way
j) noise

5 a) *water*
b) news
c) glasses
d) luggage
e) eggs
f) scissors
g) loaf
h) police officer/policeman/
policewoman

Unit 31

1 a) *Have you ever visited the United Kingdom?*
b) On our trip, we visited Canterbury Cathedral.
c) Love is a wonderful thing.
d) Pets are not permitted in this hotel.
e) A rabbit is a small wild furry animal with long ears./Rabbits are small wild furry animals with long ears.
f) New York is in the United States of America.
g) The judge sent David to prison for a month.

2 a) – b) a c) an/– d) a/an e) a/–
f) a/a/a g) –/– h) –/a

3 a) *is an*
b) in a
c) Parking
d) Jim is at
e) is the conductor
f) to the station on
g) A frog is a small amphibious

Unit 32

1 a) *the* f) the/the
b) the/the g) a
c) an/the h) a
d) An i) a
e) the/the j) the/the

2 a) *plays the piano*
b) help the
c) bike is the
d) is at the
e) was about the life
f) only goal of the match was scored by the
g) the last day of the
h) the tallest in the

3 a) *The/the/the* f) the/a/the
b) the/– g) A/a/a
c) a/the h) the/the
d) the/the i) the/the/the
e) the/the/a j) a/the

Units 31 and 32 mixed

1 a) *The/a/–* e) The/the/the
b) –/the/a f) –/the/an/–
c) a/–/the g) –/the/a
d) the/a/a h) a/the/the

2 a) *Could you get a loaf of bread from the baker's?*
b) Milk is good for children.
c) John is at work at the moment.
d) We travelled to Italy by car.
e) Have you got a brother or sister?
f) The war between the two countries was the longest in history.
g) Who was the first astronaut who landed on the moon?
h) The Nile is the longest river in the world.

3 a) *We travelled there on the train.*
b) This one is the largest.
c) Clara is a (professional) singer.
d) The unemployed often feel depressed.
e) Anna is learning to play the guitar.
f) Mike works in an office.
g) Marie comes from France.
h) David is still at work.

4 a) *George was the*
b) you have a dog at
c) a chemistry
d) The present (that/which) my friends
e) is the capital of
f) The first lesson tomorrow is
g) the phone for you
h) The film (that/which) we saw last night

5 1) *A* 2) a 3) a 4) – 5) – 6) the
7) – 8) – 9) a 10) – 11) the
12) a 13) the 14) a 15) a
16) an 17) – 18) – 19) a 20) –

Unit 33

1. a) *no*   e) either
   b) each   f) both tyres
   c) Not one g) all
   d) Some   h) none of

2. a) *not one* f) Each
   b) no   g) all/each
   c) neither   h) none
   d) All   i) both
   e) every   j) either

3. a) *Every dog in the garden was barking.*
   b) Not a single person came to the meeting.
   c) Some of the members of the class were late.
   d) None of my friends has got a car.
   e) Neither of these chairs is comfortable.
   f) There were no boys in the class.
   g) All we want to do is listen to a few cassettes.
   h) Both books are interesting.

4. a) *None of these books is interesting.*
   b) All you have left is ten minutes.
   c) Neither of the hotels was suitable.
   d) Not a single person replied to my letter.
   e) Both Paul and his brother David are ill.
   f) All of the team played well.
   g) Every house in the street was searched by the police.
   h) Some of the questions in the test were difficult.

5. a) *1* b) 2 c) 2 d) 1 e) 1 f) 2
   g) 2 h) 2

Unit 34

1. a) *a large old green plastic bag*
   b) two square wooden tables
   c) a beautiful red silk dress
   d) a pair of antique silver jugs
   e) a small plastic bowl
   f) a long winding country road
   g) some dirty old football boots
   h) a long yellow cotton skirt
   i) a pair of old blue trousers
   j) a glass of cold freshly squeezed orange juice

2. a) *boiling*   f) fantastic
   b) gigantic   g) worried
   c) tired   h) warmer
   d) cool   i) bored
   e) exciting   j) interested

3. a) *The old couple lived happily together.*
   b) You have worked hard.
   c) Chris and Paul walk slowly.
   d) George plays the piano well.
   e) Sue dances gracefully.
   f) Kate is not well/doesn't feel well.
   g) Michael skated wonderfully.
   h) Mary writes carefully.

i) David slept badly.
j) Ann completed the course successfully.

4. a) *happy*   f) fast
   b) well   g) quite
   c) hardly   h) hard
   d) good   i) terrible
   e) ill   j) extremely

5. a) *Peter has been working very hard.*
   b) My sister bought me a lovely blue woollen sweater.
   c) This book I'm reading is excellent/extremely good.
   d) David felt bad because he was tall and thin.
   e) Everyone in the team played well.
   f) Too much exercise can make you feel tired.
   g) Paula felt happy when her exams were over.
   h) Harry has never arrived late at school.
   i) One boxer hit the other really hard on the chin.
   j) I'm not really interested in this car.

Unit 35

1. a) *as tasty as*
   b) the most interesting
   c) oldest
   d) than
   e) worse
   f) tallest
   g) as hard as
   h) worse
   i) longer than
   j) more quietly

2. a) *the longest*
   b) less entertaining
   c) faster than
   d) the hottest
   e) better than
   f) just as tall as
   g) more difficult
   h) as large as
   i) not as big as/just as big as
   j) the worst

3. a) *as good a runner as David (is)*
   b) tallest in the class
   c) more than me/than I have
   d) as good as we expected
   e) longer than Jane's (hair)
   f) noisiest student in the school
   g) as interesting as this one (is)
   h) go faster than this
   i) more expensive (than this one)
   j) eat as much as George (did)

4. a) *just as/as*
   b) the most
   c) more,less/than/did
   d) more
   e) than/the
   f) the least

g) just as/as
h) less/than
i) more/than/does
j) as/as

5. a) *Could you talk more slowly, please?*
   b) This film is not as frightening as the last one we saw.
   c) Sam is the best cook in the class.
   d) You have eaten more than me/than I have.
   e) Small shops are not as convenient as supermarkets.
   f) Skiing is more exciting than skating.
   g) Alan works just as hard as Richard (does).
   h) Jack's brother is more interested in football than he is.
   i) Everyone else in the family is older than Bill.
   j) I didn't run as fast as you did.

6. a) *biggest*   i) harder
   b) greatest   j) –
   c) –   k) –
   d) –   l) –
   e) –   m) –
   f) fatter   n) –
   g) smallest   o) wider
   h) longest

Unit 36

1. a) *3* b) 5 c) 8 d) 1 e) 4 f) 2
   g) 6 h) 7

2. a) *The central heating system needs seeing to.*
   b) Let's drop in on Julia while we are here.
   c) We're heading for Paris.
   d) Our hotel room looks out onto the main road!
   e) Two children started playing, and then the others joined in.
   f) We called on my aunt on her birthday.
   g) I'm afraid that we've run out of eggs.
   h) Kate will call for you at 6.30.
   i) Nobody understood what I was getting at.
   j) I can't put up with so much air pollution.

3. a) *Brian takes after his mother.*
   b) We've run out of food!
   c) Mike and Tom don't get on well.
   d) Jean is very good at dealing with people.
   e) The handlebars on my bike need seeing to.
   f) Julia was very ill, but she's got over it now.
   g) What exactly are you getting at?
   h) Paul's new school didn't live up to his expectations.

4 a) *didn't live up to*
b) drop in on
c) run out of
d) get on with
e) caught up with
f) looking forward to
g) keep up with
h) cut down on

Unit 37

1 a) *wash*   e) try
b) look   f) fill
c) set   g) turned
d) put   h) dropped

2 a) *3* b) 8 c) 1 d) 6 e) 4 f) 5
g) 2 h) 7

3 a) *Turn the lights off when you leave the school.*
b) You should look this word up in a dictionary.
c) The athletics meeting was put off for a week.
d) The doctor told David to give up football.
e) Could you fill in this form?
f) Jack turned up half-way through the lesson.
g) We can put you up for a week.
h) Helen is getting on well in her English class.

4 a) *Paula grew up in Uruguay.*
b) As soon as it was dawn, we set off.
c) Parachuting is dangerous so you should give it up.
d) Martin clears up his room/clears his room up every morning.
e) How do you turn on the computer/turn the computer on?
f) Can I try on these shoes/try these shoes on?
g) Carol looked up the dates/ looked the dates up in an encyclopedia.
h) Skating is a great sport. When did you take it up?

Problems, Errors, Consolidation 4

1 a) *better* e) best
b) each   f) for
c) hard   g) no
d) some   h) is

2 1) *d* 2) a 3) c 4) a 5) d 6) d
7) b 8) c 9) b 10) a 11) b
12) d 13) c 14) b 15) c

3 a) *of these classrooms is very large*
b) until the end of April
c) smoking is allowed in this cinema
d) some advice
e) waited as long as you have
f) 2.00
g) classroom must be kept clean
h) on foot

i) go any further along this road
j) in time to save the burning house

4 a) *I can put you up.*
b) Harry can't put up with loud music.
c) Peter is getting on well at university.
d) I'll clear up the room if you do the washing up.
e) We're making for Madrid.
f) Why don't you look up this word/look this word up in the dictionary?
g) Jane takes after her father.
h) Sue's father is trying to give up smoking.

5 1) ✓ 2) *the* 3) it 4) a 5) was
6) ✓ 7) ago 8) much 9) the
10) more 11) one 12) ✓ 13) after
14) after 15) up 16) once 17) the

6 a) *the* b) – c) – d) the e) for
f) – g) lot h) much i) the j) any
k) the l) the m) the n) a
o) either

7 a) *Not a single person picked up the litter.*
b) Paul has been learning Hungarian since 1997.
c) There is no cheese in the fridge.
d) The rich are not necessarily happy.
e) Jane draws beautifully.
f) This is the worst film I have ever seen.
g) Helen stayed in Paris until July.
h) Are you interested in opera?

8 a) *much/than*   f) all/both
b) the/than   g) Both/in
c) the/a   h) as/as
d) not as   i) until/by
e) some/much   j) best/ever

9 a) *I'm really interested in travel.*
b) Kate's brother is a doctor.
c) I had/ate some food with Jack, and after that I went home.
d) Milk is good for you.
e) Can you give me some advice?
f) I've looked in the box. Everything is broken, I'm afraid.
g) They will have finished the new hospital by the end of March./They won't have finished the new hospital until the end of March.
h) There's a police officer/policeman/policewoman waiting outside.
i) I come to class on foot.
j) Your hair is very beautiful.

Unit 38

1 a) *Jim can't afford to go to the cinema twice a week.*
b) David wishes to leave the room.
c) Are you waiting to use the phone?
d) I'd really like to go swimming on Saturday.

e) Everyone decided to put off the football match.
f) Emma pretended to leave, but waited outside.
g) Jack agreed to meet me at the beach.
h) My bike seems to have something wrong with it.
i) The director refused to answer Helen's phone call.
j) What exactly do you intend to say to Mrs Dawson?

2 a) *loves*   f) continued
b) afford   g) bear
c) happen   h) offered
d) expected i) pretended
e) learned j) prefers

3 a) *to let me leave early*
b) singing for an hour without stopping
c) (that) you have passed the exam
d) to do well
e) to do in the summer/this summer
f) clearing up my room
g) to go to the cinema with me
h) to get married
i) to see you later
j) to do this evening

4 a) *seems* f) refused
b) hate   g) chose
c) asked   h) like
d) want   i) decides
e) hopes   j) agreed

5 a) *What do you intend to do?*
b) I can't bear getting up early!
c) I expect to see you in the morning.
d) Tom refused to help.
e) Pat learned to drive when he was young.
f) I offered to help Joe.
g) Ellen couldn't afford the ticket.
h) Susan promised to be back at 6.00.

Unit 39

1 a) *to lock* e) to open
b) to have   f) to take
c) talking   g) sky-diving
d) being   h) starting

2 a) *Do you fancy*
b) The boy admitted that he had
c) that you are wrong
d) I suggest
e) David keeps
f) Do you mind
g) Imagine
h) Paula denied
i) I can't help
j) We saw the building

3 a) *chose*   e) denied
b) afford   f) admitted
c) mind   g) decided
d) meant   h) fancy

4 a) *try* e) denied
  b) pretended f) practise
  c) expect g) imagine
  d) meant h) refused

5 a) *forget* e) kept
  b) means f) stand
  c) admit g) remember
  d) stop h) tried

Unit 40

1 a) *from* e) to h) on
  b) of f) about i) for
  c) to g) for j) at
  d) for

2 a) *Dick was bored with his work.*
  b) This town reminds me of Glasgow.
  c) Paula knows a lot about biology.
  d) I'm looking for the art gallery.
  e) I'm fond of cream cakes.
  f) Sue is married to Adrian.
  g) Dina is kind to animals.
  h) Ugh! This cake tastes of rubber!
  i) Lisa is jealous of you!
  j) I feel excited about our new house!

3 a) *interested in archaeology*
  b) angry with you
  c) ready
  d) good at geography
  e) upset by the bad news
  f) about my dog last night
  g) rely on Sue
  h) bike to Jack for the weekend
  i) of the dark
  j) full of people

4 a) *explain/to* f) apologized/for
  b) laughed at g) remind me of
  c) belonged to h) succeeded in
  d) depends on i) wait for
  e) paid for j) talking about

5 a) *4* b) 7 c) 5 d) 2 e) 8 f) 1
  g) 6 h) 3

Unit 41

1 a) *anyone* e) anything
  b) anything f) Someone
  c) nothing g) anything
  d) someone h) No one

2 a) *do anything*
  b) knows Mary better than I do
  c) was late yesterday
  d) nothing/no work
  e) ask you something
  f) here drinks
  g) replied when I phoned
  h) someone going to drive us there

3 a) *enjoy yourselves*
  b) dresses himself
  c) asking myself
  d) behave ourselves
  e) hurt myself

  f) express herself
  g) introduce myself
  h) blame yourself
  i) talk/myself
  j) cut himself

4 a) *There is something in the box.*
  b) Everyone was dancing.
  c) Something has annoyed/is annoying me.
  d) There is nothing to eat.
  e) There is no one in the office.
  f) Everybody likes Helen.

5 a) *Everybody*
  b) anything/something
  c) Something
  d) someone
  e) themselves
  f) One
  g) Everything
  h) Nothing

6 a) *Someone spoke to me, but I can't remember their name.*
  b) Everything in the garden has been growing a lot lately.
  c) Carol didn't do anything yesterday.
  d) There isn't anyone waiting for you.
  e) Peter and Kate enjoyed themselves at the party.
  f) You fill in an application form, and then you wait for an answer./One fills in an application form, and then one waits for an answer.

Unit 42

1 a) *hers* e) theirs h) my
  b) her own f) your i) our
  c) yours g) his j) its
  d) mine

2 a) *Tell Susan it's Mary's turn, not hers.*
  b) Alice's younger brother's called Bill.
  c) Tim's sandwiches were tastier than ours.
  d) The film's beginning is good but its ending is weak.
  e) Are these keys yours or hers?
  f) Kate fills in the patients' record cards at the doctor's.
  g) When it's raining, everybody's raincoats get wet.
  h) The manager's assistant reads all the customers' letters.
  i) Your sister's dog runs faster than ours.
  j) One's our teacher's car and the other's a visitor's.

3 a) *football boot/cheese sandwich*
  b) shop window/coat pocket
  c) garden gate/bicycle lamp
  d) department store/country cottage
  e) fire engine/rock singer
  f) post office/pencil sharpener
  g) football ground/school report
  h) shop assistant/railway station

  i) food mixer/pocket money
  j) street market/power failure

4 a) *sister's friend*
  b) Sam's shoes
  c) friend of mine
  d) This is my favourite television
  e) are your teachers'
  f) Have you got a tin
  g) are our neighbours'
  h) I put my books on the kitchen
  i) new umbrella of mine
  j) This is not my

5 a) *There are two bus-stops near my house.*
  b) Our cat sleeps all day in its bed.
  c) Have you met Jane's sister?
  d) Creatures like these live at the bottom of the sea/the sea bottom.
  e) This book is mine.
  f) I noticed these shoes in a shop window.
  g) Everybody's drawings were better than ours.
  h) Are these gloves yours or mine?/Are these your gloves or mine?
  i) The house stands on its own at the end of the street.
  j) Those are two friends of my father's.

Unit 43

1 a) *instead of* f) since
  b) either g) both
  c) also h) yet
  d) such as i) too
  e) except j) even

2 a) *Paula visited the castle and the museum, too.*
  b) Everyone was on time except Jack.
  c) I said it was raining but, in fact, it isn't!
  d) Helen couldn't play, since she had hurt her leg.
  e) In my view, smoking is bad for you.
  f) I ate the chocolate cake as well as the lemon pie.
  g) Jim played in goal instead of his brother.
  h) In conclusion, I'd like to thank the head teacher, Ann Coles.
  i) I have written twice, yet I have not received a reply.
  j) We can either wait for the bus or take a taxi.

3 1) *c* 2) b 3) a 4) d 5) d 6) c
  7) b 8) d 9) a 10) b

4 a) *except* e) instead
  b) as well as this f) actually
  c) Personally g) such as
  d) both h) either

5 a) *5* b) 9 c) 3 d) 7 e) 1 f) 4
  g) 10 h) 2 i) 8 j) 6

Unit 44

1 a) *1* b) 2 c) 2 d) 2 e) 3 f) 1
  g) 1

2 a) *'First of all, who is going to carry the suitcase?' asked Sue.*
  b) Kate said she would be on time, but I didn't believe her.
  c) Jack said that he had missed the train, got lost, and been arrested.
  d) When the bell rang, our teacher stood up and said, 'Stop writing, please.'
  e) 'On the other hand, we could go to the cinema, couldn't we?' said David.
  f) 'Hello Alan,' said Tina. 'How do you feel today?'
  g) If I were you, I'd ask for some help, or perhaps start again.
  h) The old stadium was eventually demolished: very few people went there, and it was becoming dangerous.

3 a) *We're meeting Uncle David on Tuesday evening at eight.*
  b) Last February I met Mrs Wilkinson for the first time.
  c) Tim lives in the south of France near Cannes.
  d) We saw a great film at the ABC called 'The Remains of the Day'.
  e) Carol works as the manager of a tourist agency.
  f) We went to a party at Mrs Harrisons' house on New Year's Eve.
  g) Julia's reading 'A Portrait of a Lady' by Henry James.
  h) When Jean met the Prime Minister she asked some difficult questions.

Unit 45

1 a) *deciding*   g) their
  b) swimming   h) beautiful
  c) photo   i) receipt
  d) question   j) beginning
  e) whistle   k) psychiatrist
  f) known   l) successful

2 a) *phone/received*
  b) whistle/field
  c) successfully/physics
  d) know/knife
  e) thief/leaving
  f) question/listening
  g) beginning/view
  h) columns/beautifully

3 a) *controlling*   g) upsetting
  b) thickening   h) hooking
  c) gripping   i) writing
  d) choosing   j) improving
  e) flying   k) swimming
  f) making   l) riding

4 Dear Tina,
    I am sorry that I have not written to you for so long. I'm afraid I've been very busy at school, and I haven't had much time for writing letters. Last week I finished my examinations, so now I'm getting ready to go on holiday.
    I was wondering whether you would like to come to stay for a few days? You can meet my friends, and we could all go swimming. The weather is really good now here in Italy, and I'm sure you will enjoy yourself.
  Best wishes,
    Maria

5 a) *tomorrow*   g) necessary
  b) Wednesday   h) disappointed
  c) advertisement i) weather/whether
  d) neighbour   j) remember
  e) through   k) library
  f) grateful   l) answer

Unit 46

1 *a/q* b/g c/m d/j e/k f/p h/o i/r l/n

2 a) *stare*   e) fare
  b) practise   f) quite
  c) thorough   g) aloud
  d) advice   h) too

3 a) ✓ b) – c) ✓ d) – e) ✓ f) ✓ g) – h) ✓ i) – j) ✓ k) ✓ l) – m) – n) – o) –

4 Dear Maria,
    Thanks for your letter and your invitation to Italy! I have never travelled abroad before, and I am really looking forward to staying with you and your family. I have spoken to my parents and they have agreed. They say they are going to phone soon to discuss the arrangements.
    I've decided to have some Italian lessons so that I can practise when I come to Italy. I'd like you to write some simple sentences for me. Please note my new address. We moved last week and now I've got a much bigger bedroom.
  Best wishes,   Tina

5 a) *vegetable*   g) interesting
  b) language   h) biscuit
  c) queue   i) ceiling
  d) receive   j) different
  e) people   k) knowledge
  f) beautiful   l) independent

Problems, Errors, Consolidation 5

1 a) *hers*   e) anything
  b) to help   f) spending
  c) in   g) at
  d) as   h) anything

2 1) *b* 2) d 3) d 4) a 5) c 6) b
  7) a 8) d 9) c 10) b 11) b
  12) d 13) a 14) c 15) c

3 a) *except Tim*
  b) knows this town better than Helen (does)
  c) the twins' gloves
  d) to carry my bag
  e) rely on Peter
  f) friend of my brother's
  g) started snowing yesterday evening
  h) no one/nobody in the classroom
  i) closing the window
  j) calculator to Bill

4 1) ✓ 2) *that* 3) take 4) me 5) it
  6) for 7) been 8) got 9) ✓
  10) for 11) or 12) it 13) they
  14) ✓ 15) have 16) with 17) it

5 a) *for*   i) forgotten
  b) her   j) even
  c) of   k) something
  d) nobody   l) Either
  e) started   m) kept
  f) hers   n) saw
  g) seemed   o) Someone
  h) with

6 Dear David,
    It was great to hear from you after so long. I enjoyed hearing all your news. I didn't realize that you had spent a year abroad. You must have had a really good time in Greece. I've decided to go there next summer. Perhaps we could go together.
    I've had a fantastic year at college. The work is harder than the work we did at school, but it's more interesting. I'm studying business administration and computer science at the moment. I've also made lots of new friends.
    I'm thinking of coming to Bristol for a few days to visit my sister. Would you like to meet? You could show me the sights and we could talk about our old schooldays.
    Why don't you give me a ring and we could discuss it. It would be wonderful to see you again.
  Best wishes,
    Ellen Wilson

7 a) *Instead of*   f) as well
  b) every single   g) yours
  c) in fact   h) herself
  d) In conclusion   i) on/in
  e) of my/mine   j) even

Vocabulary answers

2 Word formation

1 a) *uninteresting*
b) disadvantage
c) unfortunately
d) impatient
e) disappear
f) incorrect
g) unemployed
h) disagree
i) misunderstanding
j) disappointed

2 a) *overslept*   f) outplayed
b) underwear   g) rewrite
c) international   h) overcooked
d) overcoat   i) renew
e) underline   j) underpaid

3 a) *friendship*
b) foreigner
c) childhood
d) stewardess
e) teenager
f) spoonful
g) neighbourhood
h) handful
i) machinery
j) booklet

4 a) *inhabitants*
b) boredom
c) building
d) accommodation
e) refusal
f) actor
g) employee
h) imagination
i) cooker
j) advertisement

5 a) *shortness*   f) thoroughness
b) friendliness   g) happiness
c) darkness   h) silliness
d) loneliness   i) thinness
e) tiredness   j) sickness

6 a) *rainy*   f) dangerous
b) snakelike   g) difficulty
c) musical   h) foolish
d) homeless   i) heroic
e) motherly   j) successful

3 Word formation

1 a) *tired*   f) confusing
b) disappointing g) exhausting
c) frightening   h) interested
d) embarrassed   i) surprised
e) bored   j) annoying

2 a) *unlikely*   f) dislike
b) shortage   g) sleepy
c) impossible   h) unusual
d) photography   i) cheerful
e) useful   j) kindness

3 a) *unusually*
b) surprisingly
c) Interestingly
d) successfully
e) beautifully
f) thoroughly
g) awfully
h) unsuccessfully
i) unnecessarily
j) obviously

4 a) *uncomfortable*
b) independent
c) reusable
d) disappointment
e) relationship
f) unselfish
g) unhealthy
h) uncontrollable
i) unshrinkable
j) inexperienced

5 a) *receipt*   e) Marriage
b) politician   f) application
c) depth   g) knowledge
d) patience   h) explanation

6 a) *theft*   f) bravery
b) belief   g) vanity
c) suspicion   h) ability
d) length   i) frozen
e) angry   j) qualifications

4 Expressions

1 a) *high*   f) being
b) spare   g) on
c) time   h) matter
d) pass   i) in
e) tell   j) lose

2 a) *made*   e) burst   h) paid
b) had   f) told   i) caught
c) took   g) got   j) lost
d) spent

3 a) *facts*   f) mad
b) mess   g) temper
c) breath   h) secret
d) alone   i) leaf
e) difference   j) discussion

4 a) *a bird*   f) a pig
b) a bat   g) nails
c) life   h) a picture
d) a cucumber   i) rain
e) pie   j) houses

5 a) *have an early night*
b) take it easy
c) take a day off
d) have fun
e) have nothing to do
f) sleep like a log
g) feel dog tired
h) get ready

6 a) *life*   f) sound
b) soul   g) down
c) wide   h) seek
d) round   i) then
e) time   j) day

5 Compound words

1 a) *footpath*   e) haircut
b) paper clip   f) sunglasses
c) shoelace   g) headache
d) timetable   h) lamp-post

2 a) *science fiction*
b) walking stick
c) school report
d) alarm clock
e) air-conditioning
f) birthday party
g) central heating
h) washing machine

3 a) *bottle top*
b) shop window
c) bicycle pump
d) school entrance
e) sweet wrapper
f) bathroom mirror
g) television screen
h) shed door
i) pocket money
j) door handle

4 a) *hairdrier*
b) dishwasher
c) stain remover
d) fire extinguisher
e) pencil sharpener
f) bottle opener
g) lawn mower
h) food mixer
i) water heater
j) coffee maker

5 a) *day-dreamer*
b) shopkeeper
c) sunbather
d) baby-sitter
e) weightlifter
f) fire-fighter
g) bank manager
h) holidaymaker

6 a) *income* f) downpour
   b) upset g) outdoors
   c) roundabout h) outskirts
   d) downstairs i) Underground
   e) overcoat j) upbringing

6 Money and shopping

1 a) *second-hand*
  b) can't afford it
  c) pay you back
  d) save up
  e) in debt
  f) annual income
  g) in a sale
  h) be well-off

2 a) *earns* e) by cheque
  b) wages f) receipt
  c) borrowed g) change
  d) cash h) owe

3 a) 6 b) 5 c) 7 d) 2 e) 4 f) 1
  g) 8 h) 3

4 a) *packet* e) box
  b) tube f) bar
  c) tin g) bunch
  d) carton h) loaf

5 1) *c* 2) a 3) d 4) c 5) b 6) d
  7) a 8) d 9) a 10) b 11) c
  12) a 13) c 14) b 15) d

6 a) *pocket money*
  b) shop window
  c) cash desk
  d) cut price
  e) bookshop
  f) department store
  g) bank account
  h) shop assistant
  i) traveller's cheques
  j) carrier bag

7 Living space

1 a) *cushion* e) curtains
  b) socket f) carpet
  c) radiator g) drawer
  d) pillow h) settee

2 a) *4* b) 5 c) 6 d) 1 e) 3 f) 2
  g) 8 h) 7

3 a) *glass*/pane of glass
  b) cloth/towel
  c) door/gate
  d) ground/floor
  e) library/bookcase
  f) wall/fence
  g) fireplace/chimney
  h) stair/step

4 a) *at home* f) cupboard
  b) stairs g) at/in
  c) wash-basin h) a bath
  d) ceiling i) housework
  e) cook/cooker j) cellar

5 a) *bedroom* f) dishwasher
  b) armchair g) keyhole
  c) washbasin h) ashtray
  d) dustbin i) downstairs
  e) flowerbed j) bookcase

6 a) *put* d) takes g) looks
  b) move e) turn h) drop
  c) get f) finish

8 Personal matters

1 a) *angry* f) bored
  b) embarrassed g) cheerful
  c) polite h) bad-tempered
  d) lazy i) upset
  e) sensible j) nervous

2 a) *smile* e) cry
  b) nod f) cheer
  c) complain g) shake his head
  d) shout h) whistle

3 a) *unreliable*
  b) impatient
  c) uninterested
  d) dishonest
  e) unfriendly
  f) inexperienced
  g) impolite
  h) unhelpful
  i) inconsiderate
  j) unco-operative

4 a) *disappointed* f) exhausted
  b) annoyed g) jealous
  c) terrified h) excited
  d) glad i) fascinating
  e) ashamed j) selfish

5 a) *longing for*
  b) give up
  c) put me off
  d) get on my nerves
  e) fancy
  f) fed up with
  g) are fond of
  h) let me down

6 a) *mood* f) heart
  b) Thanks g) conscience
  c) trouble h) temper
  d) voice i) hand
  e) tears j) death

9 Family and friends

1 a) *husband* f) single
  b) couple g) friendship
  c) children h) elder
  d) twin i) engaged
  e) alike j) housewife

2 a) *relations/relatives*
  b) acquaintance
  c) birth
  d) greeting
  e) engagement
  f) celebration

  g) marriage
  h) resemblance
  i) behaviour
  j) death

3 a) *adults* f) young
  b) dead g) circle
  c) wedding h) relatives
  d) daughter i) home
  e) old j) birthday

4 a) 6 b) 9 c) 10 d) 8 e) 1 f) 7
  g) 5 h) 2 i) 3 j) 4

5 a) *5* b) 4 c) 7 d) 1 e) 8 f) 6
  g) 2 h) 3

6 a) *in* e) after
  b) away f) over
  c) on and off g) against
  d) on h) out

10 The body and clothes

1 a) *waist* e) shoulder
  b) wrist f) ankle
  c) thumb g) toes
  d) nails h) forehead

2 1) *c* 2) b 3) b 4) a 5) d 6) c
  7) d 8) b 9) a 10) b 11) d
  12) c 13) a 14) d 15) c

3 a) *fit* e) suit
  b) dress up f) disguise
  c) wear g) put on
  d) look h) go with

4 a) *sleeve* e) shorts
  b) dress f) skirt
  c) suit g) blouse
  d) cap h) sock

5 a) *tongue* f) heart
  b) hair g) head
  c) face h) leg
  d) foot i) hand
  e) arms j) eye

11 Everyday problems

1 a) *had* f) flooded
  b) crashed g) blocked
  c) injured h) collided
  d) collapsed i) sank
  e) exploded j) trapped

2 a) *prescription* e) pain
  b) temperature f) chemist's
  c) get over g) flu
  d) heal h) sore throat

3 a) *traffic jam*
  b) air pollution
  c) power failure
  d) parking ticket
  e) train strike
  f) car park
  g) bus-stop
  h) rush hour

i) water shortage
j) city centre

4 a) +k b) +n c) +m d) +j e) +l
f) +p g) +i h) +o

5 a) *6* b) 10 c) 9 d) 8 e) 7 f) 5
g) 3 h) 1 i) 2 j) 4

6 a) *bandage*   e) ward
b) hospital   f) surgeon
c) patient   g) blood
d) operation   h) ambulance

12 Travel and holidays

1 1) *c* 2) d 3) a 4) d 5) b 6) b
7) a 8) c 9) a 10) d 11) c
12) b 13) b 14) d 15) a

2 a) *information*   e) reservation
b) runway   f) cancellation
c) departure   g) airport
d) landing   h) takeoff

3 a) *down* e) on   h) back
b) off   f) for   i) out
c) up   g) with j) after
d) in

4 a) *7* b) 3 c) 10 d) 8 e) 1 f) 4
g) 9 h) 2 i) 6 j) 5

5 a) *ancient*   f) suntanned
b) seasick   g) reasonable
c) popular   h) exhausted
d) relaxing   i) warm
e) local   j) open

6 a) *resort*   f) station
b) breakfast   g) stop
c) walk   h) village
d) holiday   i) hostel
e) ticket   j) cheques

13 Interests and free time

1 a) *beat*   f) going
b) applauded   g) drew
c) enter for   h) spends
d) holding   i) enjoy
e) performed   j) missed

2 a) *spectators* f) group
b) athletes   g) audience
c) fans   h) viewers
d) team   i) cast
e) members   j) competitors

3 a) *prize*   f) ticket
b) medal   g) exhibition
c) queue   h) rod
d) tyre   i) line
e) whistle   j) screen

4 a) *knock*   f) go
b) turn   g) make
c) join   h) stand
d) live   i) drop
e) put   j) fall

5 1) *b* 2) c 3) b 4) a 5) d 6) d
7) a 8) b 9) a 10) c 11) d
12) c 13) b 14) a 15) d

6 a) *7* b) 6 c) 8 d) 3 e) 1 f) 2
g) 5 h) 4

14 Places

1 1) *b* 2) d 3) c 4) a 5) c 6) d
7) a 8) b 9) b 10) c 11) d
12) a 13) c 14) d 15) a

2 a) *station*   f) part
b) junction   g) place
c) hall   h) traffic
d) block   i) zone
e) crossing   j) centre

3 a) *rural*   e) international
b) neighbouring   f) local
c) isolated   g) crowded
d) capital   h) urban

4 a) *square*   f) view
b) countryside   g) Parking
c) beach   h) country
d) ground   i) stop
e) footpath   j) lane

5 a) *playground*   e) footpath
b) crossroads   f) roadside
c) roundabout   g) outskirts
d) car park   h) footbridge

6 a) *castle*
b) caravan
c) semi-detached house
d) bungalow
e) bridge
f) terraced house
g) cottage
h) tower

15 Food and drink

1 a) *roll*   f) frozen
b) course   g) recipe
c) kettle   h) tasty
d) meal   i) cook
e) cans   j) spoon

2 a) *roast*   f) Peel
b) mix   g) fry
c) chop   h) Grate
d) bake   i) Squeeze
e) add   j) Boil

3 a) *salt*   e) chips
b) fork   f) vinegar
c) bacon   g) saucer
d) butter   h) biscuits

4 a) *slice*   e) loaf
b) bar   f) glass
c) jar   g) pinch
d) cup   h) carton

5 a) *grape*   e) pie
b) onion   f) plum
c) lettuce   g) cheese
d) lamb   h) chop

6 a) *menu*   e) waiter
b) bill   f) takeaway
c) dessert   g) book
d) dish   h) tip

7 a) *a* b) some c) a d) – e) a
f) a g) a h) – i) – j) some

16 Work and study

1 a) *pass*   f) wages
b) job   g) aloud
c) teach   h) application
d) studying   i) earns
e) marks   j) office

2 a) *heart*   e) rules
b) phone   f) date
c) practice   g) time
d) work   h) business

3 a) *education*   f) employer
b) unemployed   g) timetable
c) carelessly   h) income
d) successful   i) knowledge
e) qualifications j) employees

4 a) *look*   e) make   h) take
b) write   f) pick   i) hand
c) get   g) fill   j) stand
d) keep

5 1) *d* 2) b 3) b 4) a 5) c 6) d
7) b 8) b 9) a 10) b 11) d
12) d 13) c 14) b 15) a

6 a) *7* b) 10 c) 1 d) 9 e) 2 f) 3
g) 5 h) 6 i) 8 j) 4

17 The natural environment

1 a) *weather*   f) heatwave
b) lightning   g) storm
c) fog   h) cool
d) shower   i) soaked
e) season   j) snow

2 a) *swan*   f) mosquito
b) goat   g) rabbit
c) crab   h) giraffe
d) butterfly   i) spider
e) lizard   j) puppy

3 a) *branch*   f) thorn
b) berry   g) bark
c) root   h) blossom
d) stem   i) bud
e) leaf   j) trunk

4 a) *8* f) 10 b) 4 g) 5 c) 9 h) 3
d) 2 i) 6 e) 1 j) 7

5 1) *a* 2) c 3) d 4) c 5) a 6) b
7) b 8) c 9) d 10) b 11) a
12) d 13) b 14) d 15) c

6 a) *protect/destroy*
   b) prevent/let
   c) clean up/pollute
   d) plant/cut down
   e) recycle/waste

18 Tools and technology

1 a) *calculator*   f) tyre
   b) van   g) engine
   c) petrol   h) light
   d) electric   i) nails
   e) bulb   j) plumber

2 a) *answer machine*
   b) mobile phone
   c) sewing machine
   d) vacuum cleaner
   e) cash dispenser
   f) camera
   g) dishwasher
   h) photocopier

3 a) *ring*   e) plug   h) go
   b) blow   f) cut   i) warm
   c) wear   g) turn   j) run
   d) break

4 a) *car*
   b) electric toothbrush
   c) ladder
   d) oven
   e) frying pan
   f) saw
   g) gun
   h) cello

5 a) *handle*   f) lock
   b) battery   g) plug
   c) socket   h) dial
   d) switch   i) button
   e) key   j) wire

6 a) *pump*   f) scissors
   b) tin-opener   g) thermometer
   c) lawnmower   h) binoculars
   d) razor   i) compass
   e) hairdrier   j) iron

19 Everyday objects

1 a) *needle*   f) string
   b) glue   g) scissors
   c) penknife   h) buttons
   d) rubber band i) shoelace
   e) paper clip   j) ribbon

2 a) *notice*   f) file
   b) notepad   g) ruler
   c) eraser   h) sharpener
   d) diary   i) stamp
   e) envelope   j) dictionary

3 a) *hook*   e) curtain
   b) tablecloth   f) broom
   c) plant   g) doormat
   d) dustbin   h) fireplace

4 a) *pedestrian crossing*
   b) lamp-post
   c) pavement
   d) hedge
   e) gate
   f) kerb
   g) street sign
   h) post-box
   i) subway
   j) verge

5 a) *comb*   f) toothpaste
   b) gown   g) alarm
   c) mirror   h) towel
   d) table   i) pillow
   e) slippers   j) hanger

6 a) *washing-up*   f) saucer
   b) tap   g) bowl
   c) kettle   h) jug
   d) teapot   i) teaspoon
   e) mug   j) tray

20 People

1 a) *employer*   f) officer
   b) owner   g) painter
   c) mechanic   h) cashier
   d) manager   i) typist
   e) teacher   j) postman

2 a) *gardener*   f) carpenter
   b) guide   g) electrician
   c) plumber   h) optician
   d) photographer   i) vet
   e) dentist   j) hairdresser

3 a) *member*   f) colleague
   b) partner   g) employee
   c) flatmate   h) supporter
   d) guest   i) team-mate
   e) host   j) assistant

4 a) *crew*   f) trio
   b) society   g) group
   c) staff   h) audience
   d) queue   i) team
   e) crowd   j) cast

5 a) *inhabitants*   f) scientist
   b) politician   g) criminal
   c) citizen   h) musician
   d) guitarist   i) lawyer
   e) survivor   j) opponent

6 a) *coward*   f) expert
   b) miser   g) fool
   c) optimist   h) genius
   d) celebrity   i) pessimist
   e) favourite   j) liar